Puerto Rico
Off the Beaten Path®

Help Us Keep This Guide Up to Date

Every effort has been made by the author and editors to make this guide as accurate and useful as possible. However, many things can change after a guide is published—establishments close, phone numbers change, and facilities come under new management, etc.

We would love to hear from you concerning your experiences with this guide and how you feel it could be improved and kept up to date. While we may not be able to respond to all comments and suggestions, we'll take them to heart and we'll also make certain to share them with the author. Please send your comments and suggestions to the following address:

The Globe Pequot Press
Reader Response/Editorial Department
P.O. Box 480
Guilford, CT 06437

Or you may e-mail us at:
editorial@globe-pequot.com

Thanks for your input, and happy travels!

OFF THE BEATEN PATH® SERIES

Puerto Rico

SECOND EDITION

Off the Beaten Path®

by John Marino

Revised and updated
by Tina Cohen

The
Globe
Pequot
Press

Guilford, Connecticut

Cover and text design by Laura Augustine
Cover photo by Steve Dunwell Photography
Maps created by Equator Graphics © The Globe Pequot Press
Illustrations by Carole Drong

ISBN 0-7627-1235-X

Manufactured in the United States of America
Second Edition/First Printing

Contents

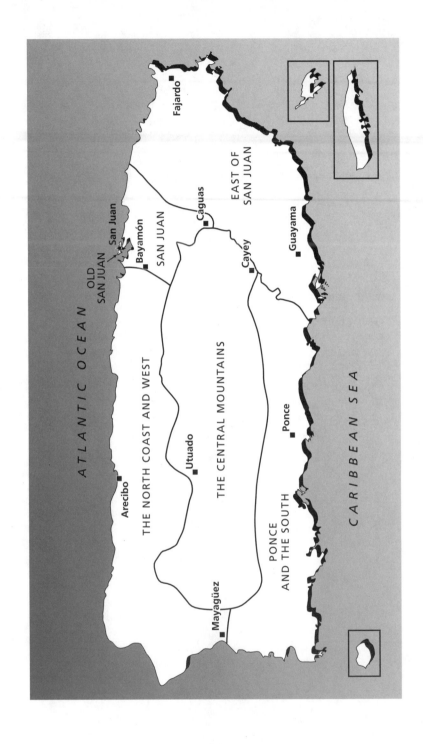

Introduction

A visitor from a country as vast as the United States initially may not understand the average Puerto Rican's feeling that his 100-by-35-mile island is majestic and vast. But he or she will likely leave feeling that *tierra boricua*, Puerto Rico, is living large indeed.

One reason for this feeling of vastness is that in Caribbean terms, a mere 30 miles often brings jarring contrasts in geography, race, political status, or language. The English-speaking island of St. Thomas is about as far from Puerto Rico's east coast city of Fajardo as Fajardo is from San Juan, for example.

Puerto Rico's dramatic and beautiful geographic diversity ranges from rain forest to beaches, from sweeping plains and valleys to mountain towns where temperatures can dip down to 50 degrees or below. The island's uniqueness also includes its land and marine treasures, like the dry forest of Guánica and two bioluminescent bays.

Equally impressive are the Puerto Ricans themselves, a spirited and exuberant people. They are friendly and unpretentious hosts, yet they are quite capable of dazzling their guests on many levels—from the tastiness of the local cuisine to the strong tradition of graphic and visual arts, to the stupendous range and joy of island music.

"Puerto Rico, U.S.A.," the tagline of the Puerto Rican government's tourism promotion campaign, is technically accurate but doesn't quite fit. While Puerto Rico has most conveniences of the modern United States and is politically part of the U.S., culturally it is a nation, and it will strike visitors as such.

Visitors will no doubt appreciate the many conveniences Puerto Rico's association with the United States affords. Travelers from the United States don't go through customs, they will be able to use English across the island, and the currency is the U.S. dollar. But the tastes, feel, and rhythms of Puerto Rico are distinctly Caribbean-Hispanic in nature, influenced by its Spanish, Taíno, and African roots.

Some visitors to Puerto Rico spend the majority of their time on the grounds of their hotel or the sun-drenched beach beside it. That just makes it all the easier to get off the beaten path and experience firsthand the charms of the place that Puerto Ricans call *la isla del encanto*, "the enchanted island."

Getting Around

San Juan has a good transportation system and is loaded with traffic jams, so it makes little sense to rent a car if you're planning on staying in the city. *Públicos* (public cars) and *la linea* (car service) travel from San Juan to most big island towns at reasonable rates (see the Old San Juan chapter). If you're leaving San Juan, especially if you're traveling to the mountains or southwestern Puerto Rico, the best way to get off the beaten path is to rent a car. Though not cheap, rentals give you the most flexibility and freedom. Most car rental agencies have offices throughout San Juan, especially in the Condado and Isla Verde tourism districts, as well as at the airport.

Comida Criolla: It's a Local Thing

Like almost everything else in Puerto Rican culture, Puerto Rican cuisine, most often called *comida criolla,* draws on the island's Taíno, African, and Spanish roots. Since the 1950s, the United States has had some influence as well. From the Taínos came yuca (cassava), *yautía* (taro root,), corn, ñame (yam), peanuts, lima beans, black-eyed peas, and fruits growing wild such as guava, soursop, and pineapple. Spaniards introduced garlic, onions, eggplant, cilantro, and chickpeas. From their Latin American exploration they also brought potatoes, papaya, avocado, cocoa, and coconuts. With African slaves came *plátanos* (plantains), *batata* (sweet potato), okra, and breadfruit. The American mainland interaction has added salads and fast foods and substituted healthier oils for the heavy use of lard.

There are two bases to Puerto Rican cooking. The first is *recaíto,* a blend of mashed garlic, chili and sweet peppers, onion, and two herbs—*recao* and cilantro—that is used in cooking beans *(habichuelas),* stews, and soups, and also used as a marinade. The other is *adobo,* a blend of dried spices rubbed on meat, poultry, and seafood before it is cooked. *Puertoriquenos* not only love their salsa music but their traditional *salsas* (sauces) accompanying the dishes at a meal. *Ajilimójili* is a sauce made with garlic, chili peppers, lemon juice, and olive oil and accompanies meats, fried fish, *tostones,* and *viandas* (root vegetables and tubers). *Sofrito* is oil blended with *recaíto,* tomato sauce, and *alcaparrado,* a mix of green olives, capers, and pimientos.

Because Puerto Rico is surrounded by water, its cuisine also draws heavily on seafood, with sea bass, red snapper, *bacalao* (salt codfish), and shellfish working their way into local cooking. But poultry is probably the most popular main course on the island, and a traditional dish is *arroz con pollo,* chicken coated with *adobo* that is sautéed, then cooked with onions, peppers, beer, *recaíto, alcaparrado,* and rice. Roasted suckling pig, *lechón asado,* is the national dish of Puerto Rico and is festively presented at holidays and family occasions.

Comida criollo also relies on native root and tuber vegetables, known as *viandas,* which include yuca, *yautía, ñame, batata,* and *apio.* Served as side dishes, *viandas* are usually steamed, boiled, or fried. *Sancocho,* a hearty Puerto Rican stew, includes *viandas* with *calabaza,* a squash similar to pumpkin, *plátanos,* corn, rice, *racaíto,* and smoked ham.

Another staple of local cuisine is the *plátano* (plantain). It is a relative of the banana. Unripe and green, the *plátano* can be sliced and fried for *tostones* or fried and mashed with olive oil and garlic to make *mofongo.* *Pasteles* are made with grated *plátanos* mixed with potato and *yautía* (taro root) that form a dough stuffed with a filling including, for example, pork and *racaíto,* which is then wrapped in plantain leaves before being boiled. The yellow, ripe *plátanos* are also cooked by frying, baking, or boiling. They can be combined with eggs, meat, and cheese.

Drawing on the variety of delectable fresh fruits, *postres* (desserts) use tropical ingredients to finish a meal with sweetness and pizzazz. Flan is the classic caramelized custard; *tembleque* is custard with coconut. Sautéed bananas can be ignited with 151-proof island rum. Mousses, tarts, and ice cream feature locally grown mango, *parcha* (passion fruit), guava, pineapple, orange, lemon, lime, papaya, mamey, or *guanabana* (soursop).

Balnearios

When somebody refers to a *balneario* (public beach), they are referring to one of the thirteen public facilities run by the commonwealth Department of Sports and Recreation (787–722–1551 or 787–724–2500). The beaches include services such as lifeguards, showers, changing rooms and lockers, bathrooms, and refreshment areas that sell everything from cold beer to seafood to breakfast. There is a $2.00 fee for parking. On weekends they are usually festive, but during the week are often absolutely tranquil, especially out on the island. Most *balnearios* are closed Mondays, meaning that access to the beach is still permitted but facilities are not open.

Public Forests

The Department of Natural and Environmental Resources administers sixteen public forests throughout Puerto Rico. All feature picnic
areas, nature exhibits, and hiking trails, and are open from 8:00 A.M.
to 5:00 P.M. Tuesday through Sunday (closed Monday for cleaning).
Camping is allowed in eight of the forests: Cambalache, Carite, Rio
Abajo, Guajataca, Susúa, Toro Negro, Vega, and Mona Island. Required
camping permits, at a charge of $4.00 per person per night, must be
purchased at the Department of Natural and Environmental Resources,
Forest Permit Division (Fernandez Juncos Avenue, just before the
entrance to the San Juan Yacht Club; 787–724–3724). Regional offices
are located at Arecibo (787–878–7279), Aguadilla (787–890–4050),
Guayama (787–864–8903), Mayaguez (787–833–3700), Ponce (787–
844–4660), and Humacao (787–852–4440).

Paradores and Mesones Gastronómicos

The Puerto Rico Tourism Company (787–721–2400) sponsors a network
of twenty-three guest houses and small hotels, called *paradores*, and a
network of more than fifty family restaurants, known as *mesones gastronómicos,* or gastronomic inns. *Paradores* rates range from $60 to $125
per night, depending on season and room size. Reservations at any mem-

Package Deals

*I*f you're traveling to Puerto Rico
from the continental U.S., take advantage of package deals through stateside travel wholesalers. Rates at
Puerto Rico's top hotels are quite steep
($250 to $350 a day and more) during winter high-season. Although sav-
ings can be found this way throughout
the year, the best deals are during off-
season (autumn or summer). Besides
holiday weekends (major U.S. and
many unique to Puerto Rico), off-season rates at five-star properties are
almost comparable to the comfortable
guest houses. It pays to shop around.
Many metro-area guest houses lower
their rates in the off-season in
response to the hotel deals. This is less
frequently done in beach towns outside of San Juan, which are filled with
vacationing sanjuaneros. In fact,
some of the better beach and mountain areas experience two tourism
seasons: a winter one driven by vacationing snowbirds and a summer one
driven by vacationing locals.

ber of the *parador* network can be made from San Juan (787–721–2884) or toll-free from out on the island (800–981–7575) or the United States (800–443–0266). The Puerto Rican Tourism Company's Web site, www.prtourism.com, has a handy section describing all the island's *paradores*, as well as other useful information for planning your trip.

The level of quality varies widely throughout the *paradores* system. And while the food has been good at all the *mesones gastronómicos* I've tried, their charms are about as wide-ranging as the *paradores*.

Centros Vacacionales

There are five vacation centers run by the commonwealth government's Recreation Development Department. Cabañas at these centers cost $65 per night and villas for up to six people are $109. Most of the lodgings are equipped with a stove, outdoor barbecue, refrigerators, bathrooms, and two bedrooms with singles and bunk beds. Guests are responsible for bringing sheets, towels, and pillows. Some centers have pools, basketball courts, and other amenities geared toward kids and families. Centers are located in Añasco, Boquerón, Maricao, Arroyo, and Humacao. Guests must make reservations in advance. For more information, contact **Compañia de Fomento Recreativo** (Oficina de Reservaciones para Centros Vacacionales), P.O. Box 9022089, San Juan, PR 00902-2089; (787) 722–1771, (787) 722–1551, or (787) 724–2500, extensions 130, 131.

Hurricane Georges

When Hurricane Georges hit Puerto Rico on September 21, 1998, no part of the island was left untouched.

Despite the storm's fury, the loss of life was small and most of the destruction was confined to poorly built wooden structures and the island's flora and fauna. Most large hotels either remained open or were back in business just weeks after the storm. Unfortunately, some of the island's smaller guest houses, especially in the mountainous interior, have not been able to bounce back as quickly.

Because of the island's tropical climate, Puerto Rico's flora and fauna will recover quickly. In fact forest reserves such as El Yunque, the

Caribbean National Forest, and Toro Negro began receiving visitors in December 1998. And the good news from forest officials is that endangered species such as the Puerto Rico parrot have weathered the storm.

Visitors to Puerto Rico will no doubt encounter some traces of the hurricane for a long time, but this shouldn't stop you from visiting this incredibly resilient island. Also, Puerto Ricans, you'll find, know how to enjoy life and manage to take everything—even natural disasters—in stride.

Tourist Help and Information

There are several sources of information available in Puerto Rico that travelers will likely find useful. A good place to start is the **Puerto Rico Tourism Company** (Paseo de la Princesa, mail to P.O. Box 902-3960, San Juan, PR 00902-3960; 787–721–2400 or toll-free 800–866–7827; open 8:00 A.M. to 4:00 P.M.). The headquarters of the government tourism agency is located in Old San Juan, and its main information center is in a yellow building on the waterfront there. The agency publishes *Que Pasá*, the government's official visitors' guide. The Tourism Company's new Web site is found at www.prtourism.com. Also look for *Bienvenidos*, published by the Puerto Rico Hotel & Tourism Association.

The San Juan Star, Puerto Rico's oldest and only English-language newspaper, will also come in handy for listings of movies, live music, theater, and other cultural and sporting events. The Thursday weekend edition is especially useful. Short-term rentals, water sports, and other services of interest are also advertised. *The Star* recently began a Spanish edition. Other Spanish daily newspapers include *El Nuevo Día*, *El Vocero*, and *Primera Hora*.

On the radio, WOSO 1040 AM is an English-language station with a news and information format.

Area Codes and Addresses

Puerto Rico has two area codes: 787 and 939. Also, most public buildings in Puerto Rico do not use standard street addresses. In general, Puerto Ricans use exact street directions much less than their U.S. counterparts. In those cases where no physical address exists, the street name and/or corner where the establishment is located is given.

Old San Juan

Old San Juan is a 7-block, mile-square city wedged between the San Juan Bay and the Atlantic Ocean and connected to the rest of San Juan by a narrow strip of land named *Puerta de Tierra,* or "land gateway." San Juan, which is what all the locals call this historic zone, is the oldest city under the U.S. flag and the second-oldest European settlement in all of the Americas. It began life in 1521 when Spanish settlers decided, over the objections of governor Juan Ponce de León, to leave their mosquito-plagued settlement in present-day Caparra for the peninsula that rises up as it narrows to split the calm bay waters from the strong Atlantic currents.

The breezy weather, which no doubt lured the first Spanish settlers, is still here today. Old San Juan, also known as the Old City, is an open, sunlit neighborhood of cleanly built Spanish colonial buildings with high ceilings and pastel-colored facades.

There's a reason writers call Old San Juan a living museum, and it has to do with the fortresses and mansions, monuments and churches, and other reminders found here of Puerto Rico's long and dramatic history. The island's recorded past dates back to Columbus's second voyage, a 1493 venture to colonize the New World. Although much less well-known than his 1492 journey of discovery, Columbus's second voyage was no less harrowing and infinitely more complicated, as it comprised seventeen ships and 1,200 men, including criminals, cartographers, astronomers, and common laborers.

Old San Juan is where you'll find some of the finest examples of sixteenth- and seventeenth-century Spanish colonial architecture in the Western Hemisphere. Many nineteenth- and early twentieth-century buildings also have been restored. Narrow stone streets, which climb from the bay to high ground overlooking the Atlantic, run through the city. Most of these streets still sport the bluish stone blocks that were imported here from Spain as ship's ballast. The streets are lined with colonial churches, residences, and mansions—all painted in pastel colors and many with wooden balconies.

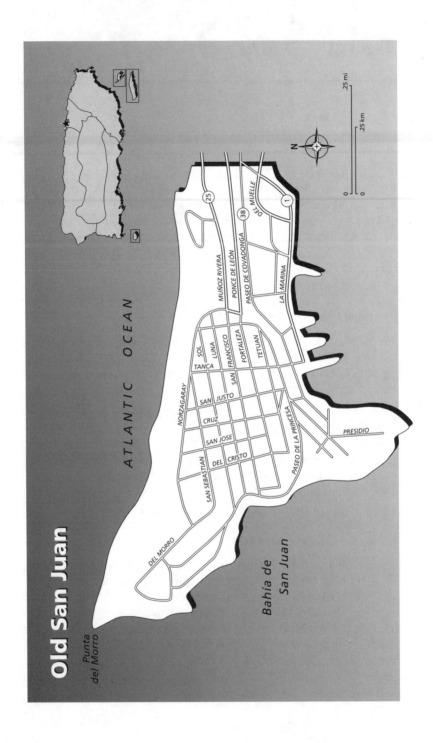

Old San Juan

Punta del Morro

ATLANTIC OCEAN

Bahía de San Juan

DEL MORRO

NORZAGARAY

SAN SEBASTIAN

DEL CRISTO

SAN JOSE

CRUZ

SAN JUSTO

TANCA

SOL

LUNA

SAN FRANCISCO

FORTALEZA

TETUAN

SAN

MUÑOZ RIVERA

PONCE DE LEON

PASEO DE COVADONGA

DEL MUELLE

LA MARINA

PASEO DE LA PRINCESA

PRESIDIO

N

25 mi

25 km

While it has a long history, San Juan is still very much a part of contemporary Puerto Rican life. It is a center of culture and art. There are fine examples of Spanish colonial and 1930s architecture. Galleries feature the best of current Puerto Rican art, and several museums offer traveling exhibits of all sorts. At night Old San Juan's clubs, restaurants, and theaters draw in visitors, while during the day its vibrant commercial sector and waterfront district do the same.

Plaza Colón

Plaza Colón greets the visitor who enters the Old City via the ocean route along Muñoz Rivera Avenue. Built in 1832, **Teatro Tapia** (La Fortaleza and Norzagaray; 787–722–0407), on the plaza's south side, is an historic structure that hosts theatrical and musical performances. The theater was named for Alejandro Tapia y Rivera, the Puerto Rican playwright. Across the street from the plaza's east side stands the **Manuel Pavía Fernández Government Reception Center for Puerto Rico's State Department,** also known as **El Casino.** The opulent structure was once the ballroom for a social club featuring the elite of San Juan society. **The Puerto Rico Olympic Committee** is housed in the adjacent neoclassical building, a former YMCA built in 1914.

Most of the residential buildings around the plaza have been successfully restored and now house diverse businesses. Ernst, the German owner of **Café Berlin** (407 San Francisco; 787–722–5205), bakes delicious breads and pastries and cooks tasty, healthy food with many organic ingredients and local produce. The **Haitian Gallery** (367 Fortaleza; 787–725–0986) sells colorful paintings and wood carvings mostly by Haitian artists.

Honoring Columbus

Plaza Colón was dedicated in 1893, the year of the 400th anniversary of the discovery of Puerto Rico by Christopher Columbus. The monument's inscription lists all of Columbus's voyages.

A revival is underway just southwest of Plaza Colón in what was formerly the not-so-nice eastern end of **La Fortaleza Street.** Some residents have even taken to making comparisons with SoHo, the trendy Manhattan arts district. But the name SoFo is not only geographically wrong, it's also unlikely to stick. Though the changes on this section of La Fortaleza Street are more modest than SoHo's emergence in the 1980s, a trend is emerging. Most of the restaurants stay open late, and both the crowd and the cuisine are on the cutting edge of style. Loud music and lively bars are the rule here.

Spearheading the movement has been the *Parrot Club* (363 Fortaleza; 787–725–7370; www.parrotclub.com). The restaurant is brightly colored, with large windows and mirrors, a long bar, and a quiet patio with tables. The food is *nuevo latino*—it blends the ingredients of traditional Puerto Rican cuisine with the influences of Taíno, Spanish, and African cookery. The place, like the food, is inventive and fun. While dinner prices can be expensive (appetizers around $6.00, and entrees from $16.00 to $18.00), prices are substantially lower at lunch. The house drink, Passion Parrot, a concoction based on passion fruit, is worth a try. This is the place to "see and be seen" in Old San Juan. Live music nightly features salsa, Brazilian, or Latin jazz.

The Gallery Café (305 Fortalezo; 787–725–8676) is a California-style bistro known for adventurous appetizers, salads, and sandwiches. Tuesday through Saturday nights feature Latin jazz, hiphop, techno, and funk; live rock bands perform Friday nights. The bar is closed on Monday.

Hotel Milano (307 Fortaleza; 787–729–9050 or toll-free 877–729–9050; www.home.coqui.net/hmilano) is the newest hotel (1999) to appear in Old San Juan. There are four floors with thirty rooms, and a restaurant on the top floor called Panorama that has great views over the city and bay. Rooms are clean and attractive, ranging in price from $80 to $135, and include a basic continental breakfast on the rooftop.

Puerto Rico's *Públicos* and *La Linea*

*P*ublic cars, known locally as **públicos,** can be found right off Plaza Colón. Públicos *are good bets for longer trips: many of them stop off at the Río Piedras market, a major* público *station, and many run on established routes.*

A special car service, known locally as **la linea,** *picks up and drops off customers. Companies are listed under* "Lineas de Carro" *in the Yellow Pages.*

One can get from San Juan to Guánica on the southwest coast of Puerto Rico for $14. The drawback is the length of time a trip can take. The rides are informal, offering door-to-door service to whomever gets on. Some people may be from remote mountain villages, while others will want to get off in the middle of a major city. Timing a trip on la linea is, therefore, a difficult proposition. Prepare for both a long trip and possibly a very cramped vehicle.

Front desk service is friendly and helpful.

Panorama Terrace Bar and Latin Grill (787–729–9050), Hotel Milano's rooftop restaurant, serves lunch and dinner with a Caribbean and international menu. Live music weekends 8:00 to 11:00 P.M.; closed Monday.

Interesting shops on Fortaleza include **Kamándula: The Bead Shop,** the place to go to have your hair braided, and **Mura's,** a small craft gallery. **Moondance** (315 Fortaleza; 787–723–0249) is also worth a look for imported artwork, jewelry, and clothing from around the world. **Storm Riders** (313 Fortaleza; 787–721–4202), a Harley-Davidson memorabilia shop, carries motorcycle accessories, leather biker clothes, handmade jewelry, irreverent T-shirts, and more.

TOP ANNUAL EVENTS

Gallery Nights,
first Tuesday of every month, at galleries throughout San Juan

Three King's Day,
January 6

Fiesta de Calle San Sebastián, mid-January

Puerto Rico Tourism Fair,
early October

Las Navidades,
early December through late January

Conveniently located next door is **Casa de la Raza** (313 La Fortaleza), a body tattoo shop that also does body piercing. If you really want a tattoo, try **Indio's Tattoo Studio** (103 Callejón del Toro/corner Luna; 787–722–0693), which has been in business for fifty-seven years.

Nearby restaurants, such as **La Chaumiére** at 367 Tetuan (787–722–3330), down the O'Donnell alleyway behind Teatro Tapia, help the sector's attractiveness. La Chaumiére is an expensive but delicious French restaurant that only serves dinner and is closed on Sunday.

Fabric and antiques shops are among the long-standing businesses here. Today you can also find food stores and shops selling crystals. **El Siglo XX,** at 355 Fortaleza (787–724–1849), is a Spanish-style *panadería,* or deli-bakery. The full-course meals here, such as tenderloin medallions in brandy sauce, paella, and filet of Dorado are recommended. Open for breakfast, lunch, and dinner, it is known for good food and good service at affordable prices.

Farther west along La Fortaleza, a more casual atmosphere prevails. **El Bar de Douglas Pub** (corner of Tanca) features an upstairs pool hall. **Don Pancho's Bar** (253 Tanca) attracts a pretty good mix of Caribbean nationals living in Puerto Rico, gringo tourists, and various ship crews from throughout the Caribbean and Latin America, not to mention the occasional scoundrel. Besides the friendly service, the place features tasty, cheap food and a jamming jukebox heavy on salsa and Dominican *bachata* and merengue.

Caribbean Deli (205 Tanca; 787–725–6695) is a great eatery specializing in American foods such as wraps, sandwiches, salads, and soups. Other features are great baked goods and a friendly staff. The changing art exhibits on the wall are for sale.

Just beyond Tanca on La Fortaleza is the *Café Tabac* (262 Fortaleza, 787–725–6785), a mahogany-lined place exuding Old World charm and featuring a wide selection of cigars, fine wines, liquors, and appetizer delicacies. Most nights there is live music, ranging from Latin jazz to salsa. Closed Sunday.

The Waterfront District

V isitors who come by bus or by water, or who take the lower route via Fernández Juncos Avenue into town (a good idea during most festivals), are more likely to first see Old San Juan's waterfront district, an area that is evolving into a tourist draw. From Plaza Colón, cross La Fortaleza Street heading south toward the bay and walk behind the Teatro Tapia to a long, wide cement staircase. Once down, take a left, then a quick right to reach the city's transportation hub, *Covadonga,* at the corner of Covadonga and Harding. Here you'll find a bus station, a public parking lot, a stand for the free municipal trolley, and a center for taxis. It's right across the street from the busiest cruise-ship piers.

Much of the waterfront district in Old San Juan and the neighboring

Taxis in San Juan

G *ood places to pick up a taxi in Old San Juan are around Covadonga, across the street at the cruise-ship piers, and next door at the Wyndham. There are standing areas on Plaza de Armas and on the southern end of Plaza Colón, along Tanca Street. Almost everywhere in the metro area can be reached for $16, and most places for significantly less.*

A new system of tourist taxis—you'll see their trademark white color—has been established that charge flat-route *fees between the airports, cruise ship ports, and tourism zones. From Old San Juan to the airport, the farthest points within the covered areas, costs $16. Extra charges apply for baggage and pick-up service. Off the standard rates, your driver should be using a meter. The airport to Isla Verde costs $8.00, while the ride to Condado, Ocean Park, or Miramar is $12.00.*

A good strategy is to combine a bus ride during the day with a cab ride back to your lodging at night.

Puerta de Tierra and Miramar districts is expected to be renovated under a proposed government plan. The ambitious project, known as the Golden Triangle, is dependent upon millions of dollars in private investments and is still in the planning stage.

The **Wyndham Old San Juan Hotel and Casino**, at 101 Marina (787–721–5100 or 800–996–3426; www.wyndham.com), opened in 1997 with a 240-room hotel featuring Dársena, a gourmet restaurant, two bars, and rooftop pool. The Wyndham has a lively casino and bar area inside, and curbside retail outlets. In fact the harbor area is growing into a separate shopping area distinct from Old San Juan. Covadonga is ringed by retail outlets occupied by local artisans, food and beverage vendors, and other producers. Try a Puerto Rico-grown and rolled cigar at **Antilles Cigar Manufacturing** (Covadonga; 787–725–5481). **Origenes Artesania** (Covadonga; 787–725–6968) has a variety of clothing and accessories, many of which are printed with Taíno symbols. There are also contemporary art, stained glass, and ceramic galleries.

Various businesses geared to the needs of international ship crews—from luxury cruise lines to military vessels—operate in this waterfront area and around Recinto Sur.

Head first to The Little House, or **La Casita** (Plaza de la Dársena; 787–722–1709). This building, dating from 1937, houses a satellite office of the Puerto Rico Tourism Company. Surrounding the structure are local artisans offering quality leatherwork, paintings, carvings, jewelry, and other creations. Open 8:30 A.M. to 8:00 P.M. Monday through Wednesday, 8:30 A.M. to 5:30 P.M. Thursday and Friday, and 9:00 A.M. to 8:00 P.M. Saturday and Sunday. There are also a variety of food and drink vendors. **Caribbean Carriage Tours,** which operates from a stand in Plaza de la Dársena, offers horse-carriage tours of the historic zone. Prices range from $30 to $60 per couple, depending on length and itinerary. Each additional person, add $10. For more information, call 787–797–8063.

Next door to La Casita is **Café Dársena.** This nice breezy spot in front of the bay is a good place to have a drink. On weekends the Puerto Rico Tourism Company often provides free concerts with local musicians at an adjacent stage here.

Immediately fronting the stage is a public plaza with cement tables under a towering shade tree around which more artisans and food vendors serving local fare are set up. Locals crowd the plaza to play dóminos. Across the street is the original office of **Banco Popular,** a restored Art Deco building from the mid-1930s; its surrounding plaza is named after

Rafael Carrión Pacheco, the bank's founder. The bank holds various art and film exhibitions, and its neon sign has worn itself into the fabric of the historic district's skyline. The strange and playful statue of a mysterious creature in front of the bank is by local artist Jorge Zeno.

Carli Cafe Concierto (787–725–4927), located at the plaza of Banco Popular at the corner of San Justo and Recinto Sur, is a lively restaurant hosted by Carli Muñoz, a talented pianist. While diners enjoy their selections from an international menu, Muñoz entertains at the Steinway, often joined by other musicians. Lunch and dinner served; closed Monday.

At 301 Cruz is the *Jules Restaurante* (787–724–6257), featuring food created by Portuguese chef Jules Himet de Oliveira. Patrons enjoy the setting as much as the meal. An intimate dining room includes an open kitchen and views to the harbor. Live music; reservations a must.

Around the corner is *Mistiko,* at 200 Tetuán (787–723–4148), a kind of adult Spencer's shop with incense, charms, crystals, and new-age music. Head up Calle Cruz in the direction of Plaza de Armas to *Club Lazer* (251 Cruz; 787–721–4479), a popular nightspot for San Juan's young and wild, as well as a mandatory watering hole for ships' crews. Club Lazer's three floors each feature a different scene. This is one of the hottest dance clubs in the city. Down Tetuán is *Saravá* (207 Tetuán; 787–725–3654), a music store with a wonderful collection of Puerto Rican and Caribbean music. Next door is an international money exchange and a good sandwich shop.

Heading up the hill along San Justo is also worthwhile. *La Mallorquina,* at 207 San Justo (787–722–3261), serves traditional Puerto Rican and Spanish food in an Old World setting. It's the oldest continuously operat-

Catch a Ferry

San Juan's huge waterfront hosts mega-cruise ships and a government-owned ferry service that runs between Old San Juan and Cataño, and Old San Juan and the Hato Rey financial district. Both stops are also connecting points to other major bus routes that push farther out into Río Piedras and western metro San Juan, like Bayamón and Cupey. The

Cataño ferry is the quickest route to tour the grounds of the local *Bacardi Rum Plant* (Highway 165, km. 2.6; 787–788–8400), which includes a tour and free samples of the rum-making process as well as a museum. Open Monday through Saturday 8:30 A.M. to 4:30 P.M. Públicos (public cabs) ply the route between the ferry and the plant.

ing restaurant in the Caribbean, dating from 1848. The indoor patio is gorgeous, and the seafood *asopao* is tops. Farther up the hill is ***Matahari,*** at 202-B San Justo (787–724–5869), which carries interesting clothing and jewelry and craftwork from around the world.

Recinto Sur, which runs west from the Banco Popular building, is known for its long string of restaurants. The classic structure across the street is the ***Old San Juan Post Office and Courthouse,*** which is currently undergoing a $28-million facelift. The complex's three-story structure, facing San Juan Bay, dates from 1914, while its seven-story annex was built in 1940. The building houses the post office, six federal courtrooms, and an office of the Resident Commissioner, Puerto Rico's sole representative to the U.S. Congress. Old San Juan's ***Hard Rock Café*** (253 Recinto Sur; 787–724–7625) is a beauty in a restored Spanish colonial house.

Beyond the post office, on the other side of the street, is Doña Fela Parking, a public parking lot open until midnight during the week, later on weekends.

How Taíno Is Boricua?

*C*onventional wisdom reckons that approximately 30,000 Taínos were living in what is now known as Puerto Rico when the Spanish arrived here on September 12, 1508. At that time Ponce de Léon, who would become Puerto Rico's first governor, peacefully exchanged greetings with Agüeybaña the Elder, the Taíno's head chief.

Just twenty-two years later, in 1530, a Spanish census reported a mere 1,200 Taínos left. While many uncounted Taínos presumably fled to the mountains, today there is a widespread belief that the number of Taíno survivors may have been greater than what was originally reported.

In 1998 a group of professors from the University of Puerto Rico went to the isolated Maricao community of Indieras, one of the last reported hold-outs of the Taíno. There the researchers searched for subjects with the dark skin, long, straight black hair, and high cheekbones typical of the Taíno. Testing only subjects whose mothers also had similar characteristics, researchers found that 70 percent showed traces of an Amerindian DNA that may prove to be handed down from a Taíno ancestry. Intrigued, the researchers took a more general sample in the city of Mayagüez, using subjects regardless of features or mother's ancestry. There they found evidence of Amerindian DNA in 50 percent of the respondents.

Although more testing is needed, researchers believe that they might be able to prove that either there were many more Taínos than were originally thought to have existed or that the Taínos survived much longer than previously thought, even to the present.

Al Dente (309 Recinto Sur; 787–723–7303; www.aldentepr.com) has good Italian food with fresh pasta and lots of fish. Thursday evenings offer live entertainment. *Yukiyu Sushi Bar & Teppan-Yaki* (311 Recinto Sur; 787–721–0653) is Puerto Rico's most famous sushi place. Non-sushi fans can also find satisfaction here. Good but pricey. *Lupi's Mexican Grill and Sports Cantina* (313 Recinto Sur; 787–722–1874) is a Tex-Mex restaurant and sports bar, famous for margaritas and fajitas with live music on weekends. They do a lot with a little bit of space. *Royal Thai* (315 Recinto Sur; 787–725–8401) serves up Thai favorites; it's possible to find fiery dishes here, but the heat has been substantially lowered to suit the local and tourist palette. Also try *Viet Nam Palace Seafood Restaurant* (332 Recinto Sur; 787–723–7539), a new Vietnamese place farther down the street. Bear left at the corner of Tetuán to get to *Casa Papyrus* (332 Tetuán; 787–722–3362), a book and music store with a nice upstairs cafe. *Cafe Zaguán* (359 Tetuán; 787–724–3476) combines a nice ambience, friendly service, and good simple food. It serves Caribbean cuisine for lunch and dinner.

The *San Juan Bay* is among the Caribbean's busiest, carrying half the region's commercial trade as well as more than one million cruise-ship visitors each year. Beyond the stage that fronts the bay and where free concerts take place is the *Old Spanish Customs House* (La Puntilla; 787–729–6977), called the *Aduana*, an impressive ornate structure built in 1925. Today it serves as a U.S. Customs House, but no tours are given. Farther back along the bay is *El Arsenal de la Marina* (La Puntilla; 787–724–1877 or 787–724–5949). A former Spanish naval station and arsenal, it now hosts changing art exhibitions, such as the Puerto Rico Photojournalists Association's annual exhibition in late July. It has also held the Biennial Latin American and Caribbean Graphics Exhibition, a phenomenal show held every two years that surveys art from across the Caribbean and Latin America. Open for exhibitions 9:00 A.M. to 4:30 P.M. Wednesday through Sunday.

Past the public parking lots is *Paseo de la Princesa,* a bayside promenade that affords a good view of *la Muralla,* the original wall of the Old City, which shadows the walkway. Built in the eighteenth century, the wall is made of up-to-20-foot-thick sandstone blocks. Once surrounding the entire settlement at San Juan, it's one of the best examples of a city wall built by the Spanish in the New World.

Paseo de la Princesa recently underwent a $2.8-million renovation. The wide walkway, shaded by royal palms and caressed by a balmy breeze from across San Juan Bay, is lined with food and refreshment vendors

Old Spanish Customs House

as well as stands selling local crafts. Also look for the local fishing club and the adjacent fried-fish turnover stands farther down as the promenade nears the bay.

On the right is *La Princesa* (Paseo de la Princesa; 787–721–2400), a restored nineteenth-century prison that today houses the *Puerto Rico Tourism Company.* The building also hosts an impressive gallery of local art (787–723–0692), which is open to the public weekdays from 9:00 A.M. to 4:00 P.M. On Sundays, local musicians gather here from 5:30 to 7:00 P.M. to salute the sunset and passersby with a serenade.

Look for the statue of the beloved *Doña Fela,* Felisa Rincón de Gautier, the mayor of San Juan from 1946 to 1968. Toward the bay the promenade is dominated by the towering bronze fountain statue by Spaniard Luis Sanguino. Unveiled as part of the 1993 festivities celebrating Columbus's discovery of Puerto Rico, *Raíces,* or Races, depicts the Taíno Indian, African, and Spanish origins of the Puerto Rican people.

The promenade cuts right as it encounters the bay beyond the fountain and winds through an area of perfectly placed, shaded benches. At night there is an impressive view of the twilight sky over Cataño. Armed with fishing rods, people of all ages frequent the small wooden dock that is home to several fishing boats.

> **Trivia**
>
> *One hundred and seventy governors have called* **La Fortaleza** *"home."*

The promenade ends at the **San Juan Gate,** the only remaining of six original entrances to the Old City, whose heavy wooden doors were once shut down at sunset for security. Today the area is one of the most tranquil spots in Puerto Rico. Beyond the ice-cone vendors who frequent the gate is palatial **La Fortaleza,** built in 1540, the oldest governor's mansion still in use in the Americas. Located at the far western end of La Fortaleza Street, it was originally used as a fortress. Tours of the structure and its surrounding

The Raíces fountain

gardens (both overlooking the San Juan Bay) are given in Spanish and English (787–721–7000, extensions 2211 or 2358). Open weekdays, except holidays, 9:00 A.M. to 4:00 P.M.; free admission.

Back up the hill in the other direction is the **Plazoleta de la Rogativa,** a nice plaza with a striking statue and an impressive perch overlooking the bay with a gorgeous view of La Fortaleza. The statue, **La Rogativa,** was created in 1971 by Australian-born sculptor Lindsay Daen, who first heard the story that would serve as his inspiration from his Puerto Rican

San Juan's Historic Jewel

*F*or decades Old San Juan was allowed to fall into decay. Fortunately, in the 1960s, Ricardo Alegría stepped in. The historian, professor, and founder of the Institute of Puerto Rican Culture led a drive to give the historic sector the treatment it deserved. His ongoing plan has been largely successful.

The restored architecture, which assures 20-foot-high rooms open to air and sunlight, is riveted with a contem-

porary spirit. Today Old San Juan is teeming with art galleries, bars, restaurants, and a diverse lot of merchants, but it also maintains quiet residential stretches and hidden wonders down its narrow walkways. It is one of the liveliest and most active parts of San Juan, day and night. And yet there are parks and walkways that remain eternally quiet. The district becomes especially lively during Christmas, elections, major holidays, and special events.

wife's grandmother. The statue, which depicts a bishop surrounded by a group of praying females with torches held high, commemorates the night of April 30, 1797, when the women of San Juan routed the British (see Divine Inspiration, below).

Above the small park the road splits in front of the **Casa Rosada,** or Pink House, which was built by the Spanish as an army barrack in 1812. Today it houses a daycare center.

The upper road passes below the fabulous gardens of **Casa Blanca** (1 San Sebastián; 787–724–5477), or the White House, the home of the Ponce de León family for 250 years. In fact Casa Blanca is the oldest continuously occupied residence in the Western Hemisphere and San Juan's oldest standing building. The gardens tumble out over the vast stone wall that runs along the road while tall trees tower above, bringing a welcome reprieve from the sun and making a good home for the flocks of tropical birds that fill the area with music. Even if you don't enter the gardens, a stroll below them will give you a taste of the experience, especially if it occurs while one of the garden's security employees is belting out an aria as he strolls around the gardens, a rare instance of true pleasure in the workplace. Open Tuesday through Saturday 9:00 A.M. to 4:45 P.M. Garden open same hours, including Sunday. Admission $2.00 for adults.

Also on the grounds are two museums. The **Juan Ponce de León Museum** (787–724–4102) at Casa Blanca is dedicated to the island's

Divine Inspiration

*O*n April 17, 1797, the British Navy, commanded by General Abercrombie, laid siege to San Juan. In response, Puerto Rico's Governor, Don Ramón de Castro, suggested to the city's bishop that a religious procession be held in order to receive divine inspiration to help the Spanish defend their port city.

On April 30, while the men stood by their guns in the fortresses of San Juan, the women of San Juan gathered for a procession dedicated to

Saint Úrsula and the 11,000 virgins.

That night, British sentries reported unusual activity in San Juan—the sound of bells crashing and reports of light flowing from the city. It was the women of San Juan, torches in hand, following the bishop through the streets. But General Abercrombie thought otherwise, surmising that the Spanish had doubled their strength and were preparing an attack. With his troops beset by dysentery and fatigue, he ordered a retreat.

first governor (de León died in battle in 1521, the year the house was built as a gift from King Charles I). The de León family occupied Casa Blanca until 1779, when the house was sold to the Spanish government. In the beginning of its life, the house guarded Spanish settlers from attacks by the Carib Indians, and by the end it was the home of the commander of the U.S. Army. It was declared a national historic monument in 1968. The other museum, the **Taíno Indian Ethno-Historic Museum,** has exhibits and examples of jewelry, artifacts, and a miniature replica of a Taíno village. The museums have the same hours as Casa Blanca.

Two Fortresses and the Boulevard

Norzagaray Avenue, also known as "The Boulevard," is one of the most beautiful roads in Old San Juan. The main thoroughfare ribbons along the curving Atlantic and runs between two fortresses.

Once you walk up the path passing under the gardens, you'll catch a glimpse of San Felipe del Morro, or *El Morro* (Norzagaray Avenue; 787–729–6960). The impressive Spanish fortress occupies the tip of the peninsula on which Old San Juan sits—an anvil bluff towering over the entrance of San Juan Bay. El Morro was built in 1540 to guard against sea attack. Several subsequent restorations and expansions resulted in its current form by 1787. You can learn all about the secrets of the castle's six levels of defense and more in its museums and exhibits. Open daily 9:00 A.M. to 5:00 P.M.

Trivia
*In 1825 the pirate **Cofresi** was executed at El Morro.*

The sprawling *San Cristóbal Fortress* (Norzagaray Avenue; 787–729– 6960) was built to guard against land attacks and is located a good hike away down Norzagaray Avenue. Although it is the larger of the two forts, rising 150 feet above sea level, its expansive design lacks El Morro's drama. What began in 1634 as a small fortification subsequently grew by its completion in the 1780s to a network of fortifications sprawling across 27 acres. Built to guard against land attacks, its inner sanctum was protected by five large rooms separated by 10-foot-wide walls connected by moats and tunnels. The dramatic views of San Juan and the coastline alone make the fort worth visiting. And make sure you check out the view of La Garita del Diablo, or *Devil's Sentry Box,* a small stone watchtower overlooking the surging Atlantic. Admission for both fortresses (United Nations Heritage sites run by the U.S. National Park Service) is a single charge of $2.00, $1.00 for senior citizens; children under 12 are free. Open 9:00 A.M. to 5:00 P.M. daily.

Devil's Sentry Box, San Cristóbal

The grounds of El Morro extend to overlook the **San Juan Cemetery,** the main resting place for several prominent Puerto Ricans. Several of the tombstones are in and of themselves dazzling sculpted works of art, and there's a small, white chapel. But the real beauty of the cemetery comes from its setting on a grassy mound of land beside the crashing Atlantic and El Morro's dramatic wall. Due to the number of muggings here, take precautions; view at a distance or with a group.

Take the Bus

*C*ovadonga is a transportation hub. Trolley service goes to Plaza de Armas, entering at San Francisco and Cristo and making stops at **La Puntilla** public parking lot (Paseo de la Princesa; 787–725–5042). Another route carries passengers to El Morro, with stops at Plaza Colón and Fort San Cristóbal.

Covadonga also serves as a center for public bus routes, which can take you to just about any area in metro San Juan. There are two major bus services: privately-owned **Metrobus** (787–763–4141), which costs 50 cents, and the government-owned **AMA bus lines** (787–250–6064), which cost 25 cents. Buses run in specific traffic lanes, which usually means a quicker ride. Look for the magenta, orange, and white PARADA signs.

Walk east from El Morro along Norzagaray Avenue to get to the **Museum of Art and History** (150 Norzagaray; 787–724–1875), which has changing shows featuring local artists as well as other arts and crafts shows. The museum's exhibition rooms fill a large courtyard—a bustling market place in 1855—with pieces ranging from the whimsical to the dramatic. The recently renovated museum will soon add a permanent exhibit on Old San Juan. There is a half-hour documentary about the history of San Juan. Open Tuesday through Sunday 10:00 A.M. to 4:00 P.M.

Gallery Inn (204 Norzagaray; 787–722–1808; www.thegalleryinn.com) is an eclectic guest house of twenty-two rooms inside a rambling 300-year-old residence run by local artist Jan D'Esopo and her husband, Manuko Gandía. The place is decorated with D'Esopo's art (all of which is for sale), numerous plants and birds, and interesting objects and antiques. Seven studios in the home are open to visitors as artists paint, silkscreen, and sculpt. Room rates range from $145 to $350, and they run the gamut from simple, one-bed affairs to three-bedroom suites with private terraces and Jacuzzis. Several rooms that front Norzagaray have outstanding ocean views, and there are communal rooftop terraces for all guests to enjoy. Continental breakfast is served, but dinners for private parties must be arranged ahead.

Walk through the Callejón two blocks to Calle Sol and turn right to get to **La Fonda El Jibarito** (280 Calle Sol; 787–725–8375), where you can feast on Puerto Rican dishes such as roast pig, codfish salad, or *mofongo*. A representation of the actual street, complete with accurate models of the facades that line it, adorns the main dining room. You'll even see the outside of the restaurant you're in on the wall. Good food at bargain prices draws locals and tourists alike to this family-run place with friendly service.

Baseball's Shining Star

*B*aseball star **Roberto Clemente** was born in Carolina on August 18, 1934. From 1955 to 1972, Clemente played for the Pittsburgh Pirates. During that time he won four National League batting titles, was the league's Most Valuable Player (1966), won twelve Gold Glove awards, and was selected to play on the All-Star team twelve times. A lifetime .317 hitter, Clemente hit 240 home runs. He obtained his 3,000th hit in 1972. That same year, he died in a plane crash en route to deliver supplies to earthquake victims in Managua, Nicaragua. He was elected to the Baseball Hall of Fame in 1973.

Further east from the Callejón along Norzagaray Avenue is *Amanda's Café* (424 Norzagaray; 787-722-0187). Directly across the street from Fort San Cristóbal, the Mexican restaurant enjoys a wonderful location with streetside tables overlooking the fortress and the ocean. The food's okay, but this place was made for drinks and appetizers—good for a first stop, a late evening snack, or a short break during a walk through the Old City. Open daily, noon to midnight. About halfway down the hill is the *Murano Glass of Venice* shop (500 Norzagaray; 787-723-4927), with an interesting art gallery, *Mariangel Galeria* (500 Norzagaray; 787-722-3081), next to it. Continuing along Norzagaray will take you down to Plaza Colón, at the entrance of the historic zone.

The first building across the huge front grounds of El Morro is the *Escuela de Artes Plásticas* (Norzagaray and El Morro Road; 725-8120), or School of Fine Arts. This is an art college that was originally constructed in 1873 as an insane asylum. After serving as a military building for the United States, it was given to the Commonwealth government, which subsequently turned it into an art school. Today it has a small shop and frequent student exhibits. The shop also sells cold bottled water and beautiful kites, both of which come in handy on the grounds of the oceanfront castle. Nearby, *La Liga de Arte de San Juan* (1 Beneficencia; 787-725-5453 or 787-722-2434), or The Arts League, gives both one- and ten-weekend courses in all of the arts, including ceramics, photography, painting, and drawing. Stop by for a schedule of offerings.

Two huge restored structures rest on either side of the renovated plaza Parque de Beneficencia. The *Asilo de Beneficencia* (787-724-5949 or 787-724-5477), a former home for the poor, now houses the headquarters of the *Institute of Puerto Rican Culture.* The Institute also features a permanent gallery on Taíno culture and art, an outstanding santos collection of carved wooden saint figures, as well as other changing exhibits. Galleries open 9:00 A.M. to 5:00 P.M. Tuesday through Sunday. Free admission.

Across the plaza stands the largest barracks built by the Spaniards in the Western Hemisphere, *Cuartel de Ballajá,* which dates from 1867. Today it houses *Las Americas Museum* (Ballajá; 787-724-5052), which strives to offer an overview of cultural offerings from throughout the New World. While a permanent exhibit features popular arts in the Americas, the museum also hosts excellent changing shows. Open Tuesday through Friday 10:00 A.M. to 4:00 P.M., weekends 11:00 A.M. to 5:00 P.M. Free admission. This venue hosts the Biennial of Caribbean and Latin American Graphic Arts.

The Roofless Museum

One abandoned building on San Sebastián has been turned into El Museo Sin Techo, or the "Roofless Museum." The museum is actually the crumbling facade of the old building, which local artists have covered with brightly colored murals and where they occasionally hang paintings. The building is marked by the two Puerto Rican flags painted on top of the building's twisted corrugated metal, and the striking portrait of independentista and National Party founder Pedro Albizu Campos. His black silhouette is etched into the building's worn sandstone wall.

Beyond Ballajá lies the recently restored **Quincentennial Plaza.** Various fountains, columns, and sculpted steps are features of the plaza, which also has underground parking. On its southern end, two columns point to the North Star. The plaza's centerpiece is a 40-foot-high totemic sculpture by artist Jaime Suárez. Built of black granite and earthen ceramics, the sculpture, erected as part of the 500th anniversary of Columbus's voyage, symbolizes the aboriginal roots of the Americas.

Casals in Puerto Rico

*Famed Spanish cellist Pablo Casals lived on San José Plaza from 1956 to 1974, in what is now the **Pablo Casals Museum** (101 San Sebastián; 787–723–9185). The museum features memorabilia including recordings, manuscripts, and the cello and piano of the master who founded Puerto Rico's annual **Casals Festival of Classical Music,** held for two weeks each June. The museum is open Tuesday through Saturday 9:00 A.M. to 5:00 P.M., and Sunday 1:00 to 5:00 P.M. Admission $1.00 adults, children 50 cents.*

Exit the plaza from the opposite side of Ballajá and go across Cristo Street to get to **San José Plaza.** In the middle of the square is a statue of Ponce de León, built from cannons captured in 1797 after an unsuccessful British attempt to take San Juan. Until it was closed for most of 1999 for renovation, the **San José Cathedral,** completed in 1539, was the second oldest church in continuous use in the New World. Open Monday through Saturday 8:30 A.M. to 4:00 P.M. Sunday mass at noon (787–725–7501). The adjacent **Convento de los Dominicos** (98 Norzaragay) is one of the oldest buildings in Old San Juan. Built in 1523, today it houses an interesting bookstore run by the Institute of Puerto Rican Culture. Open Monday through Saturday 9:00 A.M. to 5:00 P.M. For more information, call 787–721–6866.

San Sebastián Street

O ld San Juan embodies Puerto Rican history and culture more so than any other area on the island, but the historic zone pulses to a contemporary beat and gets lively when the sun goes down. In no place, perhaps, is the *ambiente* of Old San Juan captured better than on **Calle San Sebastián,** which is lined with restaurants and bars, as well as quite a few private homes in a 4-block stretch between Cristo and San Justo Streets.

Las Fiestas de la Calle San Sebastián, the biggest festival of the year, takes place on Calle San Sebastián in mid-January. Street corner rumbas, outdoor art shows, and gastronomic delights, not to mention full-blown musical acts, draw thousands from across the island. The festival marks the end of the Christmas season, known as las Navidades, *which keeps the Old City lively from late November.*

One of the best places to watch the locals in **Plaza San José** is across the street at **Nono's** (100 San Sebastián; 787–725–7819). The bar has two cable television sets tuned to the sporting event of the moment, a second-floor pool room, a great jukebox for salsa and Latin pop, and doorways opening out to the plaza. There is inexpensive American food here: burgers, onion rings, chicken-fried steaks. Open daily 11:00 A.M. to 4:00 P.M.

Old San Juan and other parts of San Juan have seen stepped up efforts by local authorities to enforce public prohibitions such as public drinking, serving minors under eighteen, and making excessive noise. This has mellowed the Old City a bit (much to the relief of residents), but the sector is still a nightlife center. The public drinking restrictions are lifted during the frequent parties and festivals held here.

San Sebastián Street is sleepy by day and energized by night. *El Patio de Sam* (102 San Sebastián; 787–723–8802), with its changing art exhibits and great collection of works by local painters, has been a favorite spot for locals and tourists since the 1950s. The menu has gone upscale over the years, but the burgers here still rule. Tiny *El Boquerón* (104 San Sebastián; 787–721–3942) has a great salsa jukebox and a knack for drawing lively crowds despite its size. Down the block on the left is *Café Culebra* (103 San Sebastián), which draws the young and restless crowd with Spanish rock music.

Amadeus (106 San Sebastián; 787–722–8635) has everything from gourmet seafood and steak dishes to light sandwiches and salads. A lively bar area features artwork on the walls and changing exhibits. *El Quinque Bar* (114 San Sebastián) has a light menu and frequent live music. *La Tortuga Bar* (corner of San José) is a favorite place to shoot pool, while across the street *Los Hijos De Borinquen* (corner of San José) has great live Puerto Rican music as well as a terrific salsa selection on the jukebox. Look for the guy with the guitar, belting out Puerto Rican classics, often with an assist from the very involved members of the crowd who use their voices and instruments. The grandfather of famed percussionist Giovanni Hildalgo, one of the most prominent figures in contemporary Latin jazz, is often his partner on percussion.

Around the corner is *Friquitín Krugger* (52 San José; 787–723–2474), a dark bar with an adjacent eatery famous for its fried crab *alcapurrias,* meat *empanadillas,* and *bacalaítos* (codfish fritters). It is open Tuesday through Sunday nights, featuring Brazilian jazz. Across the street, *La Cubanita Bar/Market* (51b San Jose; 787–725–8837) draws a bohemian crowd in the early evenings. *Café San Sebastían* (corner of Plaza Mercado) is a nice bar/pool hall that also serves selected local seafood and vegetable dishes. Its back bar, with tables and an outdoor patio (farther along Plaza Mercado Street), is also worth a look.

Rumba (152 San Sebastián; 787–725–4407) is a must, especially when there's live music, heavily tilted towards Latin jazz, salsa, and Cuban. The bands here are usually a cut above the rest, and the space and crowd are, too. *Café Seda* (157 San Sebastián; 787–725–4814) is another nice spot. *Aquí Se Puede* (at the corner, 50 San Justo; 787–724–4448) literally translates into "Here you can," and is worth the extra walk. The beloved neighborhood bar recently underwent a complete makeover and management change, but it still draws them in. Such traditions as Tuesday Opera Nights are now gone, but other standards, like great art, a jukebox, and poetry readings, continue. Island music is performed live most nights.

Cristo Street

*C*risto Street is filled with retail outlets and museums, not to mention a bar or two. *Hotel El Convento* (100 Cristo; 787–723–9020 or 800–468–2779; www.elconvento.com) is one of the more interesting properties in the Caribbean. It invites passersby with its large, open stairway, which leads into a hip Spanish tapas restaurant and a relaxed cafe bar. It's a hotel with a history. Commissioned in 1636 by King Philip IV of Spain, it served as a Carmelite convent from its opening in 1651 to its closing 250 years later in 1903. Vacant for a decade, it was next used as a dance hall, then a flophouse. In 1953 it was turned into a garage for garbage trucks. It was first turned into a hotel in 1962, when Robert

Woolworth opened up a one-hundred-room property. It now has fifty-seven rooms on its secluded top floors, which feature a beautiful dining area and a small rooftop pool and Jacuzzi. The bottom two floors host lively restaurants and bars. *El Picoteo Tapas Bar* (787–643–1597) serves pitchers of sangria and over eighty varieties of tapas. Stop for a drink and appetizer and enjoy the glitzy scene. Open Tuesday through Sunday for lunch and dinner. *Patio del Nispero* (787–723–9260) serves lunch and dinner daily with American and Caribbean cuisine. Flamenco shows presented Monday at 10:00 P.M., Tuesday at 4:30 and 10:00 P.M. *Cafe Bohemio* (787–723–9200) is a classic bistro in marble and mahogany. Serving lunch and dinner, it segues into a live music venue when the kitchen closes on Thursday, Friday, and Saturday nights. Bands include Brazilian, jazz, blues, and Latin.

Across the street from El Convento is *El Batey* (101 Cristo), a bar with a leaky roof, goofy drawings of Old San Juan characters, and graffiti and staple-gunned business cards for art. There's a pretty good gringo jukebox and a diverse crowd, from the well-connected to the down-and-out. A "hole in the wall," it is nonetheless a recommended stop—good for lunches. It stays open until 6:00 A.M. Next door, *Pablo's* draws

Not-to-be-Missed Museums

- **Casa del Libro (The Book House),** *255 Calle Cristo. This rare book museum features a large collection of early books and manuscripts, some dating back to the fifteenth century. Open Tuesday through Saturday 11:00 A.M. to 4:30 P.M. Call (787) 723–0354 for more information. Free admission.*

- **Casa de los Contrafuertes (House of Buttresses),** *101 San Sebastían. Dating back to the eighteenth century, this house is believed to be the oldest residence left in Old San Juan. Today it houses two museums, one devoted to graphic arts and one recreating a nineteenth-century pharmacy. Open Wednesday through Sunday 9:00 A.M. to 4:30 P.M. Call (787) 724–5477 for more information. Free admission.*

- **Doña Felisa Gautier de Rincón Museum,** *El Caleta de San Juan. This museum is the former residence of the beloved mayor (from 1946 to 1968). Open Monday through Friday 9:00 A.M. to 4:00 P.M. Call (787) 723–1897 for more information. Free admission.*

- **Museo del Indio (Indian Museum),** *119 Calle San José. View exhibits and ceramics and discover more about the indigenous peoples of the Caribbean region. Open Tuesday through Saturday 10:00 A.M. to 4:00 P.M. Free admission. Call (787) 724–0700, extension 4223, for more details.*

a much younger crowd, largely because of the loud Latin rock music, video games, and local grunge scene.

At 105 Cristo, a very different experience awaits the discriminating diner. *Il Perugino* (787–722–5481) is located in an artfully restored two-hundred-year-old home and has been awarded the title of Best Italian Restaurant for all of Puerto Rico for the last ten years. Dinners only, reservations suggested.

Built in 1529, the **San Juan Cathedral** (151 Cristo and Luna Streets; 787–722–0861) is the oldest cathedral in the Western Hemisphere. Originally built of straw and wood, the 1521 structure was destroyed by a hurricane in 1526. Three restorations have transformed it into its current state. The beige-and-white domed structure features a great archway, circular stairway, and Gothic vaulted ceilings. The church also boasts the tomb of Puerto Rico's first governor, Juan Ponce de León. Look for other altars, statues, and images, such as the electric-blue statue of la Virgen de Providencia, the patron saint of Puerto Rico. Open daily 8:30 A.M. to 4:00 P.M.

The nice little park out front is called Park of the Nuns. At the lower end of the park lies the **Museo del Niño,** the **Children's Museum** (150 Cristo; 787–722–3791), a good stop if you're traveling with kids. The interactive exhibits will feel like play but your kid is sure to learn something, too. Closed on Monday, the museum is open 9:00 A.M. to 3:30 P.M. Tuesday through Thursday, and Friday 9:00 A.M. to 5:00 P.M., and 12:30 to 5:00 P.M. on weekends.

Capilla del Cristo

*T*his chapel celebrates miracles. It is a tiny outdoor sanctuary adjacent to Parque de las Palomas, at the end of Calle del Cristo. Built where it is, one story attributes its location to preventing people from falling into the sea over the city wall there. But that legend is surpassed in glorious detail by the one describing a participant racing on horseback, during the eighteenth century, in San Juan Bautista festivities. Carried down Calle del Cristo by his errant horse, both plunged over the wall into the water below. Although some historical records indicate the rider died, a popular conclusion is that he miraculously survived. Hence the chapel was built, in 1753, to commemorate Christ's intercession in the saving of a life. Over the years, believers have placed milagros—tiny silver replicas of body parts—on the altar in thanks for miracles of healing in their own lives. The fence admitting visitors is open only on Tuesday 10:00 A.M. to 3:30 P.M.

San Juan Cathedral

Shopping is the name of the game farther down Cristo Street, with factory outlet stores, such as London Fog or Ralph Lauren, as well as upscale retailers. Be sure to stop at the **Spicy Caribee** (154 Cristo; 787–725–4690), a hip Caribbean condiment shop with Jamaican jerk sauce, Trinidadian curry powder, Puerto Rican coffee beans, cookbooks, vanilla extracts, preserves, hot sauces, and tropical fragrances. Open Monday through Saturday 10:00 A.M. to 6:00 P.M., Sunday 12:00 to 5:00 P.M.

Cristo Street has some of San Juan's best art galleries as well. Try the funky little **Galería Cariban** (52 Cristo; 787–722–0054), which sells everything from painted furniture to nudes on canvas. **Galería Palomas** (207 Cristo; 787–724–8904) is also worth a look. **Atlas Art Gallery**

(208 Cristo; 787-723-9987; www.atlasgalleries.com) exhibits paintings and sculpture.

Also at 154 Cristo is the restaurant *La Ostra Cosa* (787-722-2672). As the name suggests, oysters *(ostras)* are featured here, but the menu includes other seafood and meat as well. The back courtyard is considered one of the nicest outdoor dining spots in town. *Chef Marisoll Creative Cuisine* (202 Cristo; 787-725-7454) is a chic restaurant presided over by Puerto Rico's first female executive chef and winner of numerous culinary gold medals, Marisol Hernandez. She prepares classic European cooking for lunches and dinners Tuesday through Sunday; closed Monday. Reservations required.

Around the corner on Fortaleza Street, toward the governor's mansion, is *Café la Violeta* (56 La Fortaleza; 787-723-6804), one of the prettiest spots to have a drink in San Juan. Open daily 11:30 A.M. to 11:00 P.M. Sometimes there's a piano player tickling the ivories in the lavishly decorated, high-ceilinged main room. There are also more private side rooms with couches. Other eateries and cafes lie straight ahead at the end of Cristo Street, which is blocked off to traffic and filled with cafe tables and umbrellas. The street ends at *Capilla del Cristo.* This chapel lies in an awkward position, jutting out into both Cristo and Tetuán Streets. Its location has prompted authorities to close the whole stretch of Cristo to Fortaleza to vehicular traffic, making it one of the most restful areas in the historic district. To the side of the chapel, one can look over the city wall below to the Paseo de la Princesa, farther away to the La Puntilla area, and across the bay to the rough shoreline of Cataño. Next to the chapel is the *Parque de las Palomas,* or Park of the Pigeons. It's a charming place with a lovely view of the bay. If you enjoy pigeons or have children with you who will, this park lets you indulge. Hundreds roost here, are tame enough to land on visitors, and gratefully accept the snack of seeds you can purchase.

Several more shops line La Fortaleza Street from Cristo Street all the way down to Plaza Colón. Right around the corner from Cristo is the *Plastic Jungle* (101 Fortaleza; 787-723-1076), a nonviolent-toy store and great place for kids' stuff. Also poke your head into *Pareo* (101 Fortaleza; 787-724-6284), which sells sarongs and other wrap clothing.

At 104 Fortaleza is *Barrachina Village* (787-725-8239 or 800-515-3582; www.barrachina.com), a retail store, art gallery, and patio cafe in a beautiful century-old colonial building. They claim (not uncontested!) that the famous tropical concoction of coconut, pineapple, and rum—the piña colada—was first created here. You can enjoy a meal of local cuisine amid the patio's verdant setting with its resident parrots and turtles. You can also shop for fine jewelry, perfume, liquor, and island artwork, including santos. Open Monday through Saturday 9:00 A.M. to 6:00 P.M. There's a nice mini-mall at 105 Fortaleza that's definitely worth a stop, with masks, artwork, good drinks, and other fun stuff inside. *Olé* (105 Fortaleza; 787-724-2445), two gallery shops at the mall's entrance, has quality paintings, antiques, Panama hats, musical instruments, jewelry, and other artwork. Farther down Fortaleza, **Butterfly People** (152 Fortaleza; 787-723-2432; www.butterflypeople.com) draws international traffic and repeat customers, as much as for its charming cafe as for its famous mounted-butterfly gallery. In fact butterfly collectors from around the world come here to buy the artfully arranged scenes. The compositions are stunning and memorable. The restaurant serves light Puerto Rican fare; lunch is 10:00 A.M. to 6:00 P.M. Monday through Saturday.

Take a right onto San José Street to **Cronopolis** (255 San José; 787-724-1815), a bookstore and music shop with a wide selection of Puerto Rican and Caribbean material. It's also known under its former name, **The Book Store.** Next door is **Cafetería Los Amigos** (253 San José), where you'll find the best sandwiches in San Juan. This old-style cafeteria is favored by locals, makes inexpensive sandwiches and fresh orange juice, and serves up cold beer. Historic articles from Puerto Rican newspapers adorn the walls.

Plaza de Armas

Turn left at San Jose and La Fortaleza to get to **Plaza de Armas,** Old San Juan's main square since the sixteenth century. The plaza is dominated by a fountain surrounded by four statues that represent the four seasons. The statues, replicas of classical Roman sculptures of the gods, are about one hundred years old. The adjacent **Four Seasons Café** has tasty, strong local coffee, croissant sandwiches, and fruit frappes. The cafe is a popular place to drop by for coffee and while away the hours, from the early morning through the late evening. Expect to see neighborhood luminaries such as Tite Curet Alonso (who wrote much of the music that became world famous in the salsa explosion) and Rafael Tufiño (a master artist who came of age in the 1950s with his expressionistic woodcuts of Puerto Rican myths and life, and who today inspires a generation of younger artists).

On the plaza's north side is the **Alcaldía,** San Juan City Hall (787-724-7171). The building was completed in 1789 and resembles Madrid's city hall with its twin turrets, balconies, and inner courtyard. A gallery on

Qué es commonwealth?

This is the question fueling much of the debate within Puerto Rico politics (the rest has a lot to do with a person's general attitude toward the United States and Latin America).

"Commonwealth" is the current political status of Puerto Rico, which was seized by the United States more than 100 years ago during the Spanish-American War. This unique political status is a source of endless debate among Puerto Ricans, and a source of confusion among outsiders.

Puerto Rico is a Spanish-speaking Caribbean island that contains aspects of both a state of the union and a separate nation. Puerto Ricans are U.S.

citizens who receive Social Security and other federal benefits and also have been drafted to fight in U.S. wars. Yet islanders don't pay federal taxes and can't vote in presidential elections.

Supporters say that the current status, officially called Estado Libre Asociado, or "free associated state," is a "bilateral pact" between the United States and Puerto Rico that can only be changed by mutual consent. Opponents, both pro-statehood and pro-independence supporters, denounce Commonwealth as mere window dressing and claim that Puerto Rico's current status is really as a U.S. colony.

the first floor features art exhibits. Open weekdays 8:00 A.M. to 4:00 P.M.; free admission.

Aguadilla En San Juan, or de Aguadilla a San Juan (358 Cruz; 787–722–0578), depending on which sign you read, is more than a souvenir place. It has great homemade crafts, a good collection of Puerto Rican music and instruments, and local goodies and refreshments. A friendly group of people runs the place. During Christmas watch for the *coquito,* Puerto Rico's version of eggnog.

Farther up San José Street are a few more art galleries that are worth a look. Check out the workshop and exhibition space by artist Lysette Lugo.

San Francisco Street, which borders the plaza on its northern side and runs parallel to La Fortaleza Street, is also worth a stroll. Its western end is one of the nicest neighborhoods in the Old City, tree-lined and filled with pastel-colored homes with wooden balconies. Just off the plaza, as San Francisco runs between the two state department buildings, is the sidewalk cafe **Nadine's** (100 San Francisco), with gigantic Marilyn Monroe posters. It's a good spot for fruity rum drinks.

Going east along San Francisco will eventually lead you back to Plaza Colón, but there are a variety of things to see along the way. Peruvian artists have set up shop beside *La Cochera* parking lot (for which the main entrance is around the block on Luna Street). Here you'll find hand-painted, hand-carved furniture, all sorts of colorful little statues, Christmas ornaments, jewelry, and other handicraft items for sale. Check out *La Bombonera* (259 San Francisco; 787–722–0658), an old-style cafeteria that is an Old San Juan institution and still a favorite among locals. In business since 1902, it is open daily from 7:30 A.M. to 5:00 P.M. Look for authentic touches, from the original stained-glass sign in front to the brusque service of the veteran, uniformed waiters. Great Puerto Rican dishes—breakfasts and dinners. *Cafetería Mallorca* (300 San Francisco; 787–724–4607), at the corner of Tanca Street, is another formidable eatery in the Bombonera vein. This is a small restaurant with a local crowd that appreciates its authentic *criollo* cooking. This institution comes highly rated; closed Sunday. At 355 San Francisco is restaurant *La Bella Piazza* (787–721–0396), which presents authentic Italian food in an Old World setting of columns, arches, and a terrace. There is a dazzling array of fresh pastas with imaginative sauces. *Buon appetito!*

Just before Plaza Colón is *Arepas y Mucho Más* (366 San Francisco; 787–724–7776), a little joint that sells tasty Venezuelan *arepas* and a variety that ranges from breakfast to supper. Worth a try. Reggae fans will want to check out the shop next door, *Rastafari* (366 San Sebastián), selling Bob Marley T-shirts, Rasta-style caps, and an interesting collection of reggae, dub, and other Jamaican music. Cash-only transactions, and bartering is acceptable. Near Plaza Colón is *Café Puerto Rico* (208 O'Donnell; 787–724–2281), which serves traditional Puerto Rican food for lunch and dinner.

PLACES TO STAY IN OLD SAN JUAN

Gallery Inn
204 Norzagaray
(787) 722–1808;
www.thegalleryinn.com

Hotel El Convento
100 Cristo
(787) 723–9020 or
(800) 468–2779; www.elconvento.com

Hotel Milano
307 Fortaleza
(787) 729–9050 or
(877) 729–9050;
www.home.coqui.net/hmilano

Wyndham Old San Juan Hotel and Casino
101 Marina
(787) 721–5100 or
(800) 996–3426; www.wyndham.com

PLACES TO EAT IN OLD SAN JUAN

Al Dente
309 Recinto Sur
(787) 723-7303;
www.aldentepr.com

Amadeus
106 San Sebastián
(787) 722-8635

Amanda's Cafe
424 Norzagaray
(787) 722-0187

Ambrosia
250 Cristo
(787) 722-5206

Arepas y Mucho Más
366 San Francisco
(787) 724-7776

Barrachina Café
104 Fortaleza
(787) 725-8239 or
(800) 515-3582;
www.barrachina.com

The Blue
9 Plaza de Mercado
(787) 723-9962

Butterfly People Café
152 Fortaleza
(787) 723-2432;
www.butterflypeople.com

Cafe Berlin
407 San Francisco
(787) 722-5205

Café Bohemio
100 Cristo at
Hotel El Convento
(787) 723-9200

Café la Violeta
56 La Fortaleza
(787) 723-6804

Café Mallorca
300 San Francisco
(787) 724-4607

Café Nispero
100 Cristo at
Hotel El Convento
(787) 723-9236

Café Puerto Rico
208 O'Donnell
(787) 724-2281

Café Seda
157 San Sebastián
(787) 725-4814

Café Tabac
262 Fortaleza
(787) 725-6785

Café Zaguán
359 Tetuan
(787) 724-3476

Cafetería Los Amigos
253 San José

Cafetería Mallorca
300 San Francisco
(787) 724-4607

Cafetería Manolin
258 San Justo
(787) 723-9743

Caribbean Deli
205 Tanca
(787) 725-6695

Carli Café Concierto
Plaza Rafael Carrion
(787) 725-4927

Casa Papyrus
357 Tetuán
(787) 722-3362

Chef Marisoll
Creative Cuisine
202 Cristo
(787) 725-7454

Dársena
100 Brumbaugh at
Wyndham Old San
Juan Hotel
(787) 721-5100

Don Pancho's Bar
253 Tanca

El Batey
101 Cristo
(787) 725-1787

El Buen Samaritano
255 Luna
(787) 721-6184

El Patio de Sam
102 San Sebastián
(787) 723-1149

El Picoteo Tapas Bar
100 Cristo at
Hotel El Convento
(787) 643-1597

El Siglo XX
355 Fortaleza
(787) 724-1849

Friquitín Krugger
52 San José
(787) 723-2474

The Gallery Café
305 Fortaleza
(787) 725-8676

Hard Rock Café
253 Recinto Sur
(787) 724-7625

Il Perugino
105 Cristo
(787) 722-5481

Isla Bonita
100 Paseo Gilberto
Concepcion de Gracia
(787) 724-3912

Jules Restaurant
301 Cruz
(787) 724-6257

La Bella Piazza
355 San Francisco
(787) 721-0396

La Bombonera
259 San Francisco
(787) 722-0658

La Chaumiére
367 Tetuán
(787) 722-3330

La Danza
56 Fortaleza,
corner of Cristo
(787) 723-1642

La Fonda El Jibarito
280 Sol
(787) 725-8375

La Mallorquina
207 San Justo
(787) 722-3261

La Ostra Cosa
154 Cristo
(787) 722-2672

La Querencia
100 de la Cruz
(787) 725-1304

Lupi's Mexican Grill
and Sports Cantina
313 Recinto Sur
(787) 722-1874

Nono's
100 San Sebastián
(787) 725-7819

Panorama Terrace Bar and
Latin Grill
307 Fortaleza at Hotel
Milano
(787) 729-9050

Parrot Club
363 Fortaleza
(787) 725-7370

Patio del Nispero
100 Cristo at
Hotel El Convento
(787) 723-9260

Royal Thai
315 Recinto Sur
(787) 725-8401

Trois Cent Onze
311 Fortaleza
(787) 725-7959

Viet Nam Palace Seafood
Restaurant
332 Recinto Sur
(787) 723-7539

Yukiyu Sushi Bar &
Teppan-Yaki
311 Recinto Sur
(787) 721-0653

San Juan

San Juan is a diverse city made up of distinct districts. Tourists often pour into the Miami Beach–like Condado, where the pastel skyline is set against the Atlantic, and Isla Verde, where condos, hotels, restaurants, and bars along a busy beachfront give the area an almost Las Vegas–like feel.

San Juan is also Río Piedras and Santurce, two cultural and commercial centers often passed over by visitors but beloved by *sanjuaneros*. And there are places within the city, such as the Botanical Gardens or Piñones (an undeveloped beachfront area beyond Isla Verde), that feel as remote from San Juan as the Puerto Rican countryside.

Condado, Isla Verde, Río Piedras, and Santurce, as well as other San Juan districts, offer much for the visitor who wants to go off the beaten path. Although there are many hidden spots along the well-trodden beach areas, visitors with the time should venture into the heart of the city. It's a good place to discover the real Puerto Rico.

Puerta de Tierra

The word on Puerta de Tierra is that it has a sleazy waterfront, mechanic shops, strip clubs, dangerous public-housing projects, and little else. But the truth is that there is much of interest here.

Puerta de Tierra is a sliver of land dominated by the **Muñoz Rivera Park** with wide stone and mosaic walks winding through green rolling hills and blooming gardens. The park is conveniently located across from the **Escambrón Public Beach,** and a walkway connects the two. Two main thoroughfares surround the park, Muñoz Rivera Avenue, which enters San Juan along the Atlantic coast, and Ponce de León Avenue, which exits San Juan. Fernández Juncos Avenue is a two-way street that winds along the bayside waterfront. It goes past the cruise ship docks, then passes a waterfront district.

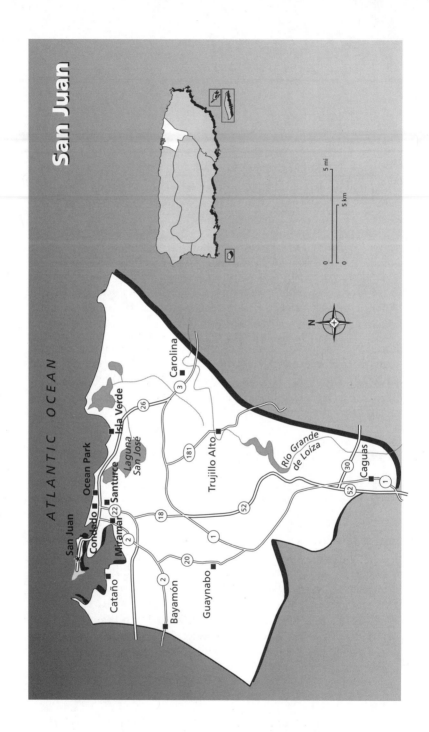

San Juan

ATLANTIC OCEAN

San Juan
Ocean Park
Condado
Isla Verde
Miramar
Santurce
Cataño
Laguna
San José
26
Carolina
3
181
Trujillo Alto
Río Grande
de Loíza
30
Caguas
1
52
52
18
1
22
2
20
Bayamón
2
Guaynabo

N

5 mi
5 km
0
0

The *Caribe Hilton* (San Gerónimo Grounds, Los Rosales Street; 787–721–0303 or 800–724–7500; www.hilton.com) was Puerto Rico's first successful hotel, and it remains one of the island's more profitable properties. Founded by Conrad Hilton in 1949, the Caribe Hilton was the first hotel in Puerto Rico designed to appeal to both business travelers and tourists. The hotel features a private beach, huge exhibition center, Japanese gardens with roaming peacocks, an enviable location, and first-rate bars and restaurants. The circular bar overlooking the pool area is a contender for the best piña colada served on the island, and some locals credit a bartender here with inventing the famous drink in 1957. The restored ruins of *Fort San Gerónimo,* which held back a British attack in 1797, are also located here, on a beautiful mount overlooking the Atlantic. It is owned by the Caribe Hilton and rented for private functions.

Beyond the hotel the first light you come to is a good point of entry for both the Escambrón Public Beach and the Muñoz Rivera Park. The park is often the scene of special events and is filled with activity on weekday mornings. Rollerbladers and skateboarders, as well as joggers and cyclists, find a welcome environment here. The park's *Peace Pavilion* was inaugurated in 1991 by Nobel Peace prize–winner Oscar Arias, the former Costa Rican president who brokered regional peace accords.

Visitors to Escambrón and related facilities use this entrance by going right at the light to get to the public parking. Pedestrians can also enter the public beach area on foot through the car exit beside the Normandie Hotel.

Turning at the light the first thing you see is the *Dumas Restaurant* (Reserve Officer's Beach Club; 787–721–3550), which serves up large portions of hearty seafood dishes with *criollo* flourishes. The back porch is the place to sit, overlooking the crashing surf.

The entire Escambrón Public Beach and adjacent sports complex (built to host the Pan-American Games in the 1960s) is due to undergo a much-needed face-lift through government plans to construct the Park of the New Millennium. At the site, the Sixto Escobar Stadium remains in use. Named after the first Puerto Rican National Boxing Association champion, the stadium hosts track and field and other sporting events, as well as the annual Heineken Jazz Fest. The palm-lined public beach is perfect for a cool dip and hanging a hammock in the shade, but expect crowds, especially on summer or holiday weekends. Outdoor freshwater showers and bathrooms are available, as well as places to barbecue. The more mobile might want to try the restaurant at the end of the public beach, **Escambrón Beach Club & Restaurant** (Escambrón Public Beach; 787–722–4785). Outside there's an open-air beach cafe serving fried food, cold beer, soft drinks, sandwiches, and hamburgers, while formal dining is available inside an air-conditioned restaurant specializing in Puerto Rican and seafood dishes. The place draws crowds all weekend, beginning Friday afternoon. The indoor restaurant features live music and dancing.

Immediately in front of the Dumas Restaurant is a small plaza that overlooks a favored spot for local surfers. The area also attracts local fishermen, both on shore and in boats.

Above the Escambrón entrance, Muñoz Rivera Avenue winds beyond the nondescript condos before coming to great views of grassy, palm-lined bluffs overlooking the surf on the Atlantic side. Across the street you'll see a white wooden shack surrounded by scores of cars. This is **El Hamburger** (402 Muñoz Rivera; 787–721–4269), serving up the best burgers in town, along with the best hot dogs, onion rings, and fries. A late-night favorite of *sanjuaneros*, El Hamburger also attracts the powerful and politically connected from the nearby capitol and the Popular Democratic Party Headquarters during the day.

El Capitolio (Ponce de León; 787–724–8979), Puerto Rico's capitol

Heineken Jazz Fest

*T*he annual **Heineken Jazz Fest,** held each May, is a Latin jazz experience under the Caribbean stars in Sixto Escobar Stadium. Here you can enjoy the region's best talent and other jazz greats at an affordable price in a comfortable environment, with good food and beverages, including the requisite ice-cold Heineken. The festival runs Thursday evening through Sunday evening (tickets $47.50 all four nights, or $18.00 per day). Each year the festival is dedicated to a different honoree. Previous honorees include Tito Puente, Eddie Palmieri, and Mongo Santamaria. Giovanni Hildalgo and David Sanborn are festival regulars. It's a good idea to come early and set up a chair (bring your own or rent one here), but the concerts are never overcrowded. The music rocks—this is Latin jazz you can dance to. For more information on the variety of special package deals available, including airfare, hotels, and concert tickets, contact the Puerto Rico Tourism Company (800–223–6530).

El Capitolio

building, is beyond the National Guard Museum and the nearby Armory. The white, domed, classically structured building built in 1929 is the seat of this U.S. commonwealth's bicameral legislature and boasts a beautiful rotunda where the Puerto Rican constitution is exhibited. A variety of mosaics, statues, and other touches makes it a worthwhile visit. Open 9:00 A.M. to 4:00 P.M. Monday through Friday, with free guided tours available on the hour.

In front of the capitol is a plaza where you'll see a contemporary stone statue of Saint John the Baptist, the patron saint of San Juan. Descend stairs to get to a surprisingly well-kept beach, good for lying in the sun, and good for swimming, too. The beach is called **Peña Pará** by residents of Old San Juan and Puerta de Tierra. The walkway then begins winding around the beginning slopes of the Fort San Cristóbal and then on into Old San Juan.

Leaving Old San Juan along Ponce de León Avenue takes you by several interesting structures clustered outside the historic district beyond the casino, in what is generally considered the last vestige of Old San Juan. The **Carnegie Library** (7 Ponce de León; 787–722–4739), shut down for years because of hurricane damage, is now back and better than ever. It's a nice spot to read international news or local history. Open 9:00 A.M. to 9:00 P.M. Monday and Wednesday, 9:00 A.M. to 5:30 P.M. Tuesday and Thursday, 9:00 A.M. to 5:00 P.M. Friday and Saturday. Also just outside of town is the **Casa de España** (Ponce de León; 787–724–1041), a blue-tiled structure with towers, built in 1935 by the Spanish expatriate community and is now used for a variety of cultural and social occasions. The building was also part of the backdrop in the movie *The Disappearance of García Lorca,* a thriller about the death of the Spanish poet.

Beyond the capitol, you pass through a small retail district. Here you'll find the **Archives and General Library of Puerto Rico** (500 Ponce de Leon; 787–722–2113), run by the Institute of Puerto Rican Culture. Books, video footage, vintage prints, and photographs are all stored here, and visitors can read up on Puerto Rican culture and even view videotapes of local films, including footage taken during the Spanish-American War. The archives are located in a building constructed in 1877. Built as a hospital, it was the last construction by Spanish colonizing the island. Call ahead for hours.

The Beach District:
Condado, Ocean Park, Isla Verde, and Piñones

The **San Geronimo Bridge** into the Condado is a favorite spot, drawing fishermen and swimmers during the day and couples taking romantic walks in the evening. It's easy to see why. The Condado Lagoon pours out to the Atlantic Ocean here, with the ruins of San Gerónimo on one side and the modern skyline of Condado on the other, and the air is always filled with the salty spray of the sea.

A trip across the bridge brings you into bustling, prosperous modernity. The **Condado** is the closest that San Juan gets to Miami Beach—a world of luxury hotels and casinos, fancy retail shops, restaurants, and towering beachfront condominiums.

The Condado is the first in a string of beach districts running from the western edge of Puerta de Tierra to beyond the airport at Piñones, the last undeveloped beachfront property within the metro area's reach. The real attraction for most visitors to the Condado is still the beach, which may pale when compared to other beaches in Rincón or Culebra, but is still quite pretty by stateside standards. A wide, white-sand beach runs for most of the way through the entire beach district. All beaches are public property in Puerto Rico, open to anyone who wants to use them, whether or not they are fronted by a large hotel or condominium.

Ashford Avenue, which begins at the bridge into the Condado, is the sector's main strip, running between the ocean and the Condado Lagoon, with modern towers on both sides. Immediately beyond the bridge is the **Condado Plaza Hotel and Casino** (999 Ashford; 787–721–1000 or 800–624–0420; www.condadoplaza.com), a modern structure sprawling over both sides of Ashford Avenue, connected by a pedestrian walkway above the Condado strip. Like most of San Juan's top-flight hotels, the Condado Plaza offers casinos, restaurants, and nightclubs. These city hotels are as attractive to San Juan residents as to the tourists staying in them. Even if you're renting more modest accommodations, think about checking out the international scene at one of the big hotels located in the Condado and Isla Verde districts. Whether you want great food in an elegant restaurant, a quiet drink at a bar with a live piano player, or a *cuba libre* (rum and coke with lime) and a monster salsa band blasting Puerto Rican classics from the 1970s, chances are you can find it at a city hotel. The atmosphere is especially lively on weekends.

The Condado Plaza's casino is one of the biggest and busiest in San Juan, and its restaurants offer quality food. The bar area usually features live bands.

Next door to the Condado Plaza is the more moderately priced and modest **Regency Hotel** (1005 Ashford; 787–721–0505 or 800–468–2823), which is so close by it almost feels like a part of its larger neighbor. The hotel also houses the well-respected **St. Moritz** restaurant (787–721–0999), known for its pastries and meats.

The tangle of streets on the other side of Ashford Avenue and extending out to the lagoon is full of interesting lodging and dining options. On the corner of Ashford is **Ajilli-Mójili** (1052 Ashford; 787–725–9195), where Chef Mariano Ortiz serves up Puerto Rican cuisine in a gourmet style with revved-up versions of local favorites like *arroz con pollo, fricasé de cabrito,* and even *bacalao*. The **Comfort Inn Tanama Princess** (1 Mariano Ramiréz Bages; 787–724–4160 or 888–826–2621; www.comfortinn.com) is a low-key alternative to the district's big oceanfront hotels.

Visitors can follow the coast of the Condado Lagoon where it winds around to Baldorioty de Castro Expressway. A nice jogging park surrounds it. Kayak rentals are available at the small parking lot at the lagoon's eastern end.

For every hotel on Condado's bustling oceanside drive, there's a guest house just off Ashford Avenue on a quiet, residential street only steps

Top Annual Events

Puerto Rican International Folklore Festival, *early January, Luis A. Ferré Performing Arts Center, Santurce*

Puerto Rico Symphony Orchestra, *January through May, Luis A. Ferré Performing Arts Center, Santurce*

Heineken Jazzfast, *late May, Sixto Escobar Stadium, Puerta de Tierra*

Casals Festival, *early June, Luis A. Ferré Performing Arts Center, Santurce*

San Juan Bautista Day, *June 23, San Juan beaches*

San Juan Cinemafest, *mid-October, San Juan*

Bacardi Arts Festival, *early November, Cataño*

away. Many of these places are still within a block of the beach and the major hotels, yet they cost significantly less. Many have pools, friendly service, and comfortable rooms. More importantly, they often offer a more intimate experience of Puerto Rico that brings visitors in contact with everyday Puerto Ricans.

Caruso Restaurant (1104 Ashford; 787–723–6876) is an elegant Italian restaurant serving gourmet dinners; reservations are required. Magdalena, which swings away from Ashford through much of the rest of the Condado before merging back into it, has some nice restaurants, too. *Ramiro's* (1106 Magdalena; 787–721–9049) is considered one of the finest restaurants on the island, with the personal cuisine of owner/chef Jesús Ramiro, described as one of the island's most creative chefs. Reservations recommended.

The *Atlantic Beach Hotel* (1 Vendig; 787–721–6900), which caters to the gay community, is a well-kept property with a deck bar overlooking the ocean and *Indiana John's Restaurant,* with deli and American menu. The nearby *Alelí by the Sea* (1125 Seaview; 787–725–5313) is a family-run guest house that has a sundeck overlooking the beach. There are nine renovated rooms with shared use of parking, living room, and kitchen.

The *San Juan Marriott Hotel & Stellaris Casino* (1309 Ashford; 787–722–7000 or 800–288–9290; www.marriotthotels.com) has a nice casino, good live entertainment in its main lounge, and good restaurants. Its simple construction has an openness that seems to allow the sea and beach into the hotel. Across the street, on the rooftop of the *Diamond Palace Hotel & Casino* (55 Condado; 787–721–0810 or 800–468–2014), is *Martino's* (787–722–5256), serving good Northern Italian cuisine in a glass-topped penthouse with a wonderful view.

El Canario operates four quality lodgings in the Condado that strive to give their customers a laid-back, Caribbean guest-house experience (all can be reached at 800–533–2649; www.canariohotels.com). Besides *El Canario by the Lagoon* (4 Clemenceau; 787–722–5058), there's *El Canario Inn* (1317 Ashford; 787–722–3861), a cozy bed-and-breakfast. Around the corner on the ocean is *El Canario by the Sea* (4 Condado; 787–722–8640), within steps of the beach. In front of the Marriott, half a block off Ashford, is *Casa del Caribe: A Tropical Bed and Breakfast* (57 Caribe; 787–722–7139), a sleepy guest house with a nice pool, patio, and plenty of shady trees.

The Condado district is one of the finer places to eat in San Juan, and this section of Ashford is one reason why. *Via Appia* (1350 Ashford;

787–725–8711) is a sidewalk cafe serving great Italian food at good prices. The quality rivals that of much more expensive establishments. From the pizza to the veal scaloppini to the sausage and pepper sandwiches, this place delivers. Pitchers of sangría or cold beer entice diners to linger and enjoy the people-watching.

Right next door is *Salud* (1350 Ashford; 787–722–0911), a health-food store with a small cafe serving vegetarian fare. *Il Grottino* (1372 Ashford; 787–723–0499) has one of the island's largest international wine selections and serves fresh pasta and appetizers in an elegant dining room or on an open-air patio. *Zabó Cocina Creativa* (14 Candina; 787–725–9494) combines a dining room in a restored turn-of-the-century country house and a bar in its renovated carriage house. It's a beautiful spot, and the food is as inventive as its name suggests: a fusion of Caribbean, Italian, and Asian flavors. The thing to do here is to "graze" on assorted appetizers that you share with your companions. *The Big Apple Deli* (1407 Ashford; 787–725–6345) is a New York–style deli and bakery with corned beef and pastrami sandwiches, bagels, and knishes like they do back in 'da boroughs.

Ashford Avenue turns into McLeary Street as Condado turns into *Ocean Park* and the sky-rise condos give way to elegant split-level beach homes interspersed with Art Deco stone beauties from the 1930s. The beach scene here is decidedly more low-key than neighboring Condado and Isla Verde. The sandy, palm-lined *beach at Ocean Park,* fronted by large homes and an occasional guest house, is a favorite spot for locals. Here you can see all the way from the high-rise–ringed beach of Condado on one side to the palm-fringed beach at the start of Piñones.

Staying in this section may offer the most complete guest-house experience, and the beach may actually be the nicest in San Juan. The young and beautiful come here to play paddleball, windsurf, or just look good. Ocean Park also draws gays and lesbians, who provide a core market for the area's guest houses. Two favorites are *L'Habitation* (1957 Italia; 787–727–2499) and *Ocean Park Beach Inn* (3 Elena; 787–728–7418).

There are two restaurants on McLeary that are neighborhood staples. *Dunbar's Pub* (1954 McLeary; 787–728–2920) serves a surprisingly wide range of tasty food, with nightly specials around a theme like sushi or Mexican. The bar, which draws a lively crowd, is the other attraction here. Also try *Kasalta's Bakery* (1966 McLeary; 787–727–7340), a fine Cuban-style bakery and deli that opens at 6:00 A.M.

The Ocean Walk Guesthouse (1 Atlantic Place; 787–728–0855) has comfortable rooms, suites, and apartments for rent. There's a pool and a nice cafe/bar in an open patio fronting the beach. The establishment caters to a largely gay crowd, but the cafe draws a wide mix of locals and tourists, including the expatriate community. It's about the best place to get a beer at the beach in San Juan. Friendly service by Pablo, Sally, and the others, as well as the reasonably priced food, is also a draw. The beach in front of the guest house is a favorite of San Juan's youth. The cafe's diverse crowd is frequently quite entertaining. The place really comes alive on sunny holiday weekend afternoons.

The atmosphere is a bit more laid back in front of the **Numero Uno Guest House** (1 Santa Ana; 787–726–5010). This is a wonderful spot with a variety of comfortable rooms and a fine restaurant/bar, **Pamela's Caribbean Cuisine** (787–726–5010). The restaurant has a Pan-Caribbean focus and serves up some of the best food in San Juan: from jerk chicken sandwiches to the fresh catch of the day with a Caribbean chutney. **Hostería del Mar** (1 Tapia; 787–727–3302 or 800–242–2767) is another beachfront guest house with a restaurant that serves health food.

The **Ultimate Trolley Beach** is a big white arch at the border of Ocean Park and Punta Las Marias. **Barbosa Park,** which is across a narrow street from the beach here, is filled with soccer players as island aficionados gather to do their thing on weekends. The track here is one of the city's top sites for rollerblading and jogging.

San Juan Night Holiday

*A*t midnight on June 23, Puerto Rico goes crazy—nowhere more so than in its capital of San Juan. Everybody, from parents with screaming kids to the most ardent lovers, hits the beach at night and then dives into the surf at midnight. This is la noche de San Juan, or the Night of San Juan.

The tradition dates back to the earliest days of Spanish rule and calls for people to walk backwards into the ocean and turn over backwards three times in the surf in a tribute to John the Baptist, the patron of San Juan and two other Puerto Rican towns.

The exercise is also thought to bring good luck for the entire year.

There's much music and drinking before, during, and after the main event, which is often one of the biggest parties around. In San Juan people usually get to the beach early, armed with radios and coolers. Hotels offer special overnight packages and top-name acts.

A nighttime beach party in San Juan is certainly magical, since beaches are usually considered unsafe after dark. If you're visiting Puerto Rico on June 23, take advantage of a nocturnal sojourn to the beach.

The beach itself looks pretty good today but still hasn't bounced back fully from 1989's Hurricane Hugo. The street that winds along the beachfront contains the last guest houses until the district of Isla Verde.

Beyond the Ultimate Trolley Beach lies **Punta Las Marías.** The beach here is almost nonexistent, and the area is best known for its stretch of restaurants on the way from Ocean Park to Isla Verde. Loiza Street is the main artery into Isla Verde. For the young crowd there's *St. Mick's Irish Pub and Restaurant* (2473 Loiza; 787–727–6620), a typical Irish pub offering a variety of beer, food, classic rock, and televised sports. *Mango's Café* (2421 Laurel; 787–727–9328) maintains a Caribbean focus, from its jerk chicken to its vegetarian Rasta burgers. Wide selection of sandwiches, very few entrees. *Che's Restaurante Argentino* (35 Caoba; 787–726–7202) serves Argentine and Italian specialties but is known for its excellent *churrasco* steaks.

The initial journey into Isla Verde is also marked by fine restaurants. *Casa Dante* (39 Isla Verde; 787–726–7310) is the place to try *mofongo,* a mashed plantain dish that is one of Puerto Rican cuisine's real triumphs. They serve it here with whatever you want, from a delicious *churrasco* to shrimp in a tomato sauce to a chicken consommé. This family favorite also serves up a tasty sangría.

Isla Verde, or green island, bears little vestige of its namesake condition, having grown into a concrete jungle two decades ago. Technically part of the municipality of Carolina, Isla Verde lies between San Juan proper and the Luis Muñoz Marín International Airport. Today it is a main boulevard lined with high-rise luxury condos and hotels, fast food joints and restaurants, and rental car agencies in small strip-malls.

Isla Verde has the fattest beach in metro San Juan, and water sports from kayaks to jet skis to parasails are available. The view from the beach is decidedly better than from the main drag, Isla Verde Avenue. The asphalt parking lots that front the hotels and condos on Isla Verde Avenue give way to grassy plazas and gardens and well-landscaped pool areas. Like elsewhere in metro San Juan, tourists and locals interact on the beach.

Off the beaten path there are still some finds. The *Casa de Playa Beach Hotel* (4851 Isla Verde; 787–728–9779 or 800–916–2272) is one beachfront guest house that is on a quiet stretch of beach. The hotel also runs a friendly, open-air beachfront bar.

Calle Tartak, farther along the strip, is a good place to enter the beach, as access is difficult through the stretch of hotels and private condos that follow. On the beachfront here is the *Hungry Sailor* (Tartak;

787–791–3017), a reasonably priced pub with friendly service, cable television, a jukebox, and a nice open-air porch.

The old Sands Hotel, now known as the **Inter-Continental San Juan Resort and Casino** (5961 Isla Verde; 787–791–6100 or 800–443–2009; www.inerconti.com), is known for its live shows, including *Legends,* with its impersonations of Hollywood and musical stars. It's also home to **Ruth's Chris Steak House** (787–791–6100), serving up the same delicious steaks as it does everywhere else it's located.

Wyndham El San Juan Hotel & Casino (6063 Isla Verde; 787–791–1000 or 800–468–2818; www.wyndham.com) was refurbished in 1999. From its high-energy casino to its dark, mahogany lobby to the circular bar and huge chandelier, El San Juan is a class act. The live entertainment in the hotel's disco, **Babylon** (787–766–7700), helps draw an exciting crowd; this is one of the best spots to take in San Juan's intoxicating nightlife. On Wednesday nights the tango returns to El San Juan, with well-dressed couples and professional dancers sashaying beneath the chandeliers. Babylon is open Thursday through Saturday nights from 9:00 P.M.

Cheaper digs can be found at the **Green Isle Inn** (36 Uno; 787–726–4330 or 800–677–8860), a block away from the beach. The rooms are equipped with kitchenettes, and the property has two pools, a bar, and a restaurant. Another affordable option at the end of Isla Verde Beach is **Hotel La Playa** (6 Amapola; 787–791–1115 or 800–791–9626; www.hotellaplaya.com), which has a big, round bar, La Playa Lounge, overlooking the ocean. **Sonny's Ocean View Terrace,** at the Hotel Empress (2 Amapola; 787–791–3083), has an enviable location on a covered dock over the ocean.

Isla Verde is also home to the **Club Gallístico de Puerto Rico** (787–791–1557), at the intersection of Gobernadores and Isla Verde Avenues. The stadium is Puerto Rico's premier spot to watch the sport of cock fighting (Saturdays, November through August). The sport may offend some, as the cocks are allowed to brutally battle each other (sometimes until the death), but it is a popular and long-standing island sport and tradition. Several similar *galleras* are located throughout the island. Bets are also made on the fights, of course, and an honor system ensures payment. All the shouting over bets and money lends the *gallera* something of the hysteria of a Wall Street trading floor.

Next door, at the Club Gallístico Annex, the good service and fine Cuban food of the **Metropol Restaurant** (787–791–4046) draws a steady clientele. It's one of their several full-service restaurants throughout the metro area.

Trivia

*In 1978 Karl Wallenda, of the **Flying Wallendas,** fell ten stories to his death while attempting a high-wire cross between two hotels in San Juan.*

The Ritz-Carlton San Juan Hotel and Casino (6961 Route 187; 787–253–1700 or 800–241–3333; www.ritzcarlton.com) is an elegant marble-white structure located around the bend from the Isla Verde strip on the way to Piñones and Loíza. A casino and a variety of restaurants are among the reasons to come here.

Located beyond Isla Verde and the airport, **Piñones** is the last untamed coastline in the San Juan area. As you cross the bridge over the Boca de Cangrejo Bay and into Piñones, the scale of things changes dramatically. The tallest objects in this skyline are palm trees, not condominiums. Populated by groves of palm trees and sea grapes, Piñones is still off-limits to big resort operators because most of its interior is wetlands. **Torrecilla Baja** is Puerto Rico's largest mangrove swamp, a dense woodland area ribboning along this area.

By day, Piñones is visited by beachcombers exploring miles of sparsely developed coastline. By night, Piñones turns into one of the city's liveliest and least-expensive entertainment alternatives and takes on a distinctly Dominican cast, with live music playing in many of the open-air clubs.

The coastal road is dotted with stands selling all manner of fried delicacies, or *frituras,* many of which have a distinctly African flavor, a result of the slaves who fled here in the 1800s to escape their Spanish rulers. Visitors acclimated to the glitzy Condado/Isla Verde tourism axis might feel as though they've entered a time warp in Piñones. Here the smell of roasting *pinchos,* the Puerto Rican shish kebab, hangs heavy in the air as does the smell of wood-burning fires, tended by women making finger foods such as *bacalaítos* (codfish fritters), *alcapurrias* (deep-fried mashed plantain-and-yuca cylinders stuffed with crabmeat or beef), and *piónono* (a fritter made with yellow plátano, cup-shaped to hold beef, chicken, or crab stuffing, and fried).

This strip of beaches winds along some ten miles of road to a bluff called **Vacía Talega,** a once infamous lovers' lane with a picture-postcard view.

Many of the open-air bars are owned by and cater to immigrants from the neighboring Dominican Republic, though Puerto Ricans and visitors from elsewhere are made to feel welcome. One of the most popular spots in Piñones is **The Reef Bar & Grill** (787–791–1374), at your first turn-off to the left after the bridge. It is one of the few places here owned by a gringo, Bob Bishop, a former NFL player who is easily recognizable behind the bar. Shaded by a tall pine tree and perched atop a rising bluff, The Reef offers one of the most dazzling views of San Juan, especially at night when the distant lights from row after row of high-rises glitter off the water. It is especially well suited for couples and tourists who don't want to venture too deep into the thicket of dimly lit nightclubs. Sunday evenings it features live music played by competent cover groups.

Adjacent to The Reef is another favored local, *La Terraza,* which serves up *criollo* food such as the house specialty, Mami's Mangú. A variation of the Puerto Rican *mofongo, mangú* is the staple food of the Dominican Republic: boiled and mashed plantains deliciously seasoned with garlic and chicken broth. Mami, the proprietor, comes from a clan of twenty-four brothers and sisters back in the Dominican Republic. La Terraza also features some of the area's best live music on Saturdays and Sundays, including top-notch performers of merengue, Dominican dance music, and its countryside counterpart, *bachata.* Sundays are especially lively, as Juan Castillo and his down-home style merengue band takes the stage. Possessed of a delirious voice and Cheshire cat smile, Castillo, a.k.a. "the Prince of the Accordion," is supported by an electric bass and ample percussion. Dancing is nonstop from 4:00 to 9:00 P.M.

Farther along the main road is *La Pocita #2,* which probably packs more decibels per square inch than any other club on the island. The atmosphere, with wall-to-wall dancing, is more like a high-school house party than a high-tech nightclub. The droopy stucco ceilings suggests the humidity level inside—a result of all those bumping bodies. If you can take the heat, you'll be treated to some uncensored dance-floor antics. Open Wednesday through Sunday.

There are a dozen or so smaller establishments within a half mile of La Pocita #2, typical of which is *La Vereda,* a clapboard and corrugated-tin structure decorated with Christmas lights, some red and gold tinsel, and shrines to the Santería god Chang, a counterpart to the Catholic icon Saint Barbara. No potted palm trees or other pretensions here, just cold beer, a cement dance floor, occasional live music, and a mature crowd. The retiree-age owners, Rey and Margarita, have a knack for making their patrons feel at home. A handwritten sign on the bandstand reads "Women not permitted to dance together," though the rule appears to be frequently flouted and rarely enforced. Stop in if you want to see real people unwind in an atmosphere that's cozy but not overcrowded. Next door is *Bebo's,* a nightclub catering to a gay and lesbian crowd.

Feel free to try the many seafood restaurants in the area, including *Soleil Beach Club* (787–726–7614), on the beach road off Route 187 right beyond the Pulpo Loco. Soleil has everything, from seafood to pasta to *churrasco.* The beachfront bar-restaurant is open evenings during the week and all day and night on weekends. A worthwhile stop.

The area also contains several famed surfing spots, the most well-known being **Aviones,** or Airplanes, because it marks the approximate spot where departing planes veer off to the north. (The only road sign is a broken surf board affixed to a shack on Route 187.) **Vacía Talega Bay,** at the end of Piñones, is a wonderful white-sand beach with palm trees and rockless waters.

Miramar

eyond the bridge to Condado lies **Miramar,** a still-fashionable neighborhood whose shabbier sectors are looking worse. There are, in effect, two Miramars: the one of luxury condominiums squeezed between Ponce de León Avenue and Baldorioty del Castro passing by the Condado Lagoon, and the other between Ponce de León and the harborside Muñoz Rivera Expressway.

Right at the bridge are San Juan's two major marinas: **Club Naútico of San Juan** (Fernández Juncos; 787–722–0177) and **San Juan Bay Marina** (Fernández Juncos; 787–721–8086). Private boat charters and group fishing trips are available.

You'll find some of the area's best deep-sea fishing right off San Juan's coast. The ocean floor here drops off dramatically, meaning big game fish are in the immediate vicinity.

It's easy to find local sports fishermen complaining about the decline in big-game fish, but the fish are still abundant, and the area continues to live up to its name, "Blue Marlin Alley." Blue marlin are most prevalent in late summer, when the Club Naútico runs a world-famous marlin competition. The area also has white marlin, yellowfin and blackfin tuna, sailfish, wahoo, and dorado, or dolphinfish.

It's a quick twenty-minute ride through San Juan Bay and out into the Atlantic to prime marlin grounds. It's literally possible to bag a big game fish in the morning and be back at dock in early afternoon. Two miles off the coast the sea floor plunges to depths of 600 feet, and 45 miles out is the awesome **Puerto Rican Trench,** with a depth of 28,000 feet.

By the way, a fishing trip is worth taking just for the view of Old San Juan and El Morro from this vantage point.

Heading out of Old San Juan down what is now Fernández Juncos Avenue you'll pass through one of Miramar's seedier districts. Immediately after curving past some of the more notorious establishments, the road winds through well-heeled neighborhoods with massive trees and stately turn-of-the-century houses intermingled with Art Deco walkups and modern condos. *Murphy's Camera & Video Repair* (909 Fernández Juncos; 787–725–1565) is a good place to know—it's one of the few camera repair shops in Puerto Rico.

Heading back through Miramar toward Old San Juan along Ponce de León Avenue is worth your while. The area on the right side, overlooking the Condado Lagoon, is one of the prettiest parts of metro San Juan. There are also several fine restaurants here. *Augusto's Cuisine* (801 Ponce de León in the Hotel Excelsior; 787–725–7700) whips up mostly French-inspired, European gourmet. Formal and expensive, but worth the price. Down the street at *Godfather's* (1426 Ponce de León; 787–721–1556), high-quality Dominican and Puerto Rico favorites such as *mofongo relleno* and *mangú* are sold at dirt-cheap prices. Also in Miramar is the *Fine Arts Cinema* (654 Ponce de León; 787–721–4288), which shows U.S. independent and European releases. The *panaderia,* or bakery (which also serves deli food and even full-course Puerto Rican, Cuban, and Spanish meals), at the corner is a good bet, as is the open-air cafe across the street. *Chayote* (603 Miramar in the Olimpo Court Hotel; 787–724–0600) is a favorite of San Juan's elite, with chef Alfredo Ayala serving up Caribbean gourmet. Ayala combines *criollo* cooking with French, Indian, African, Spanish, and Central American cuisines. This restaurant is a "can't miss." Closed Sunday and Monday.

Santurce

eyond Miramar lies *Santurce,* with its traditional downtown shopping area. To many Puerto Ricans it is still the heart and soul of San Juan. To the uninitiated this whole stretch through Santurce may be frustrating, since directions are given by the stops to a trolley that stopped running decades ago. Stop 18, for example, is at the intersection of Route 2, or Kennedy Avenue, with Ponce de León and Fernández Juncos. Also, while lack of street signs is an islandwide problem, it reaches ridiculous heights in Santurce. Even attractions such as the Museum of Contemporary Puerto Rican Art are unmarked.

Many locals come here to shop, others come here to work, and nearly everybody comes to eat. The area is loaded with *fondas* serving tasty *criollo* food. *Fondas* are restaurants frequented by the locals; family-run, they serve meals in a homey atmosphere. For island visitors, they offer the opportunity for tasty food, great prices, and wonderful ambience. There are open-air cafeterias featuring cold beer and loud jukeboxes. The area off Fernández Juncos, immediately preceding the towering sky-blue pro-statehood New Progressive Party Headquarters, is on the rise. Many of the homes are Art Deco gems that are being restored by new owners. Beyond the all-blue building of the pro-statehood party is a pink U.S. Postal Branch. To the left is Pav, a hospital, one of San Juan's best.

Continue down Fernández Juncos to get to **Sacred Heart University (Colegio Universitario Sagrada Corazón),** two blocks over on the other side of Ponce de León Avenue. If you're driving, take the left turn before the bridge into Hato Rey and then turn right at the Patio Shop. Pedestrians should get off at the bus stop before or after the curb and walk toward the university. Do not expect street signs in this neighborhood. The Patio Shop, half a block away on Fernández Juncos, is your best signpost, unless you're a local who knows it as Stop 25.

The university's pretty campus is best known for its small but well-done **Museum of Contemporary Puerto Rican Art** (Barat Building, Sacred Heart University; 787–268–0049). Here you'll find a fine permanent collection and excellent changing exhibits. Open 9:00 A.M. to 5:00 P.M. Monday through Friday, Saturday 10:00 A.M. to 4:00 P.M. Free admission.

Beyond the university the residential neighborhood spreads out over a hill toward the tough Barrio Obrero neighborhood. **La Casita Blanca** (351 Tapia; 787–726–5501) makes the area worth a trip. This is the most renowned *fonda* in San Juan. It serves reasonably priced local cuisine in a funky, Puerto Rican country-house setting, complete with an outdoor patio. This place packs them in and has received notices in *Gourmet* magazine and the *New York Times*. Look for stewed goat and other delicacies.

Once San Juan's premier commercial east–west corridor, Ponce de León Avenue is still the place for a number of the city's most popular nightclubs. Santurce's club scene runs the gamut, including straight and gay, "techno" and Top 40; **Warehouse** (1851 Ponce de León; 787–726–3337) and **Asylum** (1420 Ponce de León; 787–723–3258) are both popular with the young and hip and feature a lot of Latin pop. Both clubs are open Thursday through Sunday. Admission varies from $5.00 to $25.00, depending on the act. Sundays are traditionally gay night. **Stargate** (1 Roberto Todd Avenue; 787–725–4664) has a futuristic decor; open

José Ferrer

Thursday through Sunday nights till 4:00 A.M. This club replaced the former Egipto but remains just as popular for dancing, with its mix of Latin and gringo music.

The patch of clubs dotting de Diego Avenue just east of the performing arts center is heavily Dominican. **Music People** (318 de Diego; 787–724–2123) is a slightly upscale nightclub catering to a crowd that is mature but far from mundane. Adib, lead singer for the merengue group Conjunto Quisqueya that topped the D.R. hit charts in the 1970s and 1980s, is the club's master of ceremonies and often greets guests personally. On Thursdays, Music People pays tribute to a local performing artist, who reciprocates by improvising for the audience. Friday and Saturday nights the club's owner, Bernie Vazques, takes the stage. Merengue, *bachata,* and salsa are the rhythms of choice. Casual attire is accepted, although no jeans. Expect a modest cover charge ($5.00 to $10.00). Valet parking available.

Within half a block of Music People are several smaller, quirkier alternatives. The **Tía María Liquor Store** (326 de Diego), a few storefronts down, can be best described as an alternative bar for Puerto Rican men who prefer to keep their lifestyle choices under wraps. Local professionals and civil servants unwind after work and check their machismo at the front door. Across the street from Music People is **Margie's Little Professional Cocktail Lounge**—but don't let the name and the red lights mislead you. The women behind the bar will let you *dance* with them only for the price of a drink. Mellow but not melancholy, Margie's is typical of many Dominican pubs that cater to expatriate men who far outnumber their countrywomen in Puerto Rico. Next door to Margie's is **El Pollito #2,** a Puerto Rican–style hole-in-the-wall with cold beer and *criollo* food that manages to draw a lively crowd most Thursday and Friday afternoons and evenings. Occasional live music can be found there, usually *plena,* the spirited music born in the southern coast city of Ponce.

Further along Ponce de León Avenue is the Europa Center and the **Luis A. Ferré Performing Arts Center** (corner of Ponce de León and De Diego; 787–725–7334 or 787–725–7338), also known as **Bellas Artes.** The center was built in 1981 to host theatrical, musical, and other cultural events. A winner of architectural awards, the complex houses three theaters. If you're going to be in town, it's a good idea to check out what's happening here during your stay, since the center hosts every-thing from theater to opera to concerts by top Latin and U.S. perform-ers. It's also the home of the San Juan Symphony Orchestra. In early June the **Pablo Casals Festival** takes place here, attracting talented classical musicians from around the world.

The area between Ponce de León Avenue and Baldoriority de Castro, running from Calle Canals to the Metro movie house, is the neighbor-hood in which the **Santurce Marketplace** is found. The market itself is a great place to dine on local food or stock up on fresh fruits and veg-etables. The marketplace vendors also serve up fresh fruit frappes and other tropical drinks. There are also all sorts of other items for sale, from *Santería* (a Caribbean mix of Roman Catholicism and African religions) and religious artifacts to classic musical recordings.

The neighborhood also features several restaurants that showcase live bands on weekend nights. The area has become a favorite happy-hour spot for *sanjuaneros,* especially on Thursday and Friday evenings. Crowds thread the narrow streets, drinking cold beer and eating *empanadillas* or barbecued *pínchos,* and moving to the music, which seems to come from everywhere. Popular beers include Medalla, a light Puerto Rican brew, and Presidente, a heartier brew from the Dominican Republic.

Directly behind the marketplace, **El Popular** (205 Popular) is a no-frills restaurant that serves good, cheap food during the day. Next door, **Com-pay Cheo** (103 Capital) has live music on Wednesday through Saturday nights. **Carnicería Restaurant Díaz** (319 Orbeta, corner Dos Her-manos; 787-723-1903) has the feel of a neighborhood market and sells all sorts of drinks (try the fresh coconut juice) and Puerto Rican food, from *morcilla* sausage to fried codfish. It's a good place to base yourself while enjoying the weekend streetfest.

Across the street, **Restaurant Don Telfo** (180 Dos Hermanos; 787-724-5752) is a sit-down restaurant with reasonably priced Puerto Rican food and a great ambience with high ceilings, a mahogany bar, and a wall filled with photos of both famous and obscure satisfied cus-tomers. Next door, **El Pescador** (178 Dos Hermanos) may be one of the finest seafood restaurants in San Juan. The small restaurant is open Tuesday through Sunday from 11:00 A.M. to 6:00 P.M. Because of the restaurant's popularity, it's difficult to get a table from noon to 2:00 P.M.; try in the late afternoon.

American Vegetable Gourmet Shop (176 Dos Hermanos, 787-723-3299) is the retail outlet of this produce wholesaler. The store has a wonderful selection of Italian, Mexican, and Spanish produce, from fresh *nogales* (an edible cactus) and handmade tortillas to basil and plum tomatoes. If you're cooking in San Juan, this is the place to stock up on ingredients.

A nice vegetarian restaurant one block east of the marketplace is **Sabores Al Natural** (209 Canals; 787–722–4631). Open Monday through Thursday 11:00 A.M. to 5:00 P.M., Friday 11:00 A.M. to 8:30 P.M., and Saturday noon to 7:30 P.M.

Teatro Metro (1255 Ponce de León; 787–722–0465) is a top-flight movie house showing current-run hits. It also hosts the annual **Puerto Rico International Film Festival** and **San Juan Cinemafest,** held in October. The movie house lobby has photos of how the place (and Santurce) looked in its 1930s heyday. Next door is **Eros,** a popular nightclub that draws gays, lesbians, and straights with its DJ-ed salsa and house music (1257 Ponce de León; 787–722–1131).

Farther down Ponce de León Avenue, in an area known as Stop 15, is another row of Dominican-run pool halls and dance spots, including **El Merendero Sport Center,** which stands out thanks to the green, hand-painted coconuts adorning the facade. The front half of the Merendero is an open-air sports bar with pool tables and big-screen televisions, while the back serves as a restaurant and, on weekends, a discotheque that features quality bands from the Dominican Republic. Attire is come-as-you-are, and drinks are modestly priced.

Now open at 299 de Diego is the new **Museo de Arte de Puerto Rico** (787–977–6277). Outside, the building is 1920s neo-classical, but inside the galleries have cutting-edge technology. This five-story complex houses important works by *puertorriqueño* artists, a gallery designed for children, workshops for classes, and a 400-seat theater. A lush garden covers five acres. **Pikayo** restaurant (787–721– 6194) is here too, with Chef Wilo Benet blending French, Caribbean, and California cuisines. The museum is open Tuesday through Sunday 10:00 A.M. to 5:00 P.M., and Wednesday til 8:00 P.M. Adults $5.00, children and seniors $3.00.

Hato Rey

eyond Santurce, Fernández Juncos meets Muñoz Rivera Avenue as it turns into San Juan's "Golden Mile" banking district—a line of high-rise office towers home to some of the island's biggest names in finance and law.

Hato Rey's financial district keeps the sector lively throughout the day and well into the night. Fine restaurants are found on Ponce de León Avenue and on Franklin Delano Roosevelt Avenue into Puerto Nuevo. O'Neill Street, right off the Muñoz Rivera, one block before FDR Avenue, is also full of great restaurants. Domenech Avenue is another mecca.

Restaurants specializing in just about every major cuisine in the world operate in this sector, and many are among the best in their class on the island. Four of the best Middle Eastern restaurants in the city are located here: *Jerusalem Restaurant* (1-G O'Neill; 787-764-3265), *Tierra Santa* (284 Roosevelt; 787-754-6865), *El Cairo* (352 Ensenada; 787-273-7140) and *Al Salám* (239 Roosevelt; 787-751-6296). All serve fine Middle Eastern food in comfortable settings and feature belly dancing on weekend evenings.

Hato Rey also boasts some of the finest Mexican food. *Frida's* (128 Domenech; 787-763-4827) is especially recommended, both for its food and its rustic colonial atmosphere. An unusual ethnic mix is found in the food served at *El Zipperle* (352 Roosevelt; 787-751-4335); German and Spanish flavors combine here. This well-recommended restaurant is popular and expensive. Two Chinese restaurants, *Yuan* (255 Ponce de León; 787-766-0666) and *The Yum Yum Tree* (131 Roosevelt; 787-753-7743), draw Hato Rey execs for power lunches.

La Cueva del Chicken Inn (507 Ponce de León; 787-753-1306) has been an Hato Rey favorite for decades, renowned for its pizza, fried chicken, and barbecued skirt steak (*churrasco*). The domed, white stucco interior hasn't been fashionable in decades, but it's as cool and dark as its name implies, and the food is wonderful.

The hot spot for night life is *San Juan Chateau* (9 Chardon, 787-751-2000), considered the primo place locally for salsa and merengue!

There's much more than food and money in Hato Rey. As you enter the district along Muñoz Rivera Avenue, you can see the *Martí Coll Linear Park* (787-763-0568), a boardwalk along a mangrove canal that runs from the financial district to San Juan's *Central Park* (787-722-1646). Walkways and bicycle paths here are used by walkers and joggers. Central Park has facilities for tennis, jogging, baseball, and other activities.

Galería Botello (314 Roosevelt; 787-754-7430; www.botello.com) was founded by sculptor Angel Botella in Old San Juan, but the relocated gallery has thrived in Hato Rey as a showcase for contemporary Puerto Rican art.

The district is also home to **Plaza las Américas** (Roosevelt; 787–767–1525), the Caribbean's largest mall, drawing shoppers from across the Caribbean. The mall is also on many tourists' itineraries, not only for shopping but for its restaurants, movies, and art exhibits.

Right across the street is the **Hiram Bithorn Stadium** (787–765–5000), an outdoor baseball park, and the **Roberto Clemente Coliseum** (787–781–2258), an indoor sports complex. Puerto Rico has its own professional baseball and basketball teams that use these facilities, and they are also used for track and field and volleyball tournaments. The stadiums also host concerts, festivals, traveling amusement parks, and fairs.

Behind the stadium and coliseum is the **Muñoz Marín Park** (787–763–0568), with picnic areas, bicycle and jogging paths, miniature lakes, and beautiful gardens. The park's main entrance is on Piñero Avenue. The park also has an auditorium that gives regular presentations on the island's flora and fauna, and an open-air amphitheater that hosts reggae, pop, and jazz concerts at night.

Down Roosevelt and Piñero Avenues lies the Puerto Nuevo district, which has its own fair share of fine restaurants. **Fishes and Crabs** (301

Play Ball!

*I*f you fly into Puerto Rico at night, you'll see baseball stadiums illuminating the sky in every direction, a testament to Puerto Ricans' love of the game. Nowhere is this love more in evidence than during Puerto Rico's winter league baseball, played between November and March at **Hiram Bithorn** and stadiums across the island. The games are played on weekend nights and weekend afternoons between teams such as the Santurce Crabbers (787–274–0240 or 787–274–0247), the San Juan Senators (787–754–1300), and the Mayaguez Indians (787–834–5211).

The baseball played here is the real thing. Texas Rangers slugger Juan "Igor" González, brothers Sandy and Roberto Alomar, and Carlos Baerga are among the major-league U.S. stars who enjoy playing in front of their hometown crowd to stay in shape during the U.S. off-season. Recent comebacks by both Darrell Strawberry and Dwight Gooden were preceded by stints playing winter ball in Puerto Rico.

There are palm trees outside center field and piña coladas served in the stands. Ticket prices are less than $5.00, and cold beers are $1.50. Instead of hot dogs and pretzels, expect to see fried chicken and crab turnovers.

The play-offs are especially exciting, as fans bring various percussion instruments and perform rumbas to cheer their team to victory.

Matadero; 787–781–6570) and *Casa del Mar* (435 Andalucia; 787–782–3594) are two long-standing seafood restaurants that are favorites among locals. Casa del Mar serves until very late in the evening and often has live Latin jazz, especially on weekends.

Río Piedras

R ío Piedras is home to the University of Puerto Rico, as well as the Río Piedras Marketplace, two worthwhile reasons to come here.

The *University of Puerto Rico* (787–764–0000; www.upr.edu) campus is a sprawling, green oasis of trees, sculpted gardens, and stately buildings. A thriving bird population, including the rare Puerto Rican parrot, can be seen and heard here. The university has more than 25,000 students and faculty from throughout the world. Art openings and music and theatrical performances take place here at a handful of auditoriums. The university's *Museum of Anthropology, History and Art* (Ponce de León; 787–764–0000 extension 2452) has an informative Taíno Indian exhibit as well as Francisco Oller's masterwork, *El Velorio,* or *The Wake.* Open Monday through Wednesday and Friday 9:00 A.M. to 4:30 P.M., Thursday 9:00 A.M. to 9:00 P.M., and weekends 9:00 A.M. to 3:00 P.M. Free admission. The library has a Puerto Rico periodicals room that contains local publications—a good spot to catch up on current events or history. The campus is a wonderful attraction in itself, mixing its tropical garden feeling with a traditional collegiate ambience.

A few blocks from the pastoral campus is the *Río Piedras Marketplace* and adjacent shopping district. There's a lot of food for sale within the marketplace and in little stands lining the bustling streets that surround it. The market here is even bigger than at Santurce and offers fresh tropical fruits, vegetables, and herbs from throughout the island. Try the food stalls within the marketplace that serve fresh fruit drinks and fried *empanadas* or *pastelillos.*

There's a lively air inside the shops lining the *Paseo de Diego* pedestrian mall and other streets surrounding the marketplace, as customers and merchants haggle over prices. This area rivals Plaza las Americá, the mall in Hato Rey, as a draw for shoppers from across the Caribbean. It's not as fancy, but the prices can't be beat. *Calle Padre Colón* contains San Juan's small "Arab Quarter," with Arab import shops and the *Islamic Center of Puerto Rico.* Most of the community's members are descended from Palestinians who came here in the 1950s as merchants.

Behind the marketplace is the recently restored **Juan A. Palerm Transportation Center,** a bus, taxi, and *público* station. The best place to eat in the Río Piedras area is at **La Bodega del Hipopótamo** (880 Muñoz Rivera; 787–767–2660), located at University Avenue—the turn-off for the university and marketplace districts. Reasonable prices, an extensive menu that ranges from simple breakfast sandwiches to Spanish gourmet, and a long wine list are among its attributes. The restaurant has been a favorite of *sanjuaneros* for years.

Most visitors will want to go to the **Botanical Garden of the University of Puerto Rico** (at the traffic-congested intersection of Highway 1 and Route 847; 787–767–1710 or 787–250–0000, extension 6578), located about ten minutes away from the main campus. Once inside,

Puerto Rican Holidays

Puerto Rico is a festive place where every weekend seems a cause for celebration, with islanders heading off to the beaches or mountains or to one of the many festivals or events that occur throughout the year. All U.S. government holidays are celebrated in Puerto Rico, and there are eight local holidays honoring important Puerto Ricans or events in the island's history. These holidays are:

- *Three Kings Day, January 6*
- *Eugenio María de Hostos Day, January 11*
- *Abolition Day, March 11*
- *José De Diego Day, April 16*

- *Luis Muñoz Rivera Day, July 17*
- *Constitution Day, July 25*
- *José Celso Barbosa Day, July 27*
- *Discovery Day, November 19*

Dates with asterisks are celebrated on closest Monday.

Following a Latin American tradition, Puerto Rico's Christmas season is long and exuberant, starting in early December and lasting until Three Kings Day on January 6. While U.S. traditions such as Santa Claus and Christmas trees are popular here, there are some distinct local quirks to Christmas merrymaking in Puerto Rico. The most distinctive is the parranda, *a more rambunctious form of Christmas caroling than is known up north. Lively music is sung—usually to bongó, guitar, and guiro accompaniment—as the group goes to a friend's house, eats and drinks everything in sight, and then moves on to the home of another friend. The cycle is repeated, usually until the wee hours of the morning.*

Each town in Puerto Rico also has a weeklong annual festival to honor its patron saint. Originally religious in nature, the festivals are now more about good food and music and are often a fine place to pick up good examples of local arts and crafts. They're also a great place to hear some of the top Puerto Rican recording acts.

you'll be treated to another pastoral respite from the big city. Here on seventy-five acres are more than 200 plant species, an orchid garden with 30,000 specimens, a lotus lagoon, and extensive bamboo-lined paths. Many of the tropical and subtropical plants are from Australia and Africa. Open daily from 9:00 A.M. to 4:30 P.M., with guided tours and trail maps available. Free admission.

PLACES TO STAY IN SAN JUAN

CONDADO

Alelí by the Sea
1125 Seaview
(787) 725–5313

Arcade Inn
8 Taft
(787) 725–0668

Atlantic Beach Hotel
1 Vendig
(787) 721–6900

At Wind Chimes Inn
53 Taft
(787) 727–4153

Best Western Hotel Pierre
105 de Diego
(787) 721–1200 or
(800) 468–4549;
www.bestwestern.com

Caribe Hilton
Los Rosales
San Gerónimo Grounds
(787) 721–0303 or
(800) 468–8585;
www.hilton.com

Casa del Caribe
67 Caribe
(787) 722–7139

Comfort Inn Tanama
Princess
1 Mariano Ramiréz Bages
(787) 724–4160 or
(888) 826–2621;
www.comfortinn.com

Condado Plaza Hotel
and Casino
999 Ashford
(787) 721–1000 or
(800) 624–0420;
www.condadaplaza.com

Days Inn Condado
Lagoon Hotel
6 Clemenceau
(787) 721–0170 or
(800) 858–7407;
www.the.daysinn.com

Diamond Palace Hotel
and Casino
55 Condado
(787) 721–0810 or
(800) 468–2014

El Canario by the Lagoon
4 Clemenceau
(787) 722–5058 or
(800) 533–2649;
www.canariohotels.com

El Canario by the Sea
4 Condado
(787) 722–8640 or
(800) 533–2649;
www.canariohotels.com

El Canario Inn
1317 Ashford
(787) 722–3861 or
(800) 533–2649;
www.canariohotels.com

El Consulado
1110 Ashford
(787) 289–9191

El Prado Inn
1350 Luchetti
(787) 728–5925 or
(800) 468–4521

Embassy Guest House
1126 Sea View
(787) 725–8284

Hotel El Portal
76 Condado
(787) 721–9010

Hotel Iberia
1464 Wilson
(787) 723–0200

Hotel Normandie
Muñoz Rivera at corner of
Los Rosales
(787) 729–2929

Radisson Ambassador
Plaza Hotel and Casino
1369 Ashford
(787) 721–7300 or
(800) 333–3333;
www.radisson.com

Regency Hotel
1005 Ashford
(787) 721–0505 or
(800) 468–2823

San Juan Marriott Hotel
and Stellaris Casino
1309 Ashford
(787) 722–7000 or
(800) 288–9290;
www.marriotthotels.com

ISLA VERDE
Borinquen Royal Guest
House
58 Isla Verde
(787) 728–8400

Casa de Playa Beach Hotel
4851 Isla Verde
(787) 728–9779 or
(800) 916–2272

Casa Mathiesen
14 Uno, Villamar
(787) 726–8662 or
(800) 667–8860;
www.casamathiesen.com

Colonial Hotel and Beach
Resort
2 Tartak
(787) 253–0100 or
(888) 265–6699

Dalia 15
15 Dalia
(787) 791–3745

El Patio Guest House
87 Tres, Villamar
(787) 726–6953

Embassy Suites Hotel and
Casino
8000 Tartak
(787) 791–0505 or
(800) EMBASSY;
www.embassy–suites.com

Empress Oceanfront Hotel
2 Amapola
(787) 791–3083 or
(800) 678–0757

ESJ Towers
6165 Isla Verde
(787) 791–5151 or
(800) 468–2026;
www.esjtowers.com

Green Isle Inn
36 Uno, Villamar
(787) 726–4330 or
(800) 677–8860

Hampton Inn
Resort-San Juan
6530 Isla Verde
(787) 791–8777 or
(800) HAMPTON;
www.hampton–inn.com

Hotel La Playa
6 Amapola
(787) 791–1115 or
(800) 791–9626;
www.hotellaplaya.com

Inter–Continental San Juan
Resort and Casino (for-
merly San Juan Grand)
5961 Isla Verde
(787) 791–6100 or
(800) 443–2009;
www.interconti.com

Mango Inn
20 Uno, Villamar
(787) 726–4230 or
(800) 777–1946

Mario's Hotel and
Restaurant
2 Rosa
(787) 791–3748

Ritz–Carlton San Juan
Hotel and Casino
6961 Route 187
(787) 253–1700 or
(800) 241–3333;
www.ritzcarlton.com

Surfside Hotel
4820 Isla Verde
(787) 728–1300

Wyndham El San Juan
Hotel and Casino
6063 Isla Verde
(787) 791–1000 or
(800) 468–2818;
www.wyndham.com

MIRAMAR
Hotel Excelsior
801 Ponce de León
(787) 721–7400 or (800)
289–4274

Hotel Toro
605 Miramar
(787) 725–5150

Miramar
606 Ponce de León
(787) 722–6239

Olimpo Court Hotel
603 Miramar
(787) 724–0600

OCEAN PARK
Beach Buoy Inn
1853 McLeary
(787) 728–8119 or
(800) 221–8119

Hostería del Mar
1 Tapia
(787) 727–3302 or
(800) 742–2767

La Condesa Inn
2071 Cacique
(787) 727–3698

L'Habitation
1957 Italia
(787) 727–2499

Numero Uno Guest House
1 Santa Ana
(787) 726–5010

Ocean Park Beach Inn
3 Elena
(787) 728-7418 or
(800) 292-9208

Ocean Walk Guest House
1 Atlantic
(787) 728-0855

Tres Palmas Inn
2212 Park
(787) 727-4617 or
(888) 290-2076;
www.trespalmasinn.com

**PLACES TO EAT IN
SAN JUAN**

CONDADO
Ajili-Mójili
1052 Ashford
(787) 725-9195

Big Apple Deli
1407 Ashford
(787) 725-6345

Caruso Restaurant
1104 Ashford
(787) 723-6876

Chart House
1214 Ashford
(787) 724-0110

Cielito Lindo
1108 Magdalena
(787) 723-5597

Cobia Tapas Bar and
Seafood Grill
999 Ashford at the Condado
Plaza Hotel
(787) 721-1000,
extension 2600

Hermés Creative Cuisine
1108 Ashford
(787) 723-5151

Il Grottino
1372 Ashford
(787) 723-0499

Indiana John's Restaurant
1 Vendig at the Atlantic
Beach Hotel
(787) 721-6900

José José
1110 Magdalena
(787) 725-8496

La Patisserie de France
1504 Ashford
(787) 728-5508

Los Faisanes
1108 Magdalena
(787) 725-2801

Martino's
55 Condado at the Dia-
mond Palace Hotel
(787) 722-5256

Ramiro's
1106 Magdalena
(787) 721-9049

Ristorante Tuscany
1309 Ashford at the San
Juan Marriott Resort
(787) 722-7000,
extension 6219

Salud
1350 Ashford
(787) 722-0911

St.Moritz
1005 Ashford at the
Regency Hotel
(787) 721-0999

Sweeney's Original Scotch
'n Sirloin
1369 Ashford
(787) 729-9315

The Greenhouse
55 Condado
(787) 721-0810 or
(800) 468-2014

Urdin
1105 Magdalena
(787) 724-0420

Zabó Cocina Creativa
14 Candina
(787) 725-9494

HATO REY
Al Salám
239 Roosevelt
(787) 751-6296

El Cairo
352 Ensenada
(787) 273-7140

El Muelle
191 O'Neill
(787) 767-7825

El Zipperle
352 Roosevelt
(787) 751-4335

Frida's
128 Domenech
(787) 763-4827

Jerusalem Restaurant
1-G O'Neill
(787) 764-3265

La Cueva del Chicken Inn
507 Ponce de León
(787) 753-1306

Pikayo
300 de Diego at the Museo
de Arte de Puerto Rico
(787) 721-6194

Tierra Santa
284 Roosevelt
(787) 754-6865

Yuan
255 Ponce de León
(787) 766–0666

Yum Yum Tree
131 Roosevelt
(787) 753–7743

ISLA VERDE
Back Street Hong Kong
6063 Isla Verde at the
Wyndham El San
Juan Hotel
(787) 791–1224

Casa Dante
39 Isla Verde
(787) 726–7310

Hungry Sailor
Tartak, on the beach
(787) 791–3017

La Piccola Fontana
6063 Isla Verde at the
Wyndham El San
Juan Hotel
(787) 791–0966

La Playita
6 Amapola at the Hotel
La Playa
(787) 791–1115

Metropol (one of several
in city)
Isla Verde at the Club
Gallístico Annex
(787) 791–4046

Momoyama
5961 Isla Verde at the
Inter-Continental San
Juan Resort
(787) 791–8883

Ruth's Chris Steak House
5961 Isla Verde at the
Inter-Continental San
Juan Resort
(787) 791–6100

Sunny's Ocean View
Terrace
2 Amapola at the
Empress Hotel
(787) 791-3083

Yamato
6063 Isla Verde at the
Wyndham El San
Juan Hotel
(787) 791–8152

MIRAMAR
Augusto's Cuisine
801 Ponce de León at the
Hotel Excelsior
(787) 725–7700

Chayote
603 Miramar at the Olimpo
Court Hotel
(787) 724–0600

Godfather's
1426 Ponce de León
(787) 721–1556

**OCEAN PARK AND PUNTA
LAS MARIAS**
Che's Restaurante
Argentino
35 Caoba
(787) 726–7202

Dunbar's Pub
1954 McLeary
(787) 728–2920

Hostería del Mar
1 Tapia
(787) 727–3302

Kasalta's Bakery
1966 McLeary
(787) 727–7340

Mango's Café
2421 Laurel
(787) 727–9328

Marisquería Atlántica
2475 Loiza
(787) 726–6654

Pamela's Caribbean Cuisine
1 Santa Ana at the Numero
Uno Guest House
(787) 726–5010

St.Mick's Irish Pub and
Restaurant
2473 Loíza
(787) 727–6620

PIÑONES
La Terraza
no phone

Soleil Beach Club
Beach Road off Route 187
(787) 726–7614

The Reef Bar and Grill
(787) 791–1374

PUERTA DE TIERRA
Dumas Restaurant
Reserve Officers Beach
Club
(787) 721–3550

El Hamburger
402 Muñoz Rivera
(787) 721–4269

Escambrón Beach Club and
Restaurant
Escambrón Public Beach
(787) 722–4785

PUERTO NUEVO
Allegro Ristorante
1350 Roosevelt
(787) 273–9055

Aurorita's
303 de Diego
(787) 783–2899

Casa del Mar
435 Andalucia
(787) 782–3594

Fishes and Crabs
301 Matadero
(787) 781–6570

Margarita's Restaurante
Mexicano
1013 Roosevelt
(787) 781-8452

RIO PIEDRAS
Felix
Road 1, km. 25.1
Quebrada Cuevas Sector
(787) 720-1626

La Bodega del Hipopótamo
880 Muñoz Rivera
(787) 767-2660

Middle East Restaurant
207 Padre Colón
(787) 751-7304

SANTURCE
Carnicería Restaurant Díaz
319 Orbeta
(787) 723-1903

Compostela
106 Condado
(787) 724-6088

El Pescador
178 Dos Hermanos

El Popular
205 Capital

Havana's Cafe Restaurant
409 del Parque
(787) 725-0888

La Casita Blanca
351 Tapia
(787) 726-5501

La Casona
609 San Jorge
(787) 727-2717

Restaurant Don Telfo
180 Dos Hermanos
(787) 724-5752

Sabores Al Natural
209 Canals
(787) 722-4631

Tourist Information for San Juan

Condado Tourism Information Booth
Ashford Avenue, in front of the Condado Plaza

Luis Muñoz Marin Airport Information Center
Luis Muñoz Marin Airport, Carolina
(787) 791-1014
8:00 A.M. to 9:00 P.M. daily

East of San Juan

n la isla, a beloved term that Puerto Ricans apply anywhere outside of metro San Juan, may be as much a state of mind as any place in particular. Whether it's a silent mountain town deep in cool coffee country, a deserted Caribbean beach with glistening sand and sun, or a strip of beachfront bars blasting salsa, *en la isla* is a label that will fit anywhere beyond the fast pace, city heat, and stress of San Juan.

When leaving San Juan it's likely that you'll be heading east, since an astounding diversity of geography and areas of interest lie within the hour drive between San Juan and Fajardo on the island's northeast corner. Renting a car is the easiest way to get around *en la isla.* You could explore the entire region in a day and be back in San Juan for dinner or take advantage of the several tour companies operating day trips from San Juan to main attractions such as El Yunque, Las Cabezas de San Juan, and Fajardo.

Taking Baldorioty de Castro to the airport and then continuing onto Route 3 is the quickest way to get to the eastern part of the island. But a better way is to take Route 187, which winds through the undeveloped beachfront of Piñones at a more leisurely pace.

What Was Puerto Rico's Original Name?

From 1508 (the start of Spanish colonization) to 1510, the island was known as San Juan. It was renamed Puerto Rico in 1511.

Beyond Piñones you'll cross the majestic Río Grande de Loíza into **Loíza,** a town of 29,000 that is just 6 miles east of San Juan but has managed to maintain a separateness that belies that distance. Part of the reason for this is that until recently, the river and the massive mangrove and woodland area of Torrecilla Baja kept the area isolated. Before the bridge was built, cars were taken across the wide, gentle river by ferry.

The town was settled in the sixteenth century by African slaves brought by the Spanish to work in gold mines and then sugar plantations. When slavery was abolished in 1873, many stayed here to farm. Their African heritage is still very much alive today in Loíza, where the majority of residents are African and *Santería,* a mix of

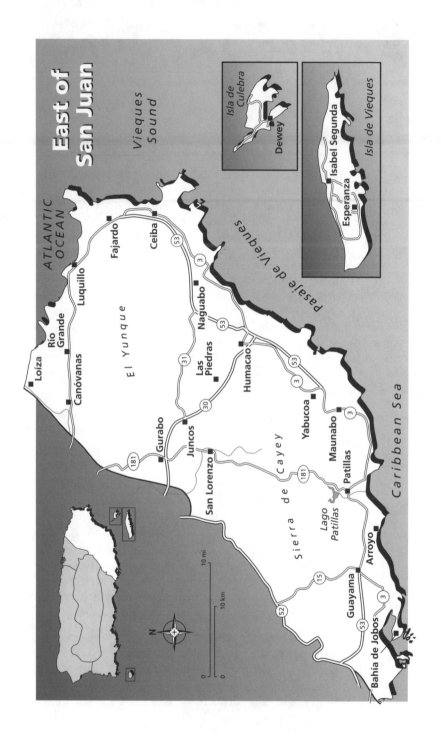

EAST OF SAN JUAN

AUTHOR FAVORITES

El Yunque (Caribbean National Forest), Palmer

Flamenco Beach, Culebra

Hacienda Carabalí, Río Grande

Las Cabezas de San Juan Nature Reserve, Fajardo

Mosquito Bay, Vieques

Sardinera fishing village, Fajardo

Sun Bay, Vieques

Roman Catholicism and African religions, is practiced. The music of choice is still the *bomba* and *plena,* which rely on percussion and a call-and-response interplay between singer and chorus that gives rise to street-corner rumba sessions.

This African heritage is most evident during the annual **Fiesta de Santiago Apóstol,** a week-long celebration beginning on July 25 that pays homage to Loíza's patron saint, Saint James. During the festival, townspeople wear costumes strikingly similar to those of West Africa's Yoruba tribe, from which many of the area's residents descended. The *vejigantes,* or masked dancers, parade through the streets wearing intricately painted and sculpted masks and colorful, shiny costumes. The masks are usually made from coconut shells and have become quite popular as works of art, both here and in galleries throughout San Juan. Loíza's town square is a shady, sleepy place fronted by rustic eateries.

Loíza's **San Patricio Church** (10 Espíritu Santo; 787–876–2229) is one of the oldest functioning parishes on the island. Originally built as a

The Goatsucker of Canóvanas

*N*ot too long ago Canóvanas was best known for its racetrack. That is until the appearance of **El Chupacabra,** or The Goatsucker.

El Chupacabra is most often described as a skinny, hairy, 4-foot-tall creature with a large head, lipless mouth, lidless eyes, and fangs. It has spiky protrusions along its backbone and webbed arms. Since first sighted in 1994, it is alleged to have killed farm animals across the Puerto Rican countryside in a particularly hideous manner that always includes completely draining the animals of their blood. Explanations as to the beast's origin range from the offspring of wild Rhesus monkeys to an alien being.

El Chupacabra is just the latest flavor in a long line of creatures that have surfaced in Puerto Rico over the last thirty years. Others have included the Moca Vampire, a bat-like being that "terrorized" the mountain town of Moca in 1975; the Comecogollo, a monkey-like creature that gorges on plátano plants; and the Creature from Fajardo's Black Lagoon, also known as garadiablo, or sea demon, which caused hysteria in the early 1970s.

Although the jury's still out on the existence of El Chupacabra, the legend lives on in song and drink, and on T-shirts and Web sites.

refuge for Spanish soldiers, it predates the town's 1719 founding—some accounts date the church to 1647. San Patricio is only open to the public during 10:00 A.M. service on Sunday. A booklet on the church's history is available for a $2.00 donation.

Route 187 spills back onto Route 3 after it passes through the congested commercial center of Carolina. In *Canóvanas, El Comandante Racetrack* (Route 3, km. 15.3; 787–724–6060; www.elcomandante.com), the largest racetrack in the Caribbean, features thoroughbred races every Sunday, Monday, Wednesday, and Friday. There are eight races every day, beginning at 2:15 P.M. to 2:45 P.M., depending on the season. El Comandante is slated to become much more than a racetrack, however. In fact the owners plan to build an amusement park along the lines of a Great Adventure with hotels. Another addition to the grounds is the *Caribbean Studios,* a new film-production studio (no tours given).

Beyond the racetrack, Route 3 passes through a more rural landscape as the *Sierra de Luquillo* mountain range rises over the road on the right side, its uppermost point usually lost in a tangle of clouds hanging over El Yunque. But the coast is just off to your left, and soon the blue water of Luquillo Beach and its sun-splashed palm trees also come into view. This juxtaposition sums up the region's unique appeal: a place that ribbons from the steaming coast to the drizzling cool of the rain forest and back again in less than an hour.

Río Grande is home to two golf courses: the *Berwind Country Club* (Route 187, km. 4.7; 787–876–3056) and the *Bahía Beach Plantation* (Route 187, km. 4.2; 787–256–5600). These are more reasonably priced

Road Food

*F*ruit and vegetable vendors are lined all along Route 3 beyond Canóvanas, and their goods are usually fresh and inexpensive. Try the roadside barbecued chicken stands. The chicken is rubbed with adobo, *a mixture of local spices, marinated, then slowly barbecued. The result is a juicy chicken, which is often served with marinated yucca* or baby green bananas, fried mashed plantains called *tostones, or amarillos, which are fried sweet bananas. Roofed, open-air bar/restaurants serve* lechón (roast pig), chicken, *and other staples of Puerto Rican food, such as* arroz con gandules *(rice with green pigeon peas). Such roadside and open-air establishments can be found throughout Puerto Rico.*

than the two championship courses at the *Westin Río Mar Beach Resort and Country Club and Ocean Villas* (6000 Río Mar; 787–888–6000 or 800–937–8461; www.westinriomar.com), which opened in 1995 as a "contemporary interpretation of a Caribbean manor house." The Westin has all the usual tourist amenities, including a nice pool area and active nightlife, but its real charm lies in its mile of pristine beachfront, which runs down toward the Luquillo public beach.

El Yunque

l Yunque, the mountainous rain forest that overtakes the *Sierra Luquillo,* has always been a special place. The Taínos revered it as a holy place that kept hurricanes at bay, and today it is the only rain forest in the U.S. National Park system, which administers and protects it as the *Caribbean National Forest.* The tropical forest sprawls over 28,000 acres covering the highest point in the Sierra Luquillo. Its green vegetation is laced with rivers and cascading waterfalls, gentle streams, and deep, cold pools. El Yunque draws 240 inches of rain annually—100 billion gallons of water.

El Yunque's water power can be seen in *Río Espíritu Santo,* Puerto Rico's largest, roughest, and only navigable river. The river tumbles down the Sierra Luquillo and becomes navigable as it reaches flat land near Route 3. It's possible to kayak or canoe the river on its way out to the Atlantic Ocean, a trip that takes a few hours and may require walking in some spots, such as around a river intake dam. Although the river depth is as low as 5 feet at some points, locals claim there are points where it reaches a 50-foot depth.

The main entrance to the Caribbean National Forest proper is in the small town of *Palmer* at Route 191. Other roads also cut through El Yunque's surroundings, including Routes 185, 186, and 956, which run off Route 3 in Canóvanas and Río Grande.

El Yunque is home to hundreds of animal species; about 225 native tree species, with types located within four distinct forest zones; and an abundance of tropical plant life,

---

Top Annual Events

Cristóbal L. Sanchez Carnival, early February, Arroyo

Luquillo Patron Saint Festival, late April, Carolina

Carolina Patron Saint Festival, late May, Carolina

Vieques Patron Saint Festival, early June, Vieques

Maunabo Patron Saint Festival, late June, Maunabo

Arroyo Patron Saint Festival, mid-July, Arroyo

Carnival, mid-July, Loíza

Festival of Typical Dishes, late November, Luquillo

Trivia

El Yunque stems from the Taíno word "Yuquiyú," the Taíno's name for their supreme creator, who lived in the mountains of the rain forest.

Puerto Rican Parrot

including 150 types of ferns, as well as exotic flowers, including fifty different types of orchids. It is also a haven for sixty-eight bird species, including the endangered and elusive bright-green Puerto Rican parrot. The Puerto Rican boa, the island's largest snake at 7 feet long, also makes his home here, as does Puerto Rico's famous singing tree frog, the *coquí*.

El Portal Tropical Forest Center (787–888–1880), a new visitors center at the park's main entrance, has an elevated walkway through the forest canopy, interactive exhibits, and written material on El Yunque's complex ecosystem. Admission is $3.00, half that for kids under twelve and seniors. Children under four are free. Open 9:00 A.M. to 5:00 P.M. daily. Three other visitor information stations are located throughout the park: the Yokahu Tower, Sierra Palma, and Palo Colorado. While it's possible to camp in the park, arrangements must be made in advance with the Forest Service.

Different forests form rings around El Yunque. The most widespread is the Tabonuco, a mix of pine forest, fern fields, and the nimble and lush Sierra palm. Above 2,000 feet the moss-covered Palo Colorado Forest begins, an area of stunted pine and moss covering less than 1,000 acres

El Yunque by Horse

*H*acienda Carabalí *(Route 992, km. 4; 787–889–5820 or 787–889–4945), just off Route 3, is a ranch that will take you on a horseback ride along the Mameyes River until it empties into the Atlantic at Luquillo's gentle shore. The tour hits the beach between the western Río Mar and the undeveloped* border area of the famed Luquillo balneario. Other trips here go through forested trails in the foothills of El Yunque. Day trips can be arranged and transportation provided by San Juan–based tour operators.
The horse ranch is also the site of an occasional concert.

that remain unseen by most visitors. The forest gets its name from the *Palo Colorado*, or Colorado tree, which is also known as a swamp cyrilla. Moss-topped, twisted dwarf pines cling to a narrow layer of soil on the highest areas of the forest, wracked by wind and more than 150 inches of rain each year.

The *El Toro* and *Tradewinds National Recreation Trail* is an 8-mile hike that begins a few hundred yards beyond the gate on Route 191 and meanders through all the distinct forest types here. Originally built in the 1930s, the rock and dirt trail takes you through damp forests of sierra palms, ferns, and red-blossomed bromeliads; grassy fields; and river streams and small falls tumbling over gigantic boulders. This trail provides excellent views of Puerto Rico's eastern coast and back to San Juan as it rises to the highest peak in the Sierra Luquillo at 3,532 feet.

Among El Yunque's premiere attractions is 85-foot-tall *La Coca Falls* (km. 8.2). Here the forest's surging runoff cascades down one of its greatest drop-offs, with barrels full of cold water crashing over moss-covered boulders. A word of caution: Drinking the water here is not recommended on account of potential bacteria.

Beyond La Coca, Route 191 passes many scenic overlooks. Off the road to the left is the *Yokahu Observation Tower,* with one of the better views of the surprisingly untarnished northeastern coast of Puerto Rico. Although there's no visitors center here, there is a small stand that sells books about the forest and other attractions. If you're lucky, you'll also spot a park ranger.

La Mina Falls, a smaller, private, swimmable waterfall, can be reached via a trail starting at the *Palma de Sierra Visitors Center* (farther along Route 191, about 0.5 mile beyond Yokahu Observation Tower). It's a good mile hike through often slippery, winding rock trails and steps. A gorgeous stone bridge has been built in front of La Mina Falls. This trip has the twin advantages of giving you a picture-perfect El Yunque respite while getting you back soon enough to drive down for an afternoon at the beach across the highway. You can also take the Big Tree Trail (0.86 mile) to view the falls.

El Yunque Trail (2.6 miles long), also from the Sierra Palma Center, is a bit more challenging but rewards the visitor with some of the park's most outstanding vistas. It leads to Los Picachos Lookout Tower, Mount Britton Lookout Tower, and finally to *El Yunque,* the anvil-shaped peak that gives the park its name. There is another tower at Pico El Yunque and other fine views from the still more remote El Yunque Rock.

La Coca Falls at El Yunque

Luquillo Public Beach is one of the prettiest in Puerto Rico. It's just down Highway 3 from El Yunque. Food vendors, showers, and bathrooms are available. The water is protected from the ocean current as it curves inland, making it a good spot for swimming and snorkeling, with coral reefs within easy reach from the shore. Off to its east side, this public beach also has a facility for the physically challenged to enjoy the beach, including a ramp down the beach and into the water, and water-ready wheelchairs.

There is incredibly good seafood at the kiosks that line Route 3 just outside the public beach at Luquillio. Some stands offer whole fresh fish to order, while others offer traditional *comida criolla* prepared in a healthy manner (no deep-frying or liberal use of other fats, and no meat products). The *arepas* stuffed with marinated conch salad at ***Monelly #55*** are highly recommended. The last kiosk on the eastern end (#65) serves cold beer and all manner of Puerto Rican food, from barbecued chicken to seafood to fried beach snacks. The tables are a good place to eat with a view to the sea. The place gets crowded on weekends and holidays and stays that way through the night, when music and dancing take over.

A bit farther along Route 3, the town of **Luquillo** has a pleasant and pretty plaza. The rain forest is also visible here and the coastline is just steps away. The **Brass Cactus Bar & Grill** (Luquillo Beach Complejo Túristico; 787–889–5735) is a good American bar and grill, with great steaks, seafood, Cajun, and Tex-Mex food in a Southwestern setting. The service is always friendly. The sporting event of the moment is on one of the numerous televisions, and often there's live rock or reggae music.

Jerry García may have passed on, but he has certainly not been forgotten at Luquillo's **Grateful Bed & Breakfast** (787–889–4919). Owner Marty Souci says the phones were ringing off the hook with calls from Deadheads in mourning on the day Jerry passed away. The guest house is nestled on five acres in the foothills of the Luquillo mountains. Take a right at El Rancho bar/restaurant on Route 3, then down the paved road to your first left. The rooms are ostensibly "free"; what you're paying for is a "daily fee for our vacation planning and guide services" (in the $50 to $90 range, depending on the season). Just tell the staff what you want to do beforehand, Marty says, and they'll figure out how to do it. Activities from canoe trips to nature hikes to

UFOs over Puerto Rico

*A*round the island, stories abound describing close encounters with unidentified flying objects. On the south coast, at La Parguera, part of Lajas, frequent reports describe low-flying spacecraft. In 1997, what was believed to be the site of a crashed UFO there was closed off to the public by the military, with no official explanation. El Yunque is often the focus of rumored sightings. In the early eighties it was widely believed Martians had landed there, and the rain forest drew crowds looking for aliens. Residents of Adjuntas, in the mountains above Ponce, reported the presence over five years of mysterious lights, as if from UFOs, traveling a path from Adjuntas to Laguna Cartagena in Lajas. Observers have described tremors, strange noises, and other inexplicable phenomena at the lagoon in Lajas.

It is tempting to attribute all of this to an overactive imagination, a kind of hysteria, or a paranoid state of mind. Paranoia would be understandable for an island with a legacy of invasions, an "alien" military presence, and a history of colonization. Why shouldn't little green creatures from somewhere else find Puerto Rico an inviting place to sightsee or make a home for themselves?

horseback riding trips can be arranged. The staff is knowledgeable about little-known areas of the adjacent El Yunque rain forest and tours to forest hideaways can be arranged.

Breakfast is on the house. There's a music room decked out with Dead memorabilia, a killer sound system, and a roomful of bootleg tapes. There are also lots of comfortable chairs and an unusual collection of wooden instruments that guests are encouraged to play.

The guest house itself is nothing fancy, but it's a nice setting. Group drumming and chanting sessions are known to occur. Among the notes I found in the guest log was this entry: "Cosmic cakes, drum circles, Bamboo Rum Punch, the rain forest and mellow times."

Fajardo

ajardo is 5 miles beyond Luquillo at Puerto Rico's northeast corner. The town's origins are as a fishing and farming village, and it became a supply port for pirate ships in the late 1700s. The town's enviable location makes it a sailing center to this day, with the *Villa Marina Yacht Harbor* (Route 987; 787–728–3450 or 787–863–5153), the large *Puerto del Rey Marina* (Route 3, km. 51.2; 787–860–1000), and several smaller marinas here. Puerto del Rey has fine amenities and long-term plans for a full-scale resort.

A huge reef at Puerto Rico's northeast corner fronts the coastline of Fajardo extending from the Cabezas of San Juan to beyond the offshore island of Culebra. The reef protects area waters from the Atlantic's full force, while the ocean's tradewinds are a sailor's delight. The calm waters are filled with marine life and reefs and are perfect for sailing, snorkeling, and scuba diving. Dozens of cays and small islands, with names like Diablos, Icacos, and Cayo Lobos, lie off Fajardo's coast. The area is also the launching point for sailing to the Eastern Caribbean.

A good way to experience Fajardo's wonderful waters is on one of the sailing day-tours leaving from town marinas. The cruises usually take place on large catamarans with anywhere from ten to twenty people. The boats make several stops to snorkel and swim, and lunch is usually served on the beach of one of the small islets. Van service from San Juan, as well as lunch, is usually included in the rate, but you can jump on a tour if you drive to Fajardo. Tours start at around $50. There are several operators at Villa Marina and Puerto del Rey. Try the *Erin Go*

Braugh (Puerto del Rey; 787–860–4401) or *Captain Jack's Catamaran* (Villa Marina; 787–863–1905). *Cpt. Jack B's Getaway* (Villa Marina; 787– 860–0861) is run by Captain Jack Becker, a veteran at this game. He's quite a character, offering free trips to Swedish flight attendants and interspersing embarrassing moments from his personal history with his take on the state of Puerto Rican affairs. He'll also tell you what's really going on, whether it's a good day to go out or not, and all about the best places to visit, depending on what you want to do.

Playa de Fajardo is a waterfront district on the town's eastern end where ferries provide service to the island municipalities of Culebra and Vieques. The *ferry terminal* is flanked by a pink stucco U.S. Customs House, which also hosts a post office and a small hotel. The ferries are operated by the Puerto Rico Ports Authority (787–863–3360 or 800–981–2005). Be forewarned—weekend tickets go fast. The *Diego Jiménez Torres Airport,* also known as the Fajardo Airport (Road 976, km. 1; 787–860–3110) further east, has air service to the Puerto Rican offshore islands, the U.S. Virgin Islands, and San Juan. It's just a fifteen-minute hop to Vieques or Culebra.

North of Fajardo's town center is the village of *Sardinera,* where fishermen still work from the central beach in town to supply the half-dozen seafood restaurants in the area. Soon the road comes to the entrance to the majestic *Wyndham El Conquistador Resort and Country Club* (Route 987, km. 3.4; 787–863–1000 or 800–468–8365; www.wyndham. com), which overlooks both the Atlantic and Caribbean seas from its 300-foot perch.

From 1968 through much of the 1970s, the original hotel on the site, also called El Conquistador, was the epitome of Caribbean splendor. Its black and stainless-steel circular casino was featured in the James Bond movie *Goldfinger,* and the hotel was a haven for U.S. celebrities and jet-setters. The hotel fell on hard times following the Middle East oil embargo and the ensuing recession, and it closed in 1977. After a few false starts, the resort reopened in 1996 after a $200-million renovation. The hotel's design draws its inspiration from several Mediterranean influences, from Sevilla's Moorish gardens to the neoclassical elegance found in northern Italian architecture.

El Conquistador is located above the charming fishing village of *Las Croabas,* which is certainly worth a trip. There are several fine seafood places in the area, but head for *La Fontanella* (Las Croabas Roads; 787–860–2480). This is an Italian restaurant opened by transplanted

Chicago restaurateurs, and the food here is the real thing: from the tomato bread to the roasted peppers and artichoke antipasto, from the lasagna Florentine to the chicken *cacciatora*. Try the *arancino*, a Sicillian rice ball stuffed with Genoa salami, pepperoncini peppers, provolone cheese, and olives. It's deep-fried, baked, and served with marinara sauce. It's listed as an appetizer but is a meal in itself. The service is low-key and very friendly, and it's a very unassuming place despite the high quality of its food. Highly recommended. Nearby on Route 987 is the Seven Seas *balneario*.

Las Cabezas de San Juan Nature Reserve (Route 987; 787–722–5882 or 787–860–2560) offers visitors 316 acres of beautiful beaches, mangrove swamps, coral reefs, and dry forest. The restored lighthouse here, with an information center and observation deck, has one of the best views on the island, extending from misty El Yunque all the way out to the Eastern Caribbean, from the smallest cays just offshore out to the island of St. Thomas. The lighthouse itself, still functioning, has been restored to its original nineteenth-century state and is itself a beauty, from its copper top to its facade to the huge *ausubo* wood beams used throughout the building.

The park's name, which translates into the "headlands of San Juan," is fitting as it occupies the northeastern corner of Puerto Rico. Much of the park can be explored over a series of elevated trails and boardwalks. There's some spectacular snorkeling right offshore. The reserve is also a lure for birds and wildlife, including endangered species such as the osprey and leatherback sea turtles. Here you'll also find *Laguna Grande,* a bioluminescent lagoon. Two-and-a-half-hour tours of the park are given three times a day, Wednesday through Sunday. Since access to the park is limited to a certain number of people each day, it is best to call

Conservation Trust

*T*he **Conservation Trust of Puerto Rico** (155 Tetuán, Old San Juan; 787–722–5882) administers Las Cabezas forest reserve as well as several other natural areas, including Guánica's Ballena coast and Ponce's Hacienda Buena Vista. The Trust, set up in 1970 as a non-profit corporation, has spent $21 million buying 15,000 acres of pristine Puerto Rican

natural beauty. Many of its holdings, such as Las Cabezas and Hacienda Buena Vista, are fully operational.

This wonderful organization deserves the support of all residents and visitors. One way to show support is to visit the organization's holdings, another is to drop by its headquarters/store in Old San Juan.

ahead for reservations (787–860–2560 or the San Juan office at 787–722–5882). Admission is $5.00 for adults, $2.00 for children. The park is administered by the Conservation Trust of Puerto Rico.

South of Fajardo lies the U.S. Navy's **Roosevelt Roads,** the biggest American naval base in the world, occupying one-quarter of Puerto Rico's east coast. The base fuels all the American and allied ships in the region and undertakes large-scale military maneuvers on the offshore island of Vieques. The base is located in **Ceiba,** which is a town that provides one less-traveled option to exploring El Yunque and the immediate area. Still, some of the following locations may be more quickly reached from San Juan via Highway 30 to Humacao. That's especially true of **Casa Cubuy** (Route 191, Naguabo; 787–874–6221) on El Yunque's southern slope, which is just as forested and full of streams as the northern side. This comfortable guest house with tropical decor and a nearby river is great for soaking. The **Ceiba Country Inn** (Route 977, Ceiba; 787–885–0471) is a bed-and-breakfast in an old family manor home. It has brightly decorated comfortable rooms with private baths and a quiet lounge.

South of Ceiba, the sleepy town of Naguabo has a picturesque harbor filled with fishing boats and nondescript restaurants serving good seafood, cold beer, and fritters. A beautiful Victorian home—the **Castillo Villa del Mar,** now a National Historic Monument—overlooks the harbor from the south. For more information on this and other Naguabo attractions, call the Municipal Tourism Office (787–874–0389 or 787–874–3040, extension 234).

Vieques and Culebra

Vieques and **Culebra** are Puerto Rico's two island municipalities. Largely unexplored by North American visitors, they are a favorite vacation spot for Puerto Ricans. The islands, often called the Spanish Virgin Islands, lie just 6 miles off Fajardo's coast.

Much of the reason the islands haven't hit the big time is that the larger of the two, Vieques, is controlled by the U.S. Navy, which has owned two-thirds of the island since 1941 and which periodically uses the land for offshore bombing practice, training maneuvers, and other operations. Access to Navy land is restricted during drills. At other times the Navy permits access to the magnificent beaches for snorkeling, swimming, and fishing. Some of Vieques's most beautiful beaches are found on the U.S. Navy–owned eastern and western ends of the island, including Green, Red, and Blue Beaches. (You will need a picture I.D. for admission at Navy checkpoints.)

The Navy's continued presence on Vieques has led to some protests and demonstrations, and many Puerto Ricans have called for the base to be closed immediately. Before making plans to travel to Vieques, you should check to see if military maneuvers are scheduled.

Another reason for the continued anonymity of these islands is the lack of large-scale, regularly scheduled commercial airline service, as well as the absence of a large hotel. Both of these situations are due to change with construction of a new resort—Martineau Bay—and expansion of the airport's present runway and service.

The 4-by-21-mile island of Vieques may be the most Caribbean part of Puerto Rico, combining dry rolling hills and pastures with coastal roads. Here egrets fly overhead as cattle lazily chew in pastures. The interior of Vieques is more hilly than its coast, with forested, winding country roads. There are fields of exotic flowers, wild horses, and mongoose. Ruins of sugar and pineapple plantations are scattered throughout the island, as are historic artifacts and archeological digs. The Taínos first called this island *Isla Nena* or *Beique,* an Amerindian word meaning "small island."

It's possible to go horseback riding through trails in the island's central hills and along the mangrove lagoons that attract over one hundred bird species. The island's more than forty beaches are among the Caribbean's finest. Many of them are isolated, accessible only by powerful jeep along dirt roads or by hiking down narrow trails. Probably the prettiest *balneario* in all of Puerto Rico is **Sun Bay,** or Sombé as locals call it, on the south coast. Vieques, like its sister island Culebra, is a water sports paradise, with excellent scuba, snorkeling, and fishing.

Isabel Segunda, the island's main town, will likely be your first point of reference. The ferry docks are located here and the airport is just outside of town. For as beautiful an island as Vieques is, its main town is only ordinary, reminiscent of nearly every other small Puerto Rican town. But if you stick around long enough, you will witness a certain relaxed pace and politeness of the people (including use of the formal pronoun, *usted*) and realize that *they* may the biggest reason this island seems like a museum of Puerto Rican yesteryear (other reasons include the absence of both traffic jams and U.S. fast-food restaurants). Vehicles can be ferried over, car rentals are available for about $50 per day, and there are also *públicos* that will take you all around the island at reasonable rates.

It was around Isabela Segunda in 1843 that the Spanish began building what would have been their last fort in the Americas. It was never completed. Today the building houses the **Fort Conde de Mirasol Museum** (787–741–1717), named after the Spanish governor there who convinced his countrymen to begin building the fortress. The museum features a permanent exhibit on the island's history, from its Taíno past to its Spanish heritage to a chronicle of the U.S. Navy's controversial presence. The museum also hosts changing shows featuring local and visiting artists, as well as frequent lectures and talks. It is open Wednesday through Sunday 10:00 A.M. to 4:00 P.M. The island's sleepy main square is where you'll find a statue of Latin America's "Great Liberator," **Simón Bolívar,** who also visited here. The statue was given to the people of

Getting to the Islands

*W*hether you fly or take the ferry to Vieques or Culebra depends on your schedule and your budget, more than anything else. The ferry, which takes forty-five minutes to Vieques and ninety minutes to Culebra, is a bargain at less than $5.00 round trip. It's actually a rather exhilarating and beautiful ride. Travelers with plenty of time may savor the ferry experience as kind of a decompression voyage, an integral part of the whole offshore experience. Island-bound passenger ferries leave from Fajardo several times each day. If you'd like to bring a car to the islands, cargo ferry service will cost you about $30 round trip. Be forewarned that the service takes longer and is a bit less reliable than passenger ferry service. You must reserve car space ahead and be in line at least one hour before departure. Call 800–981–2005 for reservations. For more information, call the ferry service (Fajardo, 787–863–0705; Vieques, 787–741–4761; Culebra, 787–742–3161).

Those with only a weekend to spend and who want to spend as much of it as possible on either island, can fly from San Juan for $50 to $70. Flying in means that you can be on Culebra's deserted Zoni beach until 4:30 P.M. and still be back in San Juan for dinner at 8:00 P.M. Many flights leave from the small Isla Grande Airport (787–729–8711) in Miramar, which is more conveniently located to Old San Juan and Condado than the international airport. Vieques Air Link (vieques-island.com/val; San Juan, 787–722–3736; Fajardo, 787–863–3020; Vieques, 787–741–8331; Culebra, 787–742–0254) provides regularly scheduled service between San Juan and Vieques, and Fajardo and Vieques. The company also provides charter service. Isla Nena (888–263–6213; San Juan, 787–791–5110; Fajardo, 787–860–3139; Vieques, 787–741–1577; Culebra, 787–742–0972) provides charter service as well as four daily flights to Culebra from San Juan and Fajardo. If you're traveling with a group, charters are a good option. Air Culebra (787–268–6951; www.airculebra.com) also flies to Culebra and Vieques from San Juan International Airport; charters only.

Usted and Tu

*I*n Spanish there are two ways to say "you," tu and usted. Tu *is generally used in informal settings, among friends and family, while* usted *is more formal and is used when addressing elders, public officials, or strangers* deserving of politeness. While usted *has fallen out of use in Puerto Rico and much of Latin America, you can still hear it on Vieques. Just another way that Vieques retains vestiges of Puerto Rico's past.*

Vieques in 1972 by the government of Venezuela (Bolívar's birthplace) in recognition of the fact that Vieques was the only Puerto Rican town visited by Bolívar.

Bravos of Boston, east of Isabel Segunda, is a beachfront area of modern Malibu Beach–style homes. The water here is clear blue and protected by a coral reef, which makes for some good snorkeling. A convenient alternative to staying on the south coast, many of the homes are available on a weekly or even weekend basis.

Most visitors head to **Esperanza,** a charming fishing village on the south coast that was once an important sugar production center. Today it is marked by its oceanfront road lined with guest houses and restaurants facing the water. The country road leading to Esperanza crosses the entire island, giving you a glimpse of the beautiful interior of the island. Right outside of Isabel Segunda is Vieques Car Rental (787–741–1037), run by Don and Betty Yoder. It has one of the largest fleets on the island as well as a small cafe that serves good diner-style food.

Before Esperanza, the road passes by **Casa del Francés** (Esperanza; 787–741–3735), a real Caribbean classic some call the "world's most laid-back hotel." It's certainly one of the most colorful. Winter rates start at $120, two meals included. The hotel is a 1910 plantation home built by a French general for his bride. Today palms, mango trees, banana plants, bamboo, as well as riotous wildflowers and orchids are scattered throughout the plantation's twelve acres. Two sweeping verandas surround the place, and the rooms are huge, high-ceilinged, and comfortable. Fine meals, which attract locals, are served on mahogany tables on a protected back porch or beside the pool beneath a towering tree that also shelters the outdoor bar. Despite the elegant digs, Casa del Francés retains the feeling of a kid's party while the parents are away. Irreverent Irving Greenblatt, who in a previous life was a Boston-based media guy, runs the place with partner Frank Celeste, who occasionally whips up Italian food in the kitchen.

There are a few interesting shops and galleries along the strip and, if you're in the mood for nightlife, you'll find a couple of rickety dance clubs and open-air bars by the beach.

The town is a center for water-sports operators, whether you want to scuba or windsurf. Sun Bay is just a fifteen-minute walk away. Beyond Sun Bay are two more secluded beaches, Media Luna and Navío. Media Luna is an ideal beach for children, where the water stays shallow for 40 feet into the bay—great for snorkeling! Navío has a small beach and a strong surf.

For listings and more information on things to do, pick up a copy of Esperanza's *Vieques Times* (153 Flamboyán, Esperanza Beach; 787–741–8508) as soon as you arrive. Check out the community's great Web site full of information, www.enchanted-isle.com, where you'll find "F.Y.I. Vieques."

If none of the restaurants or guest houses grabs your attention on your first stroll down Esperanza's main boulevard, retrace your steps—this is as cosmopolitan as Vieques gets. Rates at most inns in town start at $55. The **Amapola Inn & Tavern** (144 Flamboyán; 787–741–1382), **Bananas** (142 Flamboyán; 787–741–8700), and **Trade Winds** (787–741–8666) have clean, affordable, and comfortable rooms for rent. Bananas has a bar, loud music, and it's open late. Trade Winds is better for a quiet sit-down meal. The Amapola, right next door to Bananas, has Caribbean cuisine. **Hacienda Tamarindo** (Route 996, km. 4.5; 787–741–8525) is one of the nicest small hotels in the region, with a beautiful pool and a hilltop location overlooking the Caribbean. Rooms

Simón Bolívar

*S*imón Bolívar *(1783 to 1830) was a South American hero whose life was dedicated to uniting South America. Although he managed to create the independent republic of New Granada (where present-day Colombia is located), Bolívar's attempt to liberate Venezuela in 1815 failed, prompting him to sail to Jamaica in voluntary exile. It was there that he penned his celebrated* Jamaica Letter, *one of the documents in which he set forth*

his vision for a united republic of the Americas.

Bolívar next went on to Haiti and stopped off in Vieques in August 1816, on his way back to South America and more battles. During his week-long stay in Vieques, the Liberator and his men stocked up on supplies. Historians believe Bolívar was brought to the island by one of his generals, Antonio Valero de Bernabé, a native of Fajardo.

start at $145 for a double. The place was decorated by its owner as a swan song to a fifteen-year career as a commercial interior designer.

Overnight options include the gorgeous **Inn on the Blue Horizon** (Route 996, km. 4.2; 787–741–3318). The name says it all. The inn is on a grassy bluff overlooking Esperanza and the Caribbean. The inn has a great restaurant, **Café Blu,** and a large outdoor bar where sculpted walkways and gardens compete with the sea for the view. The bluff has a natural walkway down to a miles-long beach. The place was opened by three ex–New Yorkers who undoubtedly were as taken by the place as you will be. Rooms start at $205; call ahead for reservations at Café Blu. The **Casa Vieja Gallery** (787–741–3078), located at the entrance to the inn, is an artist-run, artist-owned gallery and working studio. The gallery shows contemporary art by local and visiting artists.

There are several other lodging and dining options outside of Esperanza. The twelve-room **Crow's Nest** (Route 201, km. 1.6; 787–741–0033) is set on five acres of rolling hillside in barrio **Florida,** the quiet middle of the island. It's just a six-minute ride from the center of town or from the beaches in Esperanza. Room rates average $85. The pool and adjoining deck have a spectacular bird's-eye view of the island's countryside. Nice grounds, and the friendly staff will help arrange all sorts of activities.

Even better is to go up to **Pilón,** in the island's hilly central region. **La Finca el Caribe** (Route 995; 787–741–0495) rightly bills itself as a "rustic getaway." There's a central guest house plus small cabins for

The Fiery Waters of Mosquito Bay

*M*osquito Bay, *on Vieques, is one of the best examples in the world of a bioluminescent bay. The shimmering waters are especially breathtaking on moonless nights. The bay's magic glow comes from the billions of tiny protozoan organisms called* pyrodinium bahamense. *At night these organisms glow, a phenomenon that increases when the water is disturbed, giving the currents a fiery look. The organisms are kept in the bay by its narrow channel. Be sure to take a swim in the glowing waters, so*

you can see their dazzling spray erupt around you.

If someone offers you a ride on a boat that is gas-powered, decline. Pollution from boat engines can kill the organisms that give the bay its glow. Most tour operators give electric boat or kayak tours, which cause no harm. Call **Island Adventures** *(787–741–0720) or* **Blue Caribe Dive Center** *(787–741–2522). To learn more about the phosphorescent bay, see the Web site www.biobay.com.*

rent. Comfortable, laid-back lodging in the heart of the country. There are also beautiful private homes for rent in the area. The community's Web site, www.enchanted-isle.com, lists many of these.

Pilón is also home to **Chez Shack** (Route 995; 787–741–2175), started by Duffy, a legendary figure who has been operating various guest houses and restaurants in Puerto Rico for the last four decades. Mondays are "Reggae Grill Night," which always draws a crowd. Another fine restaurant in an out-of-the-way spot is **La Campesina** (Route 996; 787–741–1239), which serves gourmet food in what feels like a wooden gazebo carved out of a tropical garden. If you only go to one restaurant, make it this one.

On the north coast by the airport is **Mount Pirata,** which has a cave at its summit where the ancient Taíno chief Bieque supposedly hid his people's treasures from the Spanish conquistadors. At any rate, the mount has nice views as does another spot on the north coast.

Just 7 miles long and 3 miles wide, **Culebra** is even smaller than Vieques and it's so laid-back that Vieques's Esperanza Beach seems downright cosmopolitan in comparison. Though its name means "snake," it got its name from its shape, not the presence of the reptiles. The dry island has spectacular beaches, and its lack of water run-off makes for great diving, with visibility of 60 feet or greater.

In addition Culebra has dozens of small cays and islets that make perfect stopping points on a boating trip. Magnificent reefs and hard and soft coral ridges surround the Culebra coast. Lumbering nurse sharks, tropical fish, and other sea life thrive in Culebra's shallow waters, which rarely exceed a depth of 100 feet.

Throughout the 1500s Culebra served as a hiding place for the Taínos, who fled the Spanish colonization of Puerto Rico. It then became a refuge for pirates, whose buried treasure is still said to be hidden on the island. In the late 1800s farmers growing tamarind, mango, and other tropical crops began to settle here. The U.S. Navy first established itself on Culebra shortly after the end of the Spanish-American War and left in 1975. Today Culebra is home to about 3,000 residents with many wealthy Puerto Ricans and North Americans maintaining vacation or retirement homes on the island.

In 1909 a **National Wildlife Refuge** was established in Culebra. Today more than 1,000 acres of Culebra, as well as much of its coastline and twenty-four offshore islands, are managed by the U.S. Department of Fish and Wildlife. The island teems with bird species, such as brown boobies, laughing gulls, Bahama ducks, and brown pelicans. Between

May and July the island's pristine beaches serve as a nesting ground for rare leatherback turtles. You can even go on turtle-watching expeditions, on which you quietly and patiently stand watch through the night waiting to glimpse the large creatures lumbering across the beach to bury their eggs and protect them. The *Culebra Leatherback Project* (P.O. Box 190, Culebra, PR 00775; 787–742–0015) has more information.

Several guest houses are located in the island's main town of *Dewey,* which also hosts the ferry dock, post office, town hall, and several eateries. Most of the lodgings offer transportation to the beautiful Flamenco Beach, so staying here makes a lot of sense. It's also the site for scuba and fishing expedition departures. *The Culebra Calendar* (787–742–0816) is a bilingual weekly newspaper that also puts out a handy tourist guide. Take a look at Culebra's "F.Y.I." on the Web site www.enchanted-isle.com.

In the middle of Dewey's Bay is *Pirate's Cay,* a favorite spot for holiday beach picnics. At the corner of the main road you'll find *Dewey City Hall,* with a tourist information office (787–742–3291).

Mamacíta's (66 Castallen; 787–742–0090) and *Posada La Hamaca* (68 Castallen; 787–742–3516) are two of the best places to stay in town, and they're located right next to each other on the lagoon through town. For breakfast and dinner Mamacíta's has a good restaurant on the dock overlooking the water. There are only three rooms for rent here, but they're all gorgeous. At La Hamaca there's a barbecue on the back deck for guests' use, and coolers are supplied. Both places provide transportation to Flamenco Beach.

Around the corner from these two establishments is a drawbridge over the lagoon. *The Dinghy Dock* (787–742–0581) is a restaurant on an open dock on the lagoon beside the drawbridge. The menu ranges from grilled T-bones to vegetarian specials at dinner to eggs over easy for breakfast. Around the bend, directly across the lagoon from Mamacíta's and La Hamaca, is a municipal entertainment complex with pool tables and video games. It's the scene of rowdy dance parties on weekend evenings.

Following the main road from the drawbridge will take you to *Ensenada Honda,* or Deep Bay, a favorite resting spot for Caribbean boaters. *Club Seabourne* (787–742–3169 or 800–613–1511) is a charming wooden clubhouse with high ceilings, a wooden lobby, and a screened-in dining room. The dining room, with an adjacent open-air bar, serves the best food on the island. The hotel also has the only freshwater, public swimming pool on the island.

Taking the road from the drawbridge out of town the other way leads to the airport. Bearing left at the airport takes you on the road to Flamenco Beach. *Tamarindo Estates* (787–742–3343) is an isolated hotel and restaurant down a long gravel road overlooking a beautiful coastline. The bar and restaurant here are worth visiting even if you don't stay. It has that edge-of-the-world feeling to it, with a seemingly endless empty beach fronting the property.

Crescent-shaped and palm-lined *Playa Flamenco* has a campground, bathrooms, freshwater showers, and some lodging. Most guest houses in Dewey will bring you here in the morning and take you back in the afternoon, so many guests prefer staying in town. Flamenco's white-sand beach is great for swimming. The tanks at the far end of the beach are a grim reminder of the military exercises that used to take place on these peaceful shores. Uphill a half mile from the beach is the island's highest point, *Mount Resaca,* covered by forest and giving a panoramic view of the countless cays and the Virgin Islands.

A right turn at the airport leads to secluded *Playa Zoni,* a mile-long strip of white beach that has the feeling of being your very own. I actually once found a message in a bottle on this beach. The bottle had been tossed over the side of a ship by a couple in Martinique who felt that compelling urge to connect with someone on this particular New Year's Eve. Zoni is well worth the trip, even though roads are bad and a Jeep is usually required. The snorkeling is wonderful.

Culebrita, a mile-long islet off Culebra's coast, has an old lighthouse and gorgeous beaches. It's a great spot to snorkel. The most experienced scuba operator on the island is Gene Thomas, who runs *Culebra Dive Shop* (317 Fulladoza; 787–742–0566). He's a thorough teacher who knows the waters around Culebra and its more than forty dive sites like the back of his hand.

Humacao

Humacao lies south of Ceiba along Route 3. Though the Route 3 ride is lovely, passing by sleepy farmland and towering bamboo, travelers heading directly to Humacao from San Juan might want to travel south along the Luis Ferré Expressway and then take Highway 30 east. Towns on the southeast coast are more quickly reached by taking the Expressway to Highway 53 toward Guayama. The new expressway, Highway 53, has also opened on the east coast and will get you from Fajardo to Yabucoa in thirty minutes. Following the original Route

Monkey Business

*L*ess than 1 mile offshore is **Cayo Santiago,** *a thirty-nine-acre island that is home to about 700 rhesus monkeys. The monkey colony was started under a Columbia University grant in 1938, when the first group of monkeys was brought over from India. Even though the monkeys were hit by a tuberculosis epidemic and then nearly starved to death when research money ran out during World War II, the colony is still thriving under the administration of the University of Puerto Rico's Caribbean Primate Research Center. Because the monkeys live in a natural environment but are contained on the island, scientists can study their behavior and development throughout their entire life span. More than 300 scientific articles have been written based on research conducted here, which is also credited with several breakthroughs in human medicine. To avoid disturbing the research, visitors are forbidden. But boats can be hired that anchor offshore close enough to see the monkeys, who can be seen having a good time on the beach or swinging from the trees. The Shagrada (787–852–6000, extension 17785) specializes in trips to the island leaving daily from Harbourside Dock No. 135, weather permitting.*

3 will reward you with a glimpse of a pastoral Puerto Rico.

Humacao's **Punta Santiago** (Route 3, km. 77) public beach features a miles-long beach and off-shore cays that draw crowds of locals and tourists alike. The beach is also one of the more active, with a burgeoning refreshment area and activities ranging from beach volleyball to kayaking. **Centro Vacacional de Punta Santiago** (Route 3, km. 72.4; 787–852–1660), one of the island's government-run vacation centers, is near here.

Further south is **Doral Resort at Palmas del Mar** (170 Candeloro Drive; 787–852–6000 or 800–PALMAS3; www.palmasdelmar.com), a massive 2,700-acre residential and tourism complex that's been called everything from the "New American Riviera" to the "Caribbean side of Puerto Rico." The resort boasts 3 miles of beach and another 3 miles of oceanfront cliffs and promontories. There's even a reserve of tropical forest and a lush fern garden within the grounds. The resort does seem to have it all, with a nice beach, golf course, restaurants, casino, equestrian center, and marina. There is good deep-sea fishing here, with marlin, wahoo, and tuna all up for grabs. Charters are around the same price as in San Juan ($450 to $650 for a full day). Day-long snorkeling trips to offshore cays and nearby Vieques can also be arranged. Most of these activities are open to the public by prior arrangement, and visitors should feel free to wander around the beaches and property. There's a fee for parking and use of lockers.

Casa Roig (66 Antonio López Street; 787–852–8380), a restored residence of the prominent Roig family (who made important social and economic contributions to the eastern part of the island), was constructed in 1919 by noted architect Antonín Nechodoma. Today the building operates as a museum and art gallery. Art exhibits, book presentations, and other cultural events often take place here. Open Wednesday through Friday 10:00 A.M. to 3:00 P.M.

Southeast Puerto Rico

Below Humacao, Route 3 leads to the rarely visited Southeast Puerto Rico. Here you'll pass through sugar cane fields, cow pastures, towering bamboo vegetation, lush mountains, and beautiful beaches. Although new highways have recently made this area more accessible, the southeast corner of Puerto Rico is still one of the island's more remote spots, a fact made all the more surprising by the region's beauty. The **Roig Sugar Mill** is located off Route 3. During harvest, which ends in June, one can see the stacks of cane waiting to be processed. In winter, when the cane is still high, the shifting stalks appear to change color depending on the time of day.

Yabucoa is the eastern starting point of the **Panoramic Route,** a tangle of narrow country roads running through the island's central mountain range to the west coast. (For more on this route, see the Central Mountains chapter.)

Take Route 901 outside of Yabucoa to join with Route 3 later. Here the road bucks up steep hills that offer phenomenal views of the rugged coastline and the offshore island of Vieques. **El Nuevo Horizonte** (Route 901; 787–893–5492) is a fine restaurant built on one of the road's more impressive look-outs. The restaurant has a rustic feel to it, and it serves good fresh seafood, steaks, and Puerto Rican specialties like *mofongo.* The view is incredible, with the dining room's large windows overlooking Puerto Rico's eastern coast and offshore islands.

Farther south the road begins a gradual decline through long gentle curves that eventually leads to **Maunabo,** a quiet coastal town best known for its splendid 1890s lighthouse at Punta Tuna. The beautiful coastal road ribboning through here alone is worth the trip, and many people don't stay much longer than it takes to appreciate it—perhaps taking a quick look at the lighthouse. But those who do feel the urge to stay should do so at **Playa de Emajagüas** (Route 901, km. 2.5; 787–861–6023), a family-run guest house set on a bluff overlooking a gorgeous, mostly deserted beach. There's a gazebo area with a bar and picnic tables. The guest house itself is nothing special, but the rooms are comfortable and some have windows facing the ocean. The house also has an outdoor deck where you can sit and relax during the day or at night.

The beach here is empty much of the time—fishermen use a lower beach road to make launches to the north, and a beachfront cantina open on weekends caters mostly to the area's older clientele. The scratchy jukebox carries some old classic Puerto Rican songs, romantic boleros, and early salsa. The bar's decor includes an eclectic mix of items, including a photo of John F. Kennedy Jr.

Here the beach sand is darker and heavier than elsewhere in Puerto Rico, and the surf can be quite rough. Palm trees line the lower dirt road at the base of the bluff.

Maunabo itself is a nondescript town, with the few businesses along the coastal road dedicated to the basics like food and gasoline. Like most Puerto Rican towns, it has a quaint central plaza area where you can have lunch or breakfast at one of the cafeterias in town. At **Punta Tuna** the 1890s lighthouse is one of the few still functioning in Puerto Rico. The wide sand beach here is among the nicest in the region.

Route 3 leaves Maunabo and heads into flatter coastal areas with sugar cane fields toward **Patillas,** a sleepy southeastern town. The midday heat is so strong here in summer that the town's downtown plaza seems uninhabited, as everyone is taking refuge in the dark, air-conditioned cafes, restaurants, and bars, or inside their own homes.

If you came here for the coast, you have several choices of where to stay. **Caribe Playa Resort** (Route 3; km. 112.1; 787–839–6339 or 800–221–4483; www.caribeplaya.com), is a small hotel outfitted to the max with a precious piece of coastline outside its door. It makes for an affordable weekend getaway and is quickly becoming a favorite spot for locals. Also in the neighborhood are **Caribbean Paradise Hotel** (Route 3, km. 114.3; 787–839–5885) and **Villa de Carmen Resort** (Route 3, km. 113; 787–839–7576).

The next town along the south coast, **Arroyo,** has both a *balneario* and *centro vacacional* at **Punta Guilarte** (Route 3, km. 128.5; 787–839–3565). The beach here is nice, and the weather is almost always dry and hot. The *centro vacacional* has twenty-eight cabins, thirty-two villas, forty tent sites, a swimming pool, and basketball and tennis courts.

The town also has a renovated historic train that leaves from Estación de Tren del Sur, or **Southern Train Station** (Route 3; 787–271–1574. Adults $3.00, children $2.00). The train was once used to transport sugar cane, today it transports tourists on an hour-long trip to the Santa Elena plantation in neighboring Guayama. While at the station, take a ride on **El Trolley,** which provides free service to downtown Arroyo and surrounding areas. It's a good way to see the town's historic sites. Saturdays and Sundays, 9:30 A.M. to 4:00 P.M.

Guayama, further along Route 3's trek through sugar country, is renowned as the cleanest town in Puerto Rico, most probably based on the impression given by its beautiful downtown plaza. The plaza makes a great place for lunch or a quick stroll, as it gives an almost idealized impression of small-town Puerto Rican life. It also contains some of Puerto Rico's most valuable historic architecture outside of Old San Juan.

One of the stately homes here is the birthplace of **Luis Palos Matos** (Calle Ashford), a poet who celebrated Puerto Rico's African roots. A plaque adorns the house, which is now a private residence. The **Casa Cautiño Museum** (1 Calle Palmer; 787–864–9083), right on the plaza, is named after the family who lived here when the home was built in 1887. Its exhibits of art, period furniture, and family artifacts are aimed at presenting a look at what life was really like for *los cautiños.* Open Tuesday through Saturday 9:00 A.M. to 4:30 P.M., Sundays 10:00 A.M. to 4:30 P.M. Admission $1.00; 50 cents for children and seniors.

Other historic buildings include a theater and pharmacy. The **Centro de Bellas Artes,** or Fine Arts Center (Antiguo Tribunal Superior; McArthur Street; 787–864–7765), is housed in a stately former courthouse dating from 1927. The museum features a nice collection of paintings and sculptures from the 1940s to the present. Admission is free. It's also a good spot from which to take advantage of the town's free trolley service to visit Guayama's other historic sites. The trolley runs from 9:00 A.M. to 4:00 P.M. on Sunday and is available for group tours (by prior arrangement). Call 787–864–7765 for reservations.

Guayama also has its own shore, around **Jobos Bay,** which it shares with neighboring **Aguirre,** another center of sugar country (or the little that remains of it). The protected bay is a magnet for several bird species, and its shallow waters team with microorganisms that attract fish of all kinds.

Beyond Guayama, Route 3 connects with the Luis A. Ferré Expressway (Highway 52), which is the quickest route over the Cordillera Central to San Juan.

**PLACES TO STAY
EAST OF SAN JUAN**

ARROYO
Centro Vacacional Punta Guilarte
Route 3, km. 128.5
(787) 839–3565

CEIBA
Casa Marshall
14 Las Quinta
(787) 885–4474

Ceiba Country Inn
Route 977
(787) 885–0471

CULEBRA
Club Seabourne
Punta del Soldado Road
(787) 742–3169 or
(800) 613–1511

Culebra Beach Villas
Playa Flamenco
(787) 742–0319

Culebra Dive Resort
Above Villa Muñeco
(787) 742–0129

Culebra Island Villas
South of Dewey
(787) 742–0333

Harbour View Villas
Dewey
(787) 742–3171 or
(800) 440–0070

Hotel Kokomo
66 Castalen, Dewey
(787) 742–0719

Mamacíta's
66 Castallen, Dewey
(787) 742–0090

Posada La Hamaca
68 Castallen, Dewey
(787) 742–3516

Tamarindo Estates
Playa Tamarindo
(787) 742–3343

Villa Arynar
South of Dewey
(787) 742–3145

Villa Boheme
South of Dewey
(787) 742–3508

Villa Nueva
Barriada Clark
(787) 742–0257

FAJARDO
Anchor's Inn
Route 987, km. 2.5
(787) 863–7200

Parador Fajardo Inn and Scenic Inn
Route 195, 52 Parcelas
Beltran Road
(787) 860–6000;
www.fajardoinn.com

La Familia
Route 987, km. 4.1
(787) 863–1193;
www.hotellafamilia.com

Wyndham El Conquistador Resort and Country Club
Route 987, km. 3.4
(787) 863–1000 or
(800) 468–8365;
www.wyndham.com

HUMACAO
Centro Vacacional de Punta Santiago
Route 3, km. 72.4
(787) 852–1660

Doral Resort at Palmas del Mar
170 Candeloro Drive
(787) 852–6000 or
(800) PALMAS3;
www.palmasdelmar.com

LUQUILLO
Casa Flamboyant Bed and Breakfast
(787) 874–6074

Grateful Bed and Breakfast
Off Route 3 down unmarked road at
El Rancho Bar
(787) 889–4919

Trinidad Guest House
(formerly known as
Parador Martorell)
6-A Ocean Drive
(787) 889–2710;
www.trinidadguesthouse.
com

Villa Falcon Resort
Calle 1, #8 Fortuna
(787) 889–7185

NAGUABO
Casa Cubuy Ecolodge
Route 31, 4 miles west of
Naguabo in Río Blanco
(787) 874–6221

Phillips Family Budget
Cabins
Route 191
(787) 874–2138;
www.elyunque.com

PATILLAS
Caribe Playa Beach Resort
Route 3, km. 112.1
(787) 839–6339 or
(800) 221–4483;
www.caribeplaya.com

Caribbean Paradise Hotel
Route 3, km. 114.3
(787) 839–5885

Villa de Carmen Resort
Route 3, km. 113
(787) 839–7576

RIO GRANDE
Le Petite Chalet
(787) 887–5802

Río Grande Plantation Eco
Resort
Route 956, km. 4.2
(787) 887–2779;
www.riograndeplantation.
com

Río Mar Resort Villas
Paraíso 47 Hacienda
Las Garzas
(787) 793–6195

Westin Río Mar Beach
Resort
6000 Río Mar
(Route 968)
(787) 888–6000 or
(800) 937–8461;
www.westinriomar.com

VIEQUES
Acacia Apartments
236 Acacia, Esperanza
(787) 741–1856

Amapola Inn and Tavern
144 Flamboyán, Esperanza
(787) 741–1382

Bananas
142 Flamboyán, Esperanza
(787) 741–8700

Casa Cielo
El Pilón
(787) 741–2403

Casa La Lanchita
Bravos de Boston
(800) 774–4717

Crow's Nest
Route 201, km. 1.6, Florida
(787) 741–0033

Finca Caribe
Route 995
(787) 741–0495

Hacienda Tamarindo
Route 996, km.
4.5, west of Esperanza
(787) 741–8525

Hix Island House
El Pilón
(787) 741–2302;
www.hixislandhouse.com

Inn on the Blue Horizon
Route 996, km. 4.2,
Esperanza
(787) 741–3318

La Casa de Francés
Route 996, Esperanza
(787) 741–3751

Tourist Information for East of San Juan

Naguabo Tourism Office
(787) 874–0389 or (787) 874–3040 extension 234

Fajardo Tourism Information
City Hall
(787) 863–4013

Culebra Tourism Information
City Hall
(787) 742–3291

Luquillo Tourism Information
14 de Julio
(787) 889–2225

Vieques Tourism Information
City Hall
(787) 741–5000

La Finca el Caribe
Route 995, Pilón
(787) 741-0495

La Piña Apartments
22 Acacia, Esperanza
(787) 741-2953

Martineau Bay
Gringo Beach
(787) 741-4100 or
(888) 767-3966;
www.rosewood-hotels.com

Ocean View
Isabel Segunda
(787) 741-3696

Posada Vistamar
Esperanza
(787) 741-8716

Sea Gate Hotel
Isabel Segunda
(787) 741-4661

Trade Winds
Esperanza
(787) 741-8666

YABUCOA
Palmas de Lucía
Route 9911
(787) 893-4425;
www.palmasdelucia.com

Playa de Emajagüas Guest
House
Highway 901, km. 2.5
(787) 861-6023

**PLACES TO EAT
EAST OF SAN JUAN**

CULEBRA
Club Seabourne
South of Dewey
(787) 742-3169 or
(800) 613-1511

Dinghy Dock
Dewey
(787) 742-0581

El Batey
250 Carretera
(787) 742-3828

Hart's Oasis
Dewey
(787) 742-3175

Mamacíta's
66 Castallen
(787) 742-0090

Marta's Al Fresco
Dewey
(787) 743-3575

FAJARDO
A La Banda Waterfront
Restaurant
Puerto del Rey Marina
Highway 3, km. 51.4
(787) 860-9162

Anchor's Inn
Route 987, km. 2.7
(787) 863-7200

La Fontanella
Las Croabas Roads
(787) 860-2480

Rosa's Seafood
Route 195, Tablazo 536
(787) 863-0213

Sardinera
Calle Croabas, km. 5.5
(787) 863-0320

Tulio's Seafood
Isidro Andrew #5
(787) 850-1840

HUMACAO
Chez Daniel
Palmas del Mar
170 Candeloro Drive
(787) 852-6000

Hermés Creative Cuisine
Palmas del Mar Country
Club, Route 906
(787) 285-2277

Tulio's Seafood
Isidro Andrew #5
(787) 850-1840

LUQUILLO
Brass Cactus Bar and Grill
Luquillo Beach Complejo
Turístico
(787) 889-5735

Chef Wayne
Off Route 992 on
unmarked road
(787) 889-1962

Victor's Place Seafood
2 Jesús T. Piñeiro
(787) 889-5705

MAUNABO
Los Bohíos
Route 760, km. 2.3,
beach sector
(787) 861-2545

VIEQUES
Amapola Inn and Tavern
144 Flamboyán, Esperanza
(787) 741-1382

Bananas
142 Flamboyán, Esperanza
(787) 741-8700

Café Blu
Inn on the Blue Horizon
Route 996, km. 4.2
(787) 741-3318

Café Media Luna
Isabel Segunda
(787) 741-2594

Chez Shack
Route 995, Pilón
(787) 741-2175

La Campesina
Route 996
(787) 741-1239

La Casa del Francés
Route 996, Esperanza
(787) 741-3751

Richard's Café
Antonio Mellado
(787) 741-5242

Taverna Española
Isabel Segunda
(787) 741-1175

Trade Winds
Esperanza
(787) 741-8666

Trapper John's
Crow's Nest
Route 201, km. 1.6,
Barrio Florida
(787) 741-0011

YABUCOA
El Nuevo Horizonte
Route 901, km. 9.8
(787) 839-5492

El Tivoli
Route 901, km. 3.7
(787) 893-2727

Ponce and the South

one are the days when Puerto Rico's southern coast was separated from the capital by grueling one-lane roadways through steep mountain terrain. The completion of a freeway in 1975 put the south coast within easy reach of San Juan, and a recent extension that skirts downtown Ponce has cut trips to the southwest by about forty-five minutes. Now Ponce is a quick ninety-minute drive, and almost anywhere in the southwest can be reached within another hour or so from there.

Despite increased contact with San Juan, the south still retains its own ways. This is the Caribbean side of Puerto Rico, and the south coast sizzles throughout the year. The sun is almost always strong and high, and a lavender light is cast across the grassy pastures and coastline that run through the region. This has a big effect on the pace of the days and nights here. Puerto Rico's southerners are distinct from their northern neighbors; they're used to a slower-paced, more relaxed way of life. History seems closer at hand here, where an agricultural way of life lives on in sugarcane plantations and cattle fields that punctuate the drive along the southern coast. The region's capital, *Ponce,* is a provincial city of turn-of-the-century grandeur and immaculate plazas. From Guánica to Lajas to Cabo Rojo, southwestern Puerto Rico has some of the island's best beaches. Along with large hotels and casinos, the region also has pristine natural reserves, from coastal mangroves to cliffs to dry forests.

There are many reasons to visit this region, and no one should forgo the trip—even if it's just a Ponce day-tour from San Juan. But those who come to this region to stay for a few days will definitely be rewarded. Puerto Ricans love this part of the country, and they flock here in droves during holiday weekends.

South of San Juan

eading south from San Juan means taking the Luis A. Ferré Expressway (Highway 52), which cuts through San Juan's southern suburbs and then straight over the top of the Cordillera Central mountains to the steaming southern coast.

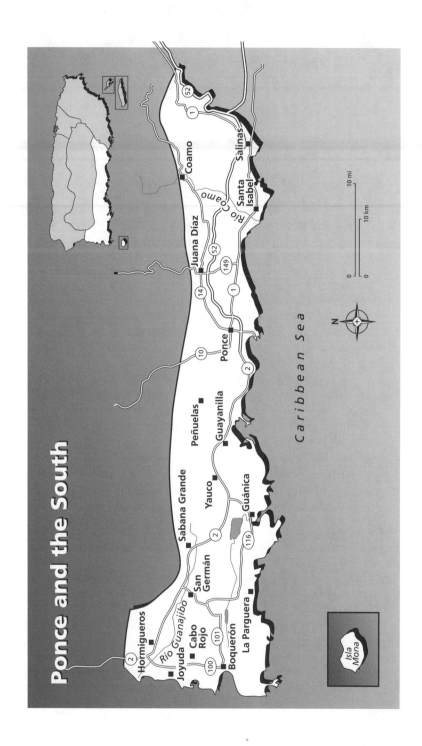

Ponce and the South

Hormigueros

Joyuda
Cabo
Rojo

Boquerón

La Parguera

San
Germán

Río Guanajibo

Sabana Grande

Yauco

Guánica

Peñuelas

Guayanilla

Ponce

Juana Díaz

Coamo

Santa
Isabel

Salinas

Río Coamo

Caribbean Sea

Isla
Mona

N

0
10 mi
0
10 km

PONCE AND THE SOUTH

The biggest points of interest on the first leg of the trip may be the three large shopping malls the expressway passes as it leaves San Juan and moves into the greater metropolitan area, which stretches clear down to Caguas. The Plaza las Américas, Montehiedra, and new Caguas Malls are good to know if you need to pick up something for your trip. Your best chance of getting in and out quickly is probably at Montehiedra. The mall is located right off the Luis A. Ferré Expressway. A sign points to the exit, right before the first toll at the outer limits of San Juan and Caguas.

When hunger strikes, go to **Martin's Barbecue and Pizzeria** (Highway 1; 787–738–1144), just off the Cayey exit, next to the Exxon station. What you miss in scenery you'll make up for in convenience. This authentic *criollo* barbecue shack serves roast pig, seasoned chicken, *mofongo,* stewed yucca, black *morcilla* sausage, and *arroz con gandules.*

Though it's only about a forty-minute drive from San Juan to the top of the central mountain range, the climatic changes are dramatic. The area is often draped in dark clouds, and it's generally much cooler here than on the coasts. As the highway soars upward, it passes lushly covered hillsides and emerald-green patches of farmland.

The descent to the Caribbean coast along the mountain range's southern side is always impressive, with the blue Caribbean Sea set back against the southern coast's vast plains and flanked by distant palms. The roadway tumbles down into the foothills that, depending on the season, are either a lunar-like terra cotta or a lush tropical green. Without fail, the hot sun blares above the blue sea, sending shimmering waves of haze across the Caribbean afternoon.

After passing over the Cordillera Central, the expressway turns into a coastal road ribboning through cattle farms and mountains. The first town you pass is **Salinas,** where you'll find **Albergue Olímpico** (Road 712, km. 3.4; 787–824–2200), a school and training center for students with Olympic potential. The center is open to visitors and includes a sports museum, mini-mall, water park, playground, and botanical gardens. Open daily 8:00 A.M. to 10:00 P.M. The Puerto Rican Museum of Sports (Road 712, km. 3.4; 787–824–2607) is open Thursday through Friday 8:00 A.M. to 5:00 P.M., Saturday and Sunday 9:00 A.M. to 6:00 P.M. The town's waterfront is known for its seafood restaurants located on open-air porches overlooking the Bahía de Rincón at

Playa Salinas. Small mangrove cays close by make for good swimming and snorkeling.

A bit farther along to the west are the famous thermal springs, *Baños de Coamo.* Take the exit for Route 153, then turn onto Route 546 and drive west for one mile. These thermal springs were revered by the ancient Taínos, and legend has it that they were the fountain of youth Juan Ponce de León was searching for. The fashionable resort that thrived here during the turn of the century drew the likes of Franklin D. Roosevelt, Alexander Graham Bell, and Thomas Edison. Open 10:00 A.M. to 5:30 P.M. Free admission. Although the public baths are free, they're not well maintained. Better to try the adjacent *Parador Baños de Coamo* (Route 546; 787–825–2186; www.banosdecoamo.com), which has a spa-like ambience. Located adjacent to the hotel, the thermal springs feed into a series of hotel pools. The springs themselves don't feel all that much different than a Jacuzzi. The real beauty of this place is in its surroundings: peaceful, tree-lined, rolling country roads that attract people who come here to jog, hike, horseback ride, and rejuvenate themselves. Be forewarned: The hotel's practice of selling day passes ($5.00 for adults, $3.00 for children; open 10:00 A.M. to 5:30 P.M.) to its pools (both spring-fed and regular) can lead to crowding on weekends. The *parador*'s exteriors are handsome, from the two-story hotel building with wraparound, wooden verandas and lattice woodwork over its facade to a Spanish-colonial stucco building that houses the restaurant, Café Puertoriqueño. Those who stay here, however, usually wind up with, at best, mixed reviews of the rooms.

Ponce

once, known as the "Pearl of the South," is the island's second-largest city. It is a pretty, provincial town that still maintains its turn-of-the century feeling, when Ponce was not only the most important city in Puerto Rico, but in much of the Caribbean as well. The city's history dates back to 1692, when it was named after Ponce de León's great grandson. It would take nearly one hundred years to become a city in its own right.

The sun-bleached city's historic zone is laced with a whimsical Caribbean architecture built from the 1850s through the 1930s, when Ponce was the rich port city of a region bursting with agricultural activity. It was also a center of intellectual life, and many poets, painters, and politicians hailed from this area.

Ponce residents initially favored a simple, colonial architectural style,

Top Annual Events

San Blas Marathon, *early February, Coamo*

Carnival, *late February, Ponce*

Sugar Harvest Festival, *mid-March, San Germán*

Carnival, *late April, Salinas*

Maví Carnival, *late April, Juana Díaz*

Danza Festival, *mid-May, Ponce*

25 de Julio *Guánica*

Bomba and Plena Festival, *early October, Ponce*

but as the city grew richer so did local tastes. In the nineteenth century, homes began displaying ornate neoclassical and Art Nouveau flourishes. Interiors were also elaborately decorated so that the sunlight coming through intricate stained-glass panels would fall in splashes of color over patterned, mosaic tile floors. Punched-tin ceilings and fixed jalousies in back corridors were also prevalent. Extremely high ceilings were adorned with wainscoting and dado, moldings, and cornices.

Until 1995 the Luis A. Ferré Expressway ended at Ponce, meaning that drivers heading for the southwest went through the city center in order to catch Highway 2. Now the road has been lengthened so that the expressway spills onto Highway 2 on the western edges of the city. While the extension only added a few miles to the expressway, it has shaved an hour off most trips by circumventing the traffic-clogged city.

Most people who want to visit Ponce, however, will still get off at the old Ponce By-Pass, a built-up roadway that runs through a modern retail district and connects the old Highway 1 and Highway 2. Here you'll find plenty of places to gas up, and roadside fruit vendors selling everything from *queñepas* to fat pineapples, depending on the season. There are also several shopping centers, with the biggest being Plaza del Caribe on Highway 2.

The Republic of Ponce

*P*onceños *will be the first ones to tell you that they're, well, different. The town's mayor is the most powerful politician in the south. In fact he works out of plush trappings that rival La Fortaleza, the governor's mansion in San Juan. Ponce is also one of Puerto Rico's few "autonomous" municipalities, a status that grants the town a wide range of oversight.*

While Ponce's rise as a shipping power always kept it better in touch with Europe than San Juan, the town is also the most African of cities, the birthplace of the bomba and plena. Ponceños still take enormous pride in their city and are more often than not unfairly criticized for doing so. Rosario Ferré offers insight in her novel **House on the Lagoon,** *where she portrays life in both Ponce and San Juan over the last century.*

To get to Ponce's historic district, take Route 133, which runs over the Río Portugues before becoming Calle Comercio, the historic district's main artery. Two bronze lions by sculptor Victor Ochoa tower over the entrance to Ponce's historic zone.

Plaza Las Delicias, also called Plaza Degetau or Plaza Central, is the main square in the historic zone. It captures the city's charm with its ultra-clean, shaded walkways and its opulent fountains and flower gardens, which give the city the appearance of a delicate pastry. Big trees hang over stone benches and antique gas lampposts, while pink granite pathways roll through the plaza. Trolleys and horse-drawn carriages ply the narrow historic streets as well-dressed *ponceños* slowly stroll in the Caribbean heat.

The plaza is dominated by the **Lion Fountain,** a bronze-and-marble fountain made for the 1939 World's Fair. It was modeled after the fountain of the same name in Barcelona, Spain. The most photographed building on the plaza is undoubtedly the **Parque de Bombas** (Plaza Las Delicias; 787–284–3338), the city's famous Victorian firehouse, which was built in 1883 as the centerpiece to an annual agricultural fair. It has red and black walls, myriad poles and cornices, and many passageways. Admission is free. Open 9:30 A.M. to 6:00 P.M., closed Tuesday.

The **Cathedral of Our Lady of Guadalupe** (Concordia and Union; 787–842–0134), named after the city's patron saint, has unique silver spiral protrusions that sparkle in the refracted heat of the Ponce afternoon. The church was built here in 1660 as a rustic chapel, but it was destroyed on several occasions by natural disasters from fires to earthquakes. The present Gothic-inspired structure was built in the 1930s.

Helpful tourist information centers are scattered throughout the downtown area. Rides in horse-drawn carriages are also offered. The attractive **Casa Alcaldía,** City Hall (787–284–4141), across from the Plaza, dates from 1840. **Hotel Meliá** (2 Cristina; 787–842–0260) is the place to stay downtown. Among its features are a rooftop terrace, friendly staff, and **Mark's at the Meliá** (Hotel Meliá; 787–842–0260), a fine restaurant by renowned local chef Mark French, which takes traditional *comida criolla* and raises it to new heights. Also on the plaza is **King's Cream** (Plaza Las Delicias; 787–843–8520), a local ice cream parlor famous for its homemade flavorful creations.

Paseo Arias is also known as the Callejón del Amor, or Lovers Lane, a pedestrian passage built in the 1920s between two banks. Today the buildings house air-conditioned mini-malls filled with African tulips and open-air cafes. The **Fox Delicias Mall** (78 Isabel), on the north end

Parque de Bombas

of Plaza Las Delicias, was built in the 1930s. The red-tile–roofed build-ing. originally a movie theater, combines Hollywood Art Deco flourishes with a Mediterranean style. It now houses a food court and stores.

Teatro La Perla (Calle Mayor; 787–843–4080) remains a center of Ponce's cultural life, with concerts, and theatrical and dance performances taking place throughout the year, as well as more low-brow (and popular) affairs such as beauty pageants. A late-afternoon stroll by here often rewards the visitor with a warm-up practice of the evening's performance. The theater was designed along the lines of New York's Carnegie Hall, and it is famous for its acoustics. The theater is graced by six Corinthian columns and was originally built in 1864 by the Italian-born Juan Bertoli Calderoni, who is considered the father of Puerto Rico's neoclassical architectural style. Bertoli also built the Ponce Creole residence that now houses the ***Museum of Puerto Rican Music*** (Calle Salud between Cristina and Isabel; 787–848–7016), where you can see displays of the Taíno, African, and Spanish instruments that have helped create the island's unique musical heritage. Open 9:00 A.M. to 4:00 P.M.(closed Monday and Tuesday).

Also worth a visit is the ***Casa Salazar,*** which houses ***The Museum of the History of Ponce*** (51-53 Isabel; 787–844–7071). The museum, which opened in 1992, traces Ponce's storied history from the time of the Taínos to the present. The 1911 building mixes Moorish and neo-classic styles and is filled with the decorative displays that typify this southern city: from its stained-glass windows, pressed-tin ceilings, and fixed-window jalousies, to its wooden and iron columns and full balconies. Open Monday through Friday 9:00 A.M. to 5:00 P.M., Saturday and Sunday 10:00 A.M. to 6:00 P.M. Closed Tuesday. Admission is $3.00 for adults, $1.00 for children.

Paseo Atocha, a pedestrian mall that is also the downtown area's main shopping district, is housed in turn-of-the-century buildings. The **Plaza del Mercado** (two blocks north of Plaza Central between Estrella and Castillos Streets) is also worth a visit. There you'll find all the heat, haggling, and liveliness you'd expect from a Caribbean market.

Another must-see is **Castillo Serrallés,** or Serrallés Castle (787–259–1774), which overlooks the city from El Vigía Hill. The mansion, built in the 1930s Spanish-revival style, was originally home to the Serrallés family, makers of Don Q rum. In 1986 the city of Ponce bought the mansion and painstakingly restored it. Today it houses a museum that attempts to replicate life in the era of the sugar barons. The museum also shows documentary films on the sugar and rum industries. Open Tuesday through Sunday 9:30 A.M. to 5:30 P.M. Admission is $3.00 for adults, $1.50 for children, and $2.00 for seniors. Forty-five-minute tours available. The mansion sits below the cross-shaped **El Vigía Observation Tower** (admission $1.00, open Tuesday through

Ponce Is Ponce

*Y*ou might hear a simple saying while you're wandering around Ponce, and it's "Ponce is Ponce." The expression aims to point up the city's uniqueness by comparing it to itself.

Nowhere is the spirit behind this saying more evident than in the city's architecture, with a sense of elegance and rich details found both in the mansions of the wealthy as well as in the most modest of homes.

Ponce boasts seven different architectural styles: Spanish colonial, European-neoclassic, superior neoclassic, as well as neoclassic Creole, Ponce Creole, town Creole, and residential Creole (all the Creole styles are closely related; their differences are indiscernible to the casual eye). What strikes most visi-

tors is the unity of Ponce's distinct architecture, with its feet firmly planted in both its European and Afro-Antillian heritages. Cristina and Mayor Streets have fine examples of wrought-iron grillwork and balconies.

*Be sure to stroll down **Isabel Street,** where many different architectural styles are present. The strong European influence here was adapted to Ponce's climate, one of the hottest in Puerto Rico. Afternoon rains are held at bay by the central mountain range. The facade of almost every building in the city is painted with pastel colors to reflect the stifling heat. The monumental 20-foot ceilings and the practice of elevating homes a few feet off the ground also help keep interiors cool.*

Sunday 10:00 A.M. to 5:00 P.M.) which affords a magnificent view. You can climb to the El Vigía neighborhood from Ponce's Plaza Las Delicias. This hilly sector overlooks the old mansions of Ponce's elite and the Caribbean sea.

If you go to one place in Ponce, go to *Jazz Nicole* (66 Calle Isabel; 787–848–5475), which serves up fine local and pasta dinners, as well as live music until well after midnight. There's jazz, Spanish rock, and *nueva trova* (a Spanish-Caribbean folk music with a socially relevant theme), depending on the night of the week. *Hollywood Café* (Boulevard Miguel Apou; 787–843–6703) is the place for rock and roll, including lots of Latin pop. The city is especially lively during the Festival of Our Lady of Guadelupe in February, when Ponce—and the whole southern coast—celebrates its African roots in song and dance.

The waterfront district of *Playa de Ponce,* sometimes referred to as El Muelle de Ponce, is a fisherman's village that lies on the opposite side of the Ponce By-Pass from the historic sector. This area (along with the adjacent waterfront wharf district of La Guancha) is loaded with casual open-air restaurants, bars, and kiosks. It is the site of concerts and other events. This is also the home of the *Ponce Yacht Club,* whose members' boats are docked just offshore.

The Ponce Art Museum

*T*he *Ponce Museum of Art* (2525 Las Américas Avenue; 787–848–0511 or 787–848–0505; www. museoarteponce.org) is the largest museum in the Caribbean and one of the most impressive. Its holdings range from European classics to contemporary Puerto Rican, with good examples of Baroque and pre-Raphaelite painting. The museum is located across from the Catholic University of Ponce. The building itself is a beauty. It was designed by Edward Durell Stone, the architect of the Museum of Modern Art in New York. The museum's collection was donated by former governor and pro-statehood New Progressive Party founder Luis Ferré.

The museum features a huge, wooden shell-shaped staircase and a series of skylit, angular galleries that give an overview of European painting from the fourteenth to nineteenth centuries. There are also traveling exhibits of contemporary art. Surrounding the staircase are such classics as Leandro Rosanno's sixteenth-century masterpiece The Flood. Other highlights include Sir Edward Burne-Jones's Sleeping Beauty, Sir Frederick Leighton's Flaming June, and Peter Paul Rubens's The Greek Magus. Open 10:00 A.M. to 5:00 P.M. daily. Adults $4.00, children $2.00, students $1.00.

At *La Guancha* you'll find a seaside boardwalk where many children's and family activities are held. While there's no beach, the waterfront area draws *ponceños* who flock here throughout the day and night to socialize. There is a large and safe parking lot, and it's possible to drive up to the water's edge. In fact as far as tourists are concerned, Ponce's biggest drawback is that it has no beach to speak of—a rarity among coastal cities.

Here you can rent boats to offshore cays such as *Caja de Muertos,* Coffin Island, which is the biggest and most popular of the offshore islands. Even when ferry service is temporarily discontinued, it's easy to rent inexpensive rides from small boats. The island has bathrooms, picnic areas, and fine swimming beaches. *Isla de Cordona,* which lies a nautical mile from La Guancha and takes less than one hour to reach, is another option for a day-trip. Although there are no public facilities, the island is much less trampled and features a nice beach and an old lighthouse. The shallow waters off both islands and the surrounding reef make for great snorkeling. Two submerged one-hundred-year-old wrecks lie just off of Cordona, and some snorkelers have found antique bottles and pottery in their explorations. San Juan–based *Las Tortugas Adventures* (787–725–5169) runs a kayaking trip to Cordona. A $75 fee provides transportation from San Juan, kayak, snorkeling equipment, and lunch, which includes drinks and beer. The tour operators set up a beachside picnic area on the island, so guests are very comfortable.

Just outside Ponce on Route 503 is the *Tibes Indian Ceremonial Center* (Route 503, km. 2.2; 787–840–5685), thought to be the oldest burial ground in the Caribbean. Ancient pre-Taíno plazas dating to A.D. 700 have been unearthed here, as well as skeletons from A.D. 200. There are also seven *bateyes,* or ball courts (where the Taínos played a soccer-like game), and two dance grounds. Both finds are cited as proof of the peaceful nature of the Taínos. Other ruins are believed to have astrological significance. The center also houses an exhibition of indigenous ceremonial objects, pottery, and jewelry. Open Tuesday through Sunday 9:00 A.M. to 4:00 P.M. Admission is $2.00 for adults and $1.00 for children and seniors.

The *Hacienda Buena Vista* (on Highway 10, north of Ponce; 787–722–5882 or 787–284–7020; www.fideicomiso.org) is a restored corn and coffee plantation that dates from 1833. It has been faithfully restored by the Conservation Trust. It's a fun trip, as you're free to wander around the plantation, which is decorated with nineteenth-century antiques and artifacts. The experience is authentic—even the waterwheels and mills function. The place is open for groups on Wednesday and Thursday and to the general public from Friday through Sunday. Spanish-language tours are given at 8:30 and 10:30 A.M. and 1:30 and 3:30 P.M., while

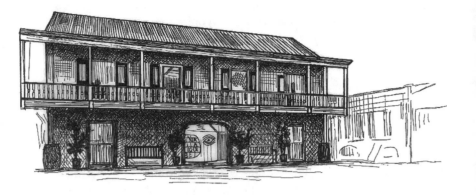

Hacienda Buena Vista

English-language tours are given at 1:30 P.M. only. Reservations are necessary for all tours. Admission is $5.00 for adults and $2.00 for children.

About 3 miles west of town lies *El Tuque,* a long stretch of beach fronting the Caribbean. It's the closest thing Ponce has to its own beach. Highway 2 westbound then passes *Las Cucharas,* a beautiful coastal area where the narrow shoreline and the highway curve in a gentle arc beside the Caribbean. On the other side of the highway is a row of famed seafood restaurants that serve fresh fish and Puerto Rican specialties. While all of them are worthy, *Pito's Seafood Café* (787–841–4977) is the most famous, with live music on weekends.

Highway 2 west of Ponce is a beautiful, rolling coastal road, with the glistening Caribbean to the left and dry, gnarled hills to the right. The one blotch on this scene is the old Corco petro-chemical plant that spreads over the Peñuelas/Guayanilla border.

The *Playa de Guayanilla,* less than 15 miles west of Ponce, is a nice place to stop and catch a real slice of Puerto Rican life. The little waterfront can be found just beyond the site of the old chemical production facility. This block-long stretch of weathered restaurants and food stands draws crowds on weekends with delicious seafood and loud music. Try *El Triangulo,* a little wood shack of a place with a fenced-in yard overlooking the waterfront. The tables are spread out in the shade of large Saint Thomas trees. Another spot worth a stop is *Brisas del Sol,* which has a good jukebox. This area, a protrusion in the staggering 3-mile-wide Guayanilla Bay, is surrounded by the Gotay and Veraco Peninsulas. It is one of the Caribbean's best naturally formed harbors.

Near the waterfront is **Parador Pichi's** (Route 132, km. 204; 787–835–3335; www.pichis.com), with a pool, fifty-eight air-conditioned rooms, and courtyard gardens. Its restaurant, **Pichi's Steakhouse and Seafood,** is a member of the government's *Mesón Gastronómico* program, known for its fine food. **La Guardarraya** (Route 127; 787–856–4222) is an impressive, informal restaurant with towering trees and enclosed-porch dining. This is strictly local fare, good and filling. The house specialty is *chuleta de Can Can* (breaded and deep fried pork chops). Also try the *arroz Mamposteao* (a fried rice concoction).

Beyond Guayanilla is the town of **Yauco,** an important coffee-growing center for over a century. In the late nineteenth century Puerto Rico's aromatic coffee was among the finest in the world, sipped in coffeehouses from Vienna to Paris to Madrid. The preeminent brand of the day was Yauco. The rise of sugar and cheaper coffee from places like Colombia replaced Puerto Rico as a major coffee exporter in the early 1900s. But Puerto Rican coffee, marked by its rich flavor, remains among the finest in the world, and Yauco coffee remains one of the best selling. Today, the cropped hills above the city are still filled with

Luchetti Lake

*O*ne good side trip is to **Luchetti Lake,** *which is about a half-hour drive up winding country roads from Highway 2. Exit the highway at Yauco Plaza and continue straight on Albizu Campos Boulevard or Route 128. As it climbs north, the road turns from four lanes to two, passing through massive bamboo and towering trees. This change happens almost instantly, and before you know it the road is overlooking dizzying drop-offs that offer precious vistas of rolling farmland and Yauco's charming center.*

You'll know when you're nearing the lake when you begin passing all manner of roadside cantinas with such magical names as El Pozo de los Milagros (the Well of Miracles) and El Vete y Vuelve (The Leave and Come Back).

Lake Luchetti, like all Puerto Rico's lakes, is an artificial lake. The lake's name comes from engineer Antonio Luchetti, who designed and constructed the dam and reservoir in 1952. Today the lake is stocked with bass, and anglers can be seen along its shores or on the roadway bridge that passes over the dam.

Since a number of the restaurants around the lake have fallen into disrepair, a picnic lunch is probably your best bet. Camping around the lake is possible with a permit from the Department of Natural and Environmental Resources (call in San Juan 787–724–3647 or 787–724–3724). There are also private lodgings available at Cabañas Muñoz (787–267–1594) and La Cabaña (787–856–2226).

coffee trees, and many former residences of the coffee barons have been elegantly restored.

It is one of the region's most charming inland cities and remains a center of agricultural activity. Here you'll find a quaint historic town center and sleepy country roads that begin as soon as you exit the highway.

Gaby's World (Route 127, km. 5.1; 787–856–2609), located right off Highway 2, bills itself as an equestrian center and recreational park. This 204-acre ranch has pony rides for kids as well as a racing course for experienced riders. The best thing is to go on a horseback tour through forests and along hillsides. Thirty-minute, one-hour, and two-hour tours are available for $10 to $40 (depending on the length). *El Caballito* restaurant (the roof-top carved wooden horse is visible from Highway 2) specializes in *comida criollo* and is open to the public from 10:00 A.M. to 10:00 P.M. (closed Tuesday).

Southwest Puerto Rico

Southwest Puerto Rico is arguably the most beautiful part of the island, filled with everything a Caribbean-bound tourist expects. The scores of beaches (many of them hidden down sandy, forested roads), and the coral reefs and cays make this one of the better places for snorkeling and swimming close to shore.

Deep-sea sports fishermen also come to the southwest to go after big game fish, such as marlin and tuna. Scuba divers relish the 100-mile-long underwater cliff that runs from Ponce to the Mona Passage. The waters here are literally teeming with fish and have good visibility.

The area's natural wonders extend to land as well. Its most famous is the Guánica Forest Reserve, a rare subtropical dry forest that looks like a giant bonsai reserve. The forest is a haven for over one hundred species of tropical birds. It tumbles down rocky cliffs to one of the most beautiful coastlines on the island.

Guánica

The coastal town of *Guánica,* the first town you'll come along on Route 116, has played a relatively unimportant role in Puerto Rican affairs since the fall of King Sugar some three decades ago. Before the arrival of the Spanish in the 1500s, the area housed a thriving Taíno community, and it was the biggest and most important *cacique,* or "gathering place," of this people. The great Taíno chief Agueybaná made his home here. Ponce de León first explored the island after landing at Guánica Bay in 1508, the start of centuries of Spanish rule and the Christianization of the island. Guánica is also where U.S. troops first landed during the Spanish-American War.

Dubbed *el pueblo de la amistad,* or the "town of friendship," Guánica lives up to its name. Asking a few questions of locals about the town's great past or its natural wonders will likely prompt long and interesting conversations with proud people wanting to share their knowledge of this special place. In fact sometimes it seems as if everybody in Guánica is an amateur historian or naturalist. The town's tourism office at city hall (corner 25 de Julio and Carlos del Rosario; 787–821–2777) might be able to recommend a guide, but asking questions along the *malecón* (waterfront promenade) may get you just as far or, with the littlest of luck, even farther.

The Back Road from Yauco

*I*f you're coming to Guánica from Yauco, avoid the main roadway and instead take quiet country Route 333. To pick it up, go underneath Highway 2 from the Yauco Plaza exit and continue straight. You'll have to pass another shopping center, Cuatro Calles, before the road returns to its country roots.

*The road then passes through shaded areas of small wooden homes and farmland with sprawling nurseries selling plants and flowers. At one point the road turns into a one-lane bridge over a trickling stream. Farther along is **El Convento de Fátima** (Calle de la Fátima, off of Route 333), a beautifully restored, active convent located at the Hacienda Santa Rita plantation. It's a beautiful place set amidst the grounds of a sugar plantation. The convent is not open to the public. Beyond the convent, the road meets up with Route 116 before coming to Guánica.*

The McDonald's at the corner of Route 116 and Guánica's main boulevard, 25 de Julio, is where to turn to get to the main town. The street is lined with charming, weather-worn wooden homes. Hardware stores and bakeries operate out of historic brick structures. The road also passes by Guánica's attractive city hall and its adjacent main square. From certain points in the town it's possible to forget if not which century, then at least which decade it is.

*25 de Julio continues on to the town's harbor area, which overlooks picturesque **Guánica Bay,** a wide mouth of protected Caribbean water between two promontories. Immediately to the right on the waterfront is a rock monument to the American invasion, placed there by the local chapter of the Daughters of the American Revolution.*

Language should not be a barrier here. Although it's true that you'll find the greatest level of English proficiency in San Juan, Guánica (like most small Puerto Rican towns) has been greatly affected by the waves of immigrants leaving the island to search for a better life stateside. Just about everyone in town has a brother, cousin, or aunt living in New York or in another stateside location and knows enough English to get by. Guánica, just like other island towns, has more than its fair share of residents who spent their productive years laboring in the United States only to return to the beloved town of their birth to retire. English is a required class in schools, and its influence among the younger generations continues to increase through cable television, Hollywood movies, and American music.

At most times the Guánica harbor is a peaceful, sleepy area, but on weekend nights it can get crowded and a bit rowdy. The *malecón* is lined with open-air bars and seafood restaurants. Try an *empanadilla de carrucho* (conch turnover) or some *escabeche de pescado* (pickled fish) at any of these places. The buildings along the harbor are graceful Caribbean colonial structures.

Following the road beyond the harbor, turn right at Marino's. The road bears left after the fishermen's dock and then leads to Route 333. Taking a left will take you back to Route 116.

Taking a right at the intersection of Route 333 will lead to one of the prettiest roads in Puerto Rico. The road climbs up in gripping curves around the hilly terrain overlooking the bay and then comes down the other side, offering cliffside vistas of the bay at each bend before flattening out to the calm, crystal-blue waters of the shoreline.

Where It All Began

*T*he advent of modern-day Puerto Rico began on July 25, 1898, with the landing of General Nelson Miles and the United States troops who would pass through this town on their march to San Juan.

To this day, almost anything you can say about the event remains impolite conversation in San Juan social circles. For starters, you can't even describe the event without showing your political cards. For independentistas, "the invasion" was the start of U.S. colonialism that has continued to this day. Pro-statehood supporters, meanwhile, see it as the long period of great benevolence under Uncle Sam.

Puerto Rican Pineapples

Guánica Bay was the site of the great exodus of Puerto Rican pineapple workers during the early 1900s, when about 5,000 islanders emigrated by ship to Hawaii to work on pineapple plantations there.

Puerto Rican pineapples are excellent—fat, sweet, and juicy. You'll know they're in season when pineapple vendors line the roadsides along the southwestern coast (spring and summer).

Halfway up the hill the road passes the ruins of an old lighthouse and Spanish fortress, both of which are barely standing. As quickly as it rises, the road drops down again, with the hot black asphalt descending into the mangrove and white-sand beachfront, the beautiful coastline running through Guánica's Caña Gorda, San Jacínto, and Ballena sectors.

One of the island's better public beaches, *Caña Gorda* (Route 333, km. 5.9), is located here. For a lively time, try the *Caña Gorda Restaurant,* a bar/cafeteria complete with a dancing area. Open 9:00 A.M. to 5:00 P.M. Next door is the *Copamarina Hotel & Beach Resort* (Route 333, km. 6.5; 787–821–0505 or 800–468–4553; www.copamarina.com), a locally owned and managed resort that is as popular with visitors as it is with Puerto Ricans. Even from a distance, with its red-roofed, open-air Caribbean architecture, this luxurious but low-key resort is a rarity in Puerto Rico, where glitz is a fact of life. Mark French, an award-winning local chef, oversees the culinary wizardry at *Copamarina's Coastal Cuisine* and the adjacent, more informal Café Las Palmas. The hotel's seventy rooms are lovely and comfortable. The complex has two pool areas and a narrow swath of white-sand beach extending from the public beach to San Jacinto's highest point overlooking the Copamarina shoreline. The resort offers all sorts of water activities, from aerobics to deep-sea scuba diving (the hotel will even arrange flexible check-in hours to suit divers' needs). In addition, on-site tour operators will take you on a number of adventures, from a nature and bird-watching tour of the nearby Guánica Forest Reserve to climbing at the famed San Sebastián canyon or a scuba adventure in Culebra. The place has game rooms and other activities for children and attracts a family crowd.

The big attraction for divers is likely the *La Parguera* sea wall, which extends from Ponce to the Mona Passage between Puerto Rico and the Dominican Republic to the west. The sea wall is a major magnet for all sorts of marine life, from nurse sharks to angel fish. There are a variety of dive sites, from challenging tunnels in the sea wall to shallow coves on its shifting top. Adventurous clients often get newly discovered dive sites named after them. Chuck Rew, who operates out of the Copamarina Hotel & Beach Resort, is one of the area's most highly recommended operators. Call him at the hotel at 787–821–0505.

One of the best places to stay in southwest Puerto Rico is just around the bend at San Jacinto Point, **Mary Lee's by the Sea** (Route 333, km. 6.7; 787–821–3600). This established lodging sits atop a beautiful point overlooking the dry forest on one side and the coastline on the other. The complex is a series of eight furnished apartments and houses.

Besides the close access to the dry forest and a nearby sand beach, both hotels offer boat transportation to the nearby offshore cay of **Gilligan's Island** or the farthest point on Ballena Beach. Both Ballena and Gilligan's offer mangrove and reef snorkeling right off their shores. Ballena is always less crowded, and it has a superior beach. Motorboats ply the ten-minute trip between the hotels and the two offshore beaches throughout the day. To avoid crowds, best to visit during the week.

Besides the boat service from the hotels, you can also catch a ferry to Gilligan's from the dock at **San Jacinto Restaurant** (next to the Copamarina Hotel). The joint offers fried seafood, beach snacks, and cold beer. Shaded tables out back overlooking the water are quite nice.

Route 333 continues beyond the San Jacinto cutoff. The inland side of the road is undeveloped land, forested flatlands, and climbing hills, all covered by a brown-green scrub forest. About a half mile after the Copamarina, the road rises to give a view of an impressive field of palm trees. This is the heart of Ballena, perhaps one of the most magnificent pieces of undeveloped land in the Caribbean.

A Puerto Rican Poet

A mong the merchants in Guánica is author **Fundador Ortiz Matos,** who sells his self-printed pamphlets of prose and poetry. One of my favorites is The Aurora Keys: Gilligan's Island, which is a heartfelt account of the history of these offshore cays.

Born in 1925 in Guánica's dry forest, Fundador has published The Aurora Keys, *three books of poems, a work of drama, and a history of local legends. He credits Don Domingo Suárez Cruz, an old newspaperman and writer who lived out by the Guánica lighthouse, for first sparking his literary flame.*

Farther along, the road bends to the right and then to the left. At this second curve lies another beach on Ballena, one of the most popular beaches along this strip. It's a favorite of surfers, and its wide beach, which spreads out for over a mile, is also perfect for a stroll. The next unnamed beach along the route is also one of the most comfortable spots to sunbathe and swim.

Eventually the road comes to a big parking lot alongside a flat cement foundation rising above the shoreline and an adjacent beach. The view from here is spectacular. The bare, flattened dirt parking lot gives way to the start of the Guánica Forest Reserve, with small twig-like plants giving rise to stunted twisted scrub trees warped by the wind and the sun. Cacti and the fat green fronds of aloe plants also punctuate the field, like a wave of etched Chinese script characters.

The *Guánica Forest Reserve* (Department of Natural and Environmental Resources, 787–724–3724 or 787–724–3647) is a United Nations Biosphere Reserve that sprawls over 9,500 acres, with 36 miles of trails and roads running through it. The two main access points are from Route 116 (turn left on Route 334) and via the coastal Route 333. Most visitors take the latter route, and many come simply to enjoy the beaches on the reserve's southern edge.

The unique look of the forest, with twisted trees and cacti spouting from red soil, stems from the area's extreme heat and dryness. Guánica is sheltered from rain clouds by the mighty back of the Cordillera Central mountain chain. Average temperature, day and night, is 79 degrees Fahrenheit. Within the forest, temperatures can vary by 10 degrees—the difference between a hillside exposed to the sun and a steep ravine in the forest shade.

Amid the cacti and forest there are also a variety of coffee plants, the white fragrant flowers of the gumbo limbo tree, and the majestic Guayacán tree, which produces one of the densest woods in the world and blooms blue flowers. Among its many treasures, the forest is home to forty-eight endangered plant species, many found in the moist ravines and caves. Half of Puerto Rico's bird species are also found here, including the endangered Puerto Rican whippoorwill, lizard cuckoos, pearly-eyed thrashers, and Puerto Rican mangos. There are also plenty of lizards, mongooses, and endangered sea turtles, too.

The reserve is divided into the dry scrub forest on the northern edge of the reserve and the coastal forest that lines the reserve's southern edge. The latter consists of deep-rooted plants whose thick stems and leaves were built to retain every drop of water. There's sea grape and giant milkweed, buttonwood mangrove, and sea blight. The grounds of the reserve are formed of limestone riddled with water holes that in some spots have formed caves and sinkholes. Off the coast, massive coral reefs have formed on the sea floor.

If you want to explore the forest, take the drive up Route 334. Most of the hiking trails run off this main route. Your first stop should be at the parking lot at road's end and the small information booth located there. This is where to pick up the Department of Natural and Environmental Resources' free *A Guide to Trails of Guánica State Forest and Biosphere Reserve*. The booklet has a map and description of the reserve's walking trails, a pretty good description of the reserve's plant and animal life, and a general overview of the weather system and terrain.

The popular **Ballena Trail** leads from the parking lot down to the beautiful coast. Bird-watching excursions and reserved tours can be arranged by Eco-Ecanto Tours at the Copamarina (787–821–0505). *Tropix Wellness Tours* (787–268–2173), run by Victor López, is one of the most active in Guánica and surrounding areas. Its renowned "Wet and Dry Tour" combines hikes through the Guánica dry forest with kayaking through coastal mangrove channels and the magnificent coast. There are also bird-watching, turtle-watching, and horseback riding tours.

Take Route 116 to visit Guánica's other half: the old sugar plantation town Ensenada and the Playa Santa beach community. Turn right at Route 325. Immediately after the underpass the road curves right and squeezes between Ensenada Bay on the left and a green hillside. Towering trees surround the stately 1930s plantation homes that overlook Ensenada Bay from the prettiest perch in town.

Ensenada was built on sugar money, and the ruins of the old Guánica Central sugar mill still dominate the place. The town's post office, hospital, clubhouse, and restaurant were all built by the owner of the sugar plantation, which was one of the world's biggest in the early part of the century. In fact for most of this century Ensenada eclipsed Guánica in importance. It is home to the island's first electric light, the first flushing toilet, and first golf course, all built for the comfort of the mill's owners.

The community never really recovered from the closure of the mill in 1980, and today fishing and a few local apparel plants provide most of the jobs here. In many ways Ensenada is a forgotten place; the economic bonanza being enjoyed elsewhere in Puerto Rico has bypassed this beautiful town.

After passing by the bay the road comes to a split. Bearing right takes you into Ensenada's sleepy downtown full of quaint shops, barbers, and bakeries, small *colmados,* or markets, churches, and schools. The charming **Ensenada Public Library** (which keeps irregular hours) was recently named a historic structure. Staying on the road out of town will lead back to Route 116, which will take you farther west along the beach route and back toward Ponce along Highway 2.

Bearing left the road winds around the grounds of the old sugar mill. The old post office, a hospital, and other plantation structures are still standing. The road then passes by a blue gymnasium and an adjacent field that is most often used as a parking lot. If you're lucky, the orange portable kiosk of **Miguelito's Pinchos** will be parked here. By all means take a break and try some of Migeulito's specialties, including fish broth soup, chicken, and pork kebobs, and a cool drink. Across the lot lies the **Parque de Las Flores,** a lovely landscaped park filled with tropical flowers. Next door is the **Club de Artesanos,** a wooden plantation structure now used as a meeting place and party hall.

The road then bears to the right as it passes into the small fishing village of **barrio Guaypao.** Most visitors driving through this area are headed toward **Playa Santa,** a low-key, slightly scruffy beach town of open-air bars and seafood snack shops. But it's a good idea to take it slow, since much lies between Guaypao and Playa Santa, which locals also call Salinas.

The main road (Route 325) from Guaypao passes dry fields filled with scrub pine, *flamboyán* trees, wild cotton, and cacti. This is the second half of the Guánica dry forest, an ecosystem related to its other half across Guánica Bay. There are a few dirt road cutoffs on the right side of the road. Although the entrances of some of these roads have been used as clandestine dumps, every dirt road between Guaypao and Playa Santa leads to hidden beaches such as Las Espaldas, Manglillo Grande, Manglillito, and La Jungla. These beaches are mostly used by locals who come here to fish and bathe, and who fill the beaches with great barbecues on summer Sundays and holiday weekends. At most other times, however, the beaches are empty. Although they are safe, there are no services available.

Right before Playa Santa the road passes **Papi's Pinchos,** a family-run seafood shack specializing in barbecued shark kebobs and marinated conch salad (open Wednesday through Sunday noon to 6:00 P.M.). The big blue monstrosity of a building facing the beach is a vacation center of the Commonwealth Employees Association. It may be an eyesore, but it does have a beautiful white-sand beach with a protected reef. Kayak rentals and other water sports are available. Any of the open-air restaurants are a good place for a snack and a cold drink, and the place is lively on weekends.

The Coastal Highway

uánica is just the start of what is Puerto Rico's most enjoyable coastal area: a series of beach towns that ring the southwest coast from Guánica to Cabo Rojo. Here the sun is at its hottest and the protected waters are among the most welcoming on the island. Route 116 is your ticket to this world.

Beyond Guánica you'll pass long rolling pastures with the massive Cordillera Central mountain range rising dramatically from the fields in the distance. The land runs into the Lajas Valley that spreads along Route 116 until entering the town of Lajas. If Puerto Rico has a big sky country, this is it.

La Parguera is the next beach community along Route 116. It's accessible by taking a left on Route 304. Before entering the village proper, a right turn takes you to *Avenida Pedro Albizu Campos,* a road that climbs a big hill overlooking the town. From the top of the road (a popular place to stop) you can see the endless cays and small islands that lie off the coast.

Because the town lacks a great beach, the thing to do is rent a boat or take one of the scheduled ferry trips to one of the offshore islands, such as *Isla Mata de Gata.* The town also makes a good base from which to explore the southwest region, with several beaches and other attractions all within a short drive.

There's a kind of honky-tonk, Jersey-shore feel to La Parguera itself, and it's a favorite of vacationing Puerto Rican families and college students. Most of the businesses are centered along Main Street, which is filled with small restaurants, hotels, and shops.

La Parguera is especially crowded on summer and holiday weekends. Particularly hopping are the *Mar & Tierra Restaurant and Bar,* as you enter town, which has pool tables, food, and a good jukebox, and the *Blues Cafe* (El Muelle Shopping Center on Avenida Los Pescadores; 787–899–4742), which often has live music and draws a younger crowd. Also try *Sangría Coño,* right across the alley to the left of the big lot from Tony's Pizza. The owner has the place decorated with newspaper articles and artwork of Puerto Rican artists, patriots, and other cultural icons from the past and present, as well as posters of local events such as the annual *Lajas Kite Festival* held each April. Pro-independence folk music, old ballads, and salsa are the music of choice. There's also assorted food and very good sangria. On weekends live merengue or salsa bands play behind the bar and in the recreation room adjacent to the town square.

A variety of casual eateries in town serve everything from pizza to sandwiches to seafood to barbecued chicken. A good choice for dinner is *La Casita Restaurant* (301 Calle Principal; 787–899–1681), right beyond the *paradores,* which specializes in seafood. Open daily from 11:00 A.M. to 10:00 P.M.

There are several lodging options in town. Two of the nicest spots are *Parador Villa Parguera* (Route 304; 787–899–7777) and the recently renovated *Parador Posada Porlamar* (Route 304; 787–899–4015 or 800–223–6530). Both are set on the water, with a small shoreline and docks. Villa La Parguera's restaurant, *El Pescador,* is also quite popular, and there are dinner shows on many nights. There are many smaller guest houses in town, as well as a few campgrounds, and several private homes are available for rent on a short-term basis.

Playita Rosada (at the end of Calle 7) is the public beach and a natural reserve run by the Department of Natural and Environmental Resources. Named after the red mangrove trees that grow along much of the water in the park, this is a very interesting area. It can get crowded, especially on weekends, and you're much better off going offshore by renting a small outboard boat or taking a tour or a scheduled trip to one of the islands, all of which are within a 4-mile-or-so distance from the shore.

Behind the parking lot at the center of town are the docks used by most of the boat operators in town, including Cancel Boats (787– 899–5891). Most boat-rental operations advertise $15-per-hour rates, but much lower prices can be negotiated for full-day excursions. Others will charge you a lower rate for a two- or three-hour tour. Boats can hold up to six. Prices are even cheaper for simple transportation to one of the offshore cays. A good idea may be to go out for a two- or three-hour snorkeling trip in the morning and then arrange for the boat to drop you off at Isla Mata de Gata, which has beaches and basic facilities like picnic areas and restrooms. *Isla Magueyes* is one of the bigger islands in the small offshore chain and is home to a group of gigantic iguanas. Stop to admire and photograph them at the University of Puerto Rico's dock (sorry, no admission for uninvited guests at this private facility).

There are also water-sports operators that can take you on fishing and scuba charters. Try **Parguera Fishing Charters** (787–382–4698) or **Paradise Scuba & Snorkeling** (787–899–7611). **Aleli Catamaran & Sailing Tours** (787–376–6447), located right at the central boat docks, offers a bunch of interesting tours with an eco-tourism bent.

Even if you don't take a daytime excursion, you'll want to come here at night to see the sparkling waters of La Parguera's **Phosphorescent Bay.** Like Esperanza's Mosquito Bay, its greenish glow is produced by the billions of microorganisms known as *pyrodinium bahamense.* Glass-bottom boats ply the bay waters in hour-long trips most nights. The waters are best seen on moonless nights. Passengers usually get into the act by leaning over the side of the boat to wave their hands and arms through the water, which brings movement to the water's glow.

La Parguera is actually part of the town of **Lajas** which, besides its valley, is known for frequent UFO sightings, as well as roving Rhesus monkeys, loose from research labs on Isla Magueyes. The UFOs, according to local news reports, appear over the Lajas lagoon with great frequency. There are even organized UFO campouts. To find out more about the UFOs, pick up *Evidencia OVNI* magazine in San Juan.

Farther west is **Cabo Rojo,** which sprawls across the island's southwest corner and encompasses several communities that are favorite vacation spots of islanders. This town, along with its neighbors, can also lay claim to some of the nicest beaches and most dramatic coastlines in Puerto Rico.

Most areas of interest lie down Route 305, which intersects with Route 116. The shaded country road passes large farms and nice homes. There's also a University of Puerto Rico agricultural post here—a farm where experiments in growing crops and raising livestock are carried out. There are a few nice spots to stop along this way, such as at **Herencia Taíno** (right on Route 305), a Puerto Rico *bohío* (hay-roofed shack) that serves local food indoors or out.

Route 305 curves into Route 303. Turn right, taking it a short distance to make a left onto Route 101. This road continues at a pastoral pass and eventually comes to Route 301, the road to Combate and the Punta Jagüey area at Puerto Rico's southwest corner, on which sits the Cabo Rojo Lighthouse.

Immediately after the turn onto Route 101, you'll pass the entrance to the **Boquerón Forest Bird Refuge,** run by the Department of Natural and Environmental Resources (DNER), where you'll find rare migratory

Cabo Rojo Lighthouse

and local birds as well as some walking trails. Fishing (tarpin and snook are common) and hunting (most commonly hunted are the ducks that fly here) are allowed. Call for DNER specifics (787–724–3647 or 787–724–3724). Open 8:00 A.M. to 4:00 P.M., closed Monday.

Boquerón

Continue about 5 miles through the Penones de Melones area along Route 101 to get to Boquerón, which is a must-visit for every traveler to this region. As you come into town, the turnoff to your left will take you to the **Playa Boquerón,** the public beach and adjacent campground. Many say that this is the best beach in Puerto Rico, and there's no doubt that it's a contender. The wide white beach is lined with palms and arcs around a clear blue bay protected by coral reefs. It also has some of the best facilities of any public beach on the island, with showers, lockers, bathrooms, and a good snack bar. If you bring a hammock, you'll likely get a nice spot in the shade between two coconut palms. There are also picnic tables and barbecue pits.

The adjacent campground, the **Centro Vacacional de Boquerón** (787–

851–1900), sometimes fills up weeks or, in the cases of high season or holiday weekends, months in advance. In any case, call the agency's San Juan Reservations Office for reservations (787–722–1771, 787–722–1551, or 787–724–2500, extension 130 or 131). The campground offers rustic, cement–bunker lodgings that are open to the sea right off the far end of Boquerón Beach. With a few creatively strung tarps, you can dramatically increase your living space, not to mention your privacy.

Continuing straight along Route 101 will take you into **Boquerón.** The town is experiencing some growing pains on account of recent development, but the funky beach-town quality is still there. Boquerón Bay has also been a favorite stopping point for boaters who can dock for free. This policy is responsible for the international feeling to the town, which is filled with boaters from around the world.

Side Trip: Cabo Rojo Lighthouse

*F**rom Route 101 (the road to Boquerón), bearing left onto Route 301 will take you out to the southwest corner of the island. The road descends to sea level and the twisted arms of the mangrove swamp tumble along the shoreline. The road will eventually lead to the **Cabo Rojo National Wildlife Refuge,** run by the U.S. Department of Fish and Wildlife (787–851–7219). The visitors' center features a nature exhibit that includes freshwater shrimp, mangrove sea turtles, and displays on the area's fauna. Rare migratory birds spotted here include the yellow-shouldered blackbird (native to Puerto Rico) and the flamingo. Open 9:00 A.M. to 5:00 P.M. (closed Monday). Free admission. The park recently acquired the adjacent (and eerie) salt flats, which house a salt mining enterprise. A musty funk usually hangs over the long mounds of salt, but it quickly dissipates as the road continues toward the coastline.*

*Drive beyond the end of Route 301, which turns into a hard-packed dirt road. You'll pass over a swizzlestick of land that passes between the Salinas and Sucia Bays. Watch out for a couple of rocky and wet patches. Brave the drive to its rocky and increasingly trail-like conclusion, and you'll come to the **Cabo Rojo Lighthouse** (not open to the public) overlooking a beautiful swimming beach in a reef-protected cove along Bahia Sucia. By all means, take your swim here and bring snorkeling gear if you have it.*

*The lighthouse was built by the Spanish in 1877. It's set atop dramatic **Punta Jagüey,** a flat-topped headland jutting out into the Caribbean and offering commanding views on every side as it drops down to sea level in sharply etched cliffs. The lighthouse has equal west–east exposure, and is at its most beautiful in the early morning and during the last rays of the day. Despite its rundown condition, the lighthouse is a fine example of colonial architecture.*

The road passes a charming plaza and then comes to a 90-degree curve at *la esquina,* the corner, the place to while away the hours sipping cool drinks and shooting the breeze at one of the open-air establishments. Try the eighty-one-year-old **Shamar Bar.** The Shamar Bar is one of the few legal establishments on the beach, since the land title stems from the Spanish crown and predates U.S. rule. In 1998 the establishment was refurbished. Rooms are now available for rent above the bar. Rooms start at $65. **Wildflowers Antiques, Cafe & Inn** (787–851–1793) is housed in a charming wooden structure across from the plaza. The rooms (starting at $75) are decorated with antiques the owners collected throughout New England, and the details, from the bedposts to the bathroom fixtures, have all been tended to. Highly recommended; it's the classiest spot in town. Nice breakfasts and lunches are served in the quaint cafe. A sports and music bar, **Guillermo's Econdite Pub** (entrance in the back), is also located in the building.

The best spot to eat in town is easily **Galloway's Bar & Restaurant** (787–254–3302), a restaurant on a porch out on Boquerón Bay. Good seafood and local food, it also has daily specials that range from comfort foods such as homemade meatloaf and roast turkey to Italian specials. The bar area draws an interesting crowd, which usually makes for entertaining and informative conversation. Food served until 10:00 P.M. on weekdays (closed Wednesday), weekends until 11:00 P.M.

The **Parador Boquemar** (787–851–2158 or 888–634–4343; www. boquemar.com), directly down the road circling back out of town in front of Galloway's, is a comfortable *parador* with a pool. The rooms are comfortable but not great. The restaurant, **La Cascada,** has a distinct decor but the service is wonderful and the food is great.

Take Route 307 up the west coast now to go through Boca Prieta, Buyé, and La Mela Beaches. Buyé Beach is lovely, but a decaying beachfront campground mars the ambience. Farther along you climb over another pine-covered mount that overlooks **Puerto Real Bay** and Elizabeth Village. A good water-sports operator, the Caribbean Reef Dive Shop (1158 Main; 787–254–4006), is located in Puerto Real. The shop offers day trips for scuba and snorkel enthusiasts of all abilities.

Playa Joyuda is a coastal town known for its beachfront restaurants. Almost all are good, so just pick out one that feels right. The town's beach isn't particularly nice, not compared to the area's other offerings anyway; the best move is to stay elsewhere and to drive into town one evening or on a rainy afternoon for a good waterfront meal.

The San Germán Region

Sabana Grande and San Germán can be reached by driving out along Route 116, but the most direct route is to continue along Highway 2 after Yauco past the Route 116 exit to Guánica. This route tumbles through the farmland of Sabana Grande, with cattle grazing in the rolling fields planted with sugarcane, *plátanos,* and other crops.

Sabana Grande means "big plain," and it is best known as the place of the **Virgin del Pozo** or Virgin del Rosario, when the Virgin Mary was reportedly sighted here by Juan Angel Collado and a group of other children in 1953. Every year religious pilgrims from across the island come here to pay homage to the Virgin Mary at the mountainside chapel built in her honor. Route 120 (which brings you into the Sabana Grande mountains) leads to the smaller Road 364, which leads to the chapel.

Farther along Highway 2 is **San Germán,** Puerto Rico's second-oldest town. Founded in 1573, this sun-bleached historical gem is set between the foothills of the Cordillera Central and the beautiful southwestern coast. Although the city is set back from the coast, most of the beaches discussed in this section can be reached in less than thirty minutes by car, and all the drives are pretty.

The best way to explore the city is to pick up the concise, one-page map and guide of San Germán prepared by Jorge Lamboy Torres. Copies are available at the wonderful old **Hotel Parador Oasis** (64 Luna; 787–892–1175 or 800–981–7575). It's a good thing it's wonderful, since it's about the only hotel in town. A pool and adjacent restaurant dining area are located in the huge courtyard. Meals here are also recommended.

Friends who have long lived in town complain about how quiet the nights are here, but that can be a tonic to the visitor aiming to get off the beaten path. San Germán, the white colonial city surrounded by verdant green hills, may be the perfect base from which to explore the whole region. The town's appeal is also boosted by the presence of **Interamerican University,** which is located above the historic zone on the western edge of the city. Founded in 1912 as the Polytechnic University, the campus is beautiful. More importantly, the student body as well as the faculty add immensely to the town's cultural life.

After turning left from Highway 2 you'll come to a traffic light at which you turn right. Follow signs for Porta Coeli. Then follow the road until you come to Photos By Ed, a photo shop in a corner-shaped stone building, at which you should bear right. Take your first right and you'll find

Porta Coeli Church

yourself at an entrance to the San Germán's historic zone. The main drag, *Calle Luna,* is usually more crowded, and there's more parking around here; try Calle Dr. Santiago Veve.

It's also a nice trek up Calle Dr. Santiago Veve, which passes historic homes on the way to the main plaza. Here is ***Porta Coeli Church,*** now known as the Porta Coeli Museum of Religious Art. Built in 1606, it is the oldest church in the United States and one of only a handful of Gothic churches in the Western Hemisphere. The church's name means "Heaven's Gate." The squat structure, sitting atop a stone staircase, opens up in a massive arcing doorway, which is made from *ausubo,* a once-common hardwood tree in Puerto Rico.

The church's impressive carved wooden altar was made in Puerto Rico during the seventeenth century and brought to the church in the 1930s after originally being placed in Old San Juan's San José Cathedral. Surrounding the altar are Dutch tiles that depict biblical scenes. The tiles were first placed in Old San Juan's San Francisco Church. Two icons inside the church honor Nuestra Señora de Monserrate, a revered saint in Puerto Rico since she appeared to island settlers in the sixteenth century. There are also examples of the religious wood carvings known as santos, which have become a specialty in Puerto Rico over the centuries.

The Victorian **Casa Morales** (not open to the public), right outside the church, is spectacular in its own right and a good example of the North American influence on Puerto Rican architecture in the early part of this century. Continuing up the hill takes you to **Plaza Santo Domingo,** which is lined with the busts of prominent San Germán citizens, many of them nationally recognized for their patriotism or for their successes in various endeavors. Also here is the town's other great church, the **Catedral de San Germán de Auxerre,** named for the French saint who is the town's patron. The church was constructed in 1739 but underwent so many substantial changes over the next one hundred years that today it mixes styles from many different time periods. Its lit, stonewashed walls are particularly impressive at night.

The historic zone is filled with businesses and residences that are every bit as intriguing as the more frequently visited Ponce and Old San Juan. Many of the residences in town date from the late 1800s and were built by rich local families. Some of my favorite buildings include the **Domínguez Pharmacy** (Calle Cruz off Dr. Veve) and **13 Calle Dr. Santiago Veve,** the home of the poet Lola Rodríguez de Tío and the patriot Ponce de León de Tío (not open to the public).

PLACES TO STAY IN
PONCE AND THE SOUTH

BOQUERÓN
Boquerón Beach Hotel
Route 101; km. 18.1
(787) 851–7110

Centro Vacacional de
Boquerón
Boquerón Public
Beach/Balneario
(787) 851–190 Cuestamar

Cofresí Beach Hotel
Route 101
(787) 254–3000;
www.cofresibeach.com

Cuestamar Hotel
Route 307, km. 7.4
(787) 851–2819

Parador Boquemar
Route 100 intersection with
Route 101
(787) 851–2158 or
(800) 634–4343

Shamar Bar–Restaurant
and Hotel
Boquerón Beach
(787) 851–0542

Wildflowers Antiques, Cafe,
and Inn
In town across from plaza
(787) 851–1793

COAMO
Parador Baños de Coamo
Route 546
(787) 825–2186;
www.banosdecoamo.com

EL COMBATE
Villas Mojacasabe
North end of town
(787) 254–4888;
www.pinacolada.com/
mojaca

EL FARO
Parador Bahía Salinas
Route 301, km. 11.5
(787) 254–1212 or
(800) 443–0266;
www.bahiasalinas.net

GUANICA
Copamarina Hotel and
Beach Resort
Route 333, km. 6.5
(787) 821–0505 or
(800) 468–4553;
www.copamarina.com

Mary Lee's by the Sea
Route 333, km. 6.7
(787) 821–3600

GUAYANILLA
Parador Pichi's
Route 132, km. 204
(787) 835–3335;
www.pichis.com

LA PARGUERA/LAJAS
Cayo Laurel Court
Avenida Pedro
Albizu Campos
(787) 899–2298

Gladys Guest House
(787) 899–4678

Hotel Casablanca
(787) 899–4250

Hotel Parador
Villa del Mar
Avenida Pedro
Albizu Campos
(787) 899–4265;
www.pinacolada.net/
villadelmar

La Jamaca Guest House
and Restaurant
Route 304, km. 3.3
(787) 899–6162

Nautilus Hotel
(787) 899–4004

Parador Posada Porlamar
Route 304
(787) 899–4015 or
(800) 223–6530

Parador Villa Parguera
Route 304
(787) 899–7777 or
(800) 443–0266;
www.villaparguera.com

Pargomar Guest House
(787) 899–4065

Viento y Vela Guest House
(787) 899–3030

PLAYA JOYUDA
Joyuda Plaza Hotel
Route 102; km. 14.7
(787) 851–8800

Parador Joyuda Beach
Route 102, km. 11.7
(787) 851–5650;
www.joyudabeach.com

Parador Perichi's
Route 102, km. 14.3
(787) 851–3131 or
(800) 435–7197

PONCE
Colonial Guest House
33 Calle Marina
(787) 843–7585

Holiday Inn Ponce
3315 Ponce ByPass
(787) 844–1200 or
(800) 465–4329

Hotel Bélgica
122 Villa
(787) 844–3255

Hotel Meliá
2 Cristina
(787) 842–0260; or
(800) 742–4276

Ponce Hilton and Casino
1150 Caribe
(787) 259–7676 or
(800) 445–8667;
www.ponce-hilton.com

SAN GERMÁN
Hotel Parador Oasis
64 Luna
(787) 892–1175 or
(800) 981–7575

**PLACES TO EAT IN
PONCE AND THE SOUTH**

BOQUERÓN
Cuesta Blanca
Route 307, km. 5
(787) 851–6899

El Papagayo
Route 100, km. 10
(787) 255–0343

Galloway's Bar and
Restaurant
Calle José de Diego
(787) 254–3302

Tourist Information for Ponce and the South

Cabo Rojo Tourism Information
(787) 254–1922 or (787) 851–7070

Guánica Tourism Office
*City Hall
corner 25 de Julio and Carlos del Rosario
(787) 821–2777*

Ponce Tourism Information
*Plaza Las Delicias
(787) 840–8044*

La Cascada
Route 101, corner of Gill
Buyé at Parador Boquemar
(787) 851–2158,
extension 185

Shamar Bar–Restaurant
and Hotel
Boquerón Beach
(787) 851–0542

EL COMBATE
Annie's Seafood Restaurant
Route 301
(787) 254–0021

Cafetería del Chopin
Calle 3
(787) 254–4005

GUÁNICA
Caña Gorda Restaurant
Balneario Caña Gorda
Route 333,km. 5.9

Copamarina's Coastal
Cuisine
Route 333, km. 6.5 at
Copamarina Hotel and
Beach Resort
(787) 821–0505,
extension 766

La Concha
C–4, Calle Principal,
Playa Santa
(787) 821–5522

Papi's Pinchos
Playa Santa

GUAYANILLA
La Guardarraya
Route 127, km. 6
(787) 856–4222

Pichi's Steak House and
Seafood
Route 132, km. 204.6
(787) 835–4140

LA PARGUERA/LAJAS
La Casita
304 Calle Principal
(787) 899–1681

La Jamaca Restaurant
Route 304, km. 3.3 at
La Jamaca Guesthouse
(787) 899–6162

Los Balcones
Route 304
(787) 899–2145

La Pared
Route 304, km. 3.3
at Posada Porlamar
(787) 899–4015,
extension 151

Parguera Blues Café
El Muelle Shopping Center,
Av. Los Pescadores
(787) 899–4742

Restaurante El Náutico
7 Calle La Parguera, Playita
Rosada
(787) 899–5237

Restaurante El Pescador
Route 304, km. 3.3 at
Parador Villa Parguera
(787) 899–3975

PLAYA JOYUDA
El Bohío
Route 102, km. 9.7
(787) 851–2755

Perichi's Restaurant
Route 102, km. 14.3, at
Parador Perichi's
(787) 851–3131

Tino's Restaurant
Route 102, km. 13.6
(787) 851–2976

Tony's Restaurant
Route 102, km. 10.9
(787) 851–2500

Vista Bahía
Route 102
(787) 851–4140

PONCE
Canda's Restaurant
Alfonso XII Street, corner
of Bonaire, Ponce Beach
(787) 843–9223

El Ancla
9 Hostas, Ponce Beach
(787) 840–2450

El Patio Colonial
Luna and Marina
(787) 848–3178

Jazz Nicole
66 Isabel
(787) 848–5475

La Montserrate Sea Port
Route 2, km. 218.6,
sector Las Cucharas
(787) 841–2740

La Terraza
Ponce Hilton,
Av. Caribe 1150
(787) 259–7676

Lupita's Mexican
Restaurant
Reina Isabel 60
(787) 848–8808

Mark's at the Meliá
Hotel Meliá
2 Cristina
(787) 842–0260

Pito's Seafood Café
Route 2, km. 2.18, sector
Las Cucharas
(787) 841–4977

SALINAS
Costa Marina
Route 701, G8 Chapin
Street, at Marina de Salinas
(787) 824–6647

La Puerta de la Bahía
298 Principal
(787) 824–1221

SAN GERMÁN
Cilantro's
Cruz and Dr. Santiago Veve
(787) 264–2735

Del Mar y Algo Mas
Plazuela Santo Domingo
at Calle Carro
636–4265

Luna Park Chicken and
Pizza
(787) 892–4230

YAUCO
El Caballito Restaurant at
Gaby's World
Route 127, km. 5.1
(787) 856–2609

Hacienda Restaurante
Campo Alegre
Route 127, km. 5.8
(787) 856–2609

The North Coast and West

De Diego Expressway (Highway 22) holds the key to Puerto Rico's western spirit as it shoots along the north coast and then leads to roads that snake around the island's magnificent northwest coast. There's much to be seen on this route, from one of the most interesting observatories in the world to an intricate underground cave system. Beautiful empty beaches are spread out in two stretches along this route; the first starts just west of San Juan and a second stretches from Camuy on the north coast to Mayagüez, Puerto Rico's third largest city, known as the Sultan of the West.

West of San Juan

There are two common ways to pick up the westbound De Diego Expressway (Highway 22) out of San Juan. One way is to travel west on Kennedy Avenue (Highway 1) on the traffic-clogged route to Bayamón, and the other is by taking Las Americas Expressway south of San Juan.

As you're passing out of Bayamón, to your left you'll notice something that looks like a huge set of colorful plastic blocks and a metal erector set. Above it are real U.S. NASA rockets, but from this distance they look like plastic models. This is the *Luis A. Ferré Science Park* (exit south from Expressway to Route 167; 787–740–6868 or 6878), with an aerospace museum, small zoo, archaeological exhibits of Taíno artifacts, and space-flight simulator (a hit with school groups). There are also art, transportation, physics, electric energy, and natural history exhibits here. The newest installation is a planetarium. The park has plenty of picnic areas, and paddle boats are available for rent at an artificial lake. From its perch at 300 feet above sea level, the science park overlooks sprawling San Juan. Open Wednesday through Friday 9:00 A.M. to 4:00 P.M., Saturday and Sunday 10:00 A.M. to 6:00 P.M. Admission is $3.00 for

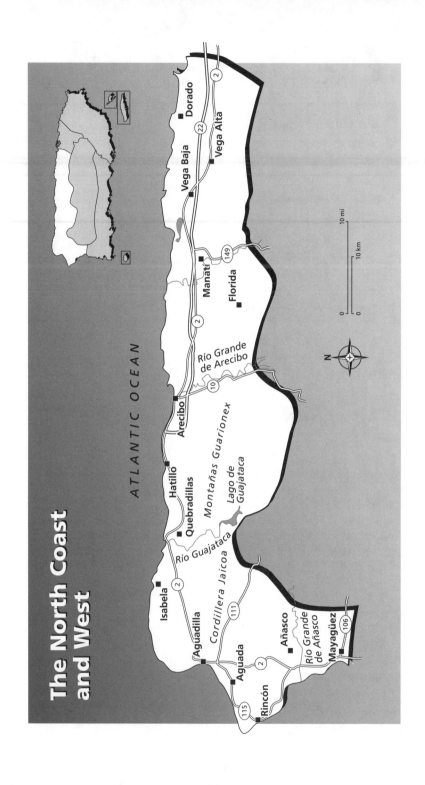

The North Coast and West

ATLANTIC OCEAN

Isabela

Aguadilla

Aguada

Rincón

Hatillo

Quebradillas

Río Guajatacoa

Cordillera Jaicoa

Montañas Guarionex

Lago de Guajataca

Arecibo

Río Grande de Arecibo

Manatí

Florida

Vega Baja

Vega Alta

Dorado

Añasco

Río Grande de Añasco

Mayagüez

N

10 mi

10 km

AUTHOR'S FAVORITES

B.O.N.U.S. Thermonuclear Energy Plant, *Rincón*

Cathedral of Our Lady of Montserrat, *Hormigueros*

La Sangría de Fido's, *Mayagüez*

Los Tubos, *Vega Baja*

Mayagüez Zoo, *Mayagüez*

Nuestra Señora de la Montserrat Church, *Moca*

children (two to twelve years old), $5.00 for adults, and $2.00 for senior citizens.

Immediately past the second toll booth is the exit for Toa Baja and **Dorado.** Route 165 exits the highway on the site of an old sugar plantation surrounded by big palms and tall flowering trees. Dorado may be growing as a tourist and residential community, but there's still a hometown feel to its downtown area (which boasts one of the few full-service libraries on the island). The road to Dorado twists through the downtown area right beyond the bridge. It's a good place to stretch your legs or grab a bite to eat. The downtown is loaded with little pizzerias, delis, and restaurants specializing in local fare. Park near **Dorado City Hall** (on your right, beside the plaza, as you enter town).

As quickly as it enters town, the road (which has become Route 698) leaves again after climbing a short hill. Soon you are driving through the shade of the massive trees and coconut palms that line the rural roadway. This road leads to two Hyatt resorts originally developed on an old plantation of the Rockefeller family. The Hyatt resorts are also the site of the **Lisa Pennfield Windsurfing School** (787–796–2188), which gives lessons and rentals for all ages and abilities.

A number of independent water sports operators in town undertake everything from scuba trips to deep-sea fishing expeditions. Try the **Dorado Marine Center** (787–796–4645). Dorado's public beach, Playa Sardinera, is just one of the beaches making up what locals call **Playa del Dorado,** a string of about six white-sand beaches. There are plenty of good seafood restaurants here including **El Malecón** (Route 693, km. 8.2; 787–796–1645), an unpretentious family-run place serving up good seafood and Puerto Rican cuisine.

West of Dorado is **Vega Baja** and the **Cerro Gordo public beach** (one of the most popular), a 2,500-foot-long beach surrounded by rows of palm trees and strange rock formations and cliffsides.

Continue west along Highway 22 to Vega Baja's other beautiful beaches. The Route 687 exit leads to the **Laguna Tortuguero Nature Reserve** (Department of Natural and Environmental Resources; 787–724–3647, in San Juan, or 787–724–3724), one of Puerto Rico's many bird havens. Beyond the inland lagoon is a beautiful palm-lined beach, one of several here protected by a coral reef running between two promontories.

Route 687 quickly becomes Route 686 as it curves close to the shoreline, running along numerous rough water beaches popular with surfers. Among them is *Los Tubos,* the site of an annual three-day summer music festival that draws a diverse group of rock, salsa, and merengue musicians and singers. *Mar Chiquita,* another attractive beach, fills up with locals on weekends.

As Highway 22 passes *Vega Alta,* the landscape becomes filled with furry green hills and cut-limestone mountains. This is the beginning of *Karst Country.* You'll know you're entering as you cross over the low-lying highway bridge beyond the Vega Bajeño exit. From Manatí into Barceloneta are more beaches that can be accessed from the exit to Route 684, such as *Pescadora de la Boca* and, farther down along Route 681, *Hallows Beach. Barceloneta* is mostly known as an industrial town. Many of the firms that have come to Puerto Rico are established here.

Arecibo

From the expressway *Arecibo* rises up like a modern Oz beyond the fertile grounds of a sugar plantation and a surging river falling from the mountains. From Highway 2 Arecibo is backed by the deep blue of the Atlantic. The coastal route along Route 681 from Barceloneta is one of the prettiest drives in Puerto Rico as it approaches Arecibo's bustling waterfront district.

Although it's one of the larger Puerto Rican cities, Arecibo usually doesn't figure on many visitor itineraries, although the attractions surrounding the city sure do. It's a shame, because there is much to recommend this north coast city, where the city's population is a bit better off than average.

The walkway along the waterfront is a good place to begin exploring the city's charms. The historic *Arecibo Lighthouse* (El Muelle, Route 681 and the waterfront; 787–817–1936) now houses the *Arecibo Lighthouse Museum* (787–879–2232). The lighthouse is still in use and was automated in 1964. The museum is located at Morrillos hilltop. From the expressway, exit on Highway 2 and take a right on Route 681 across the bridge to the waterfront. Built in 1898, the museum has a permanent exhibit of paintings, stamps, and handmade sculptures and ceramics. Open Wednesday through Sunday 10:00 A.M. to 4:00 P.M.

Although the town's once-thriving historic district is now past its prime, it still holds on to some of its charm. Arecibo was founded in 1550, and what's left of its historic district fronts this area. In the heart of the district, near the historic plaza and Paseo Victor Rojas, stands **Casa Ulanga.** This venerable and beloved structure has been used as everything from a home to a hospital to a bank, town hall, prison, and courthouse. The building takes its name from Francisco Ulanga, a Spaniard who came to Puerto Rico in 1810 and ordered the building's construction in 1850. It holds the distinction of being the first three-story building in Arecibo. Today Casa Ulanga houses the **Arecibo Cultural Center** (Calle Gonazlo Marín 7; 787–878–8015), where various cultural activities, including music, dance, and theater performances as well as art auctions, are held, mostly between 7:00 and 10:00 P.M.

Karst Country

Puerto Rico's **Karst Country** is home to some of the world's most unique geographic formations—a dramatic landscape of limestone, haystack-shaped hills (called *mogotes* by the locals), underground rivers and caves, and large conical-shaped sinkholes. The region stretches from Manatí to Isabela, with some of its most prominent traits found in the foothills and hills of the Guarionex mountain chain, just south of Arecibo. Much of Karst Country is still an almost impenetrable maze of hills and thick forest.

This Karst geography, characterized by haystack-shaped hills surrounded by deep circular depressions, was formed over millions of years by an underground river system in the limestone terrain. There are only a handful of places in the world with geography similar to this, including one area across the Mona Channel in the Dominican Republic.

These sharply etched hills are formed by land masses that have yet to sink into the porous limestone terrain. The surrounding depressions were formed through the gradual process of water pouring through limestone through the millennia. This process forms sinkholes, which form more and larger sinkholes, until at last the surface level of the area is pulled down. Over millions of years this process has given rise to this unique region. Sharp drop-offs, which have the dramatic thrust and form of mountains, stand at heights of as little as one hundred feet. This lack of height allows the area's lush green growth to cling to and cover the hills. The effect gives you the feeling of being a giant in a miniature world.

Río Camuy Cave Park

The region can be most intimately explored by descending into the extensive cave system carved out by *Río Camuy,* the world's third largest underground river. The underground cave network stretches for miles in the island's northwest region. The easiest way to explore it is to go to the 300-acre *Río Camuy Cave Park* (787–898–3100), located north on Route 129 from Route 111. The park is open from 8:00 A.M. to 5:00 P.M. Wednesday through Sunday. Guided tours go through tropical vegetation and into caves where sinkholes, subterranean streams, and giant stalactites abound. The stalactites look like delicate crystals and the cave walls are as beautiful as carved stone tapestries. The caves are 45 million years old, and the ancient tropical Río Camuy that formed them still rages through the system, like the main artery to the cave system's heart.

The park's trolleys carry visitors to the major sites, and the caves have been developed with lighting and comfortable walkways stretching throughout. Since 1989 visitors here have been thrilled by **Tres Pueblos Sinkhole,** which is located on the borders of the Camuy, Hatillo, and Lares municipalities (which is how it got its name). This natural wonder widens to 65 feet in diameter and plunges 400 feet down through the soft limestone terrain into the Río Camuy. Visitors can view it from two different platforms: one overlooking the town of Camuy and the other overlooking Tres Pueblos Cave and the river. The other major sinkhole within the park is **Cueva Clara de Empalme.**

Despite its popularity and development, much of the underground cave system remains undeveloped and much of it is still unexplored. A number of companies on the island give tours in areas beyond the park. One recommended operator is **Aventuras Tierra Adentro** (787–766–0470). Run by Rossano Boscarino, activities range from spelunking to river explorations to rafting to rappelling. Some of the trips are quite physically challenging and others are suited for beginners. All are exhilarating—a highly recommended operator.

The almost 4,000 acres of protected land in Karst Country is divided into four commonwealth forests: Cambalache, Guajataca, Vega, and Río Abajo, which is the largest, accounting for over half the total land area. Like Puerto Rico's other public forests, each features picnic areas, nature exhibits, and numerous hiking trails (be sure to first pick up a map at each area). Camping is also permitted in these four forests (at a cost of $4.00 per night), but permits must first be obtained from San Juan-based Department of Natural and Environmental Resources Miramar Division (787–724–3647 or 3724). The public forests are open from 8:00 A.M. to 5:00 P.M. Tuesday through Sunday, and are closed Mondays.

Cambalache features two camping areas. It's reached by exiting Highway 22 onto Highway 2 east of Arecibo and then taking Route 682. The entrance is at km. 6.6, next to the Job Corps. **Guajataca** has an 8-mile hiking trail, bike trail, and a lakefront beach. Take Highway 2 west of Arecibo. After the road crosses the Guajataca River, exit left on Route 446, which leads to the forest entrance. **Río Abajo** has a new camping

---

Spelunking

Spelunkers say that the cave system at **Río Camuy Cave Park** presents some of the most enjoyable spelunking spots in the world. Although much of the system remains unexplored, it has been known to locals for years. When official exploration of the caves began in 1958, local boys had knowledge of the cave system from years of hiking through parts of it. In fact the boys served as guides for the explorers. There's even evidence of Taíno remains in some of the caves.

area. Exit Highway 22 by taking a left on Highway 10. At km. 70.3, take a right on Route 621. At km. 4.4 lies the access road to the forest. *Vega* is one of the smaller camping areas in the system. It's located at km. 1.5 of Route 676, alongside the municipal cemetery.

Several attractions lie south of Arecibo. More than 800 years ago the Taínos built the recreation and worship areas of the **Caguana Indian Ceremonial Park** (Route 11, km. 12.3; 787–894–7325 or 787–724–5477), the oldest discovered burial ground in the Antilles. Take Route 10 then go right on Route 111. The thirteen-acre park features several Taíno ball courts (called *bateyes*) lined with etched stone monoliths and petroglyphs. The Taíno cut images of birds and regal people with mysterious halos and decorative jewelry into the boulders. The austere surroundings here retain the air of the Taíno gods. In fact the Taíno built the park to play a semi-religious game that is believed to be a predecessor of soccer or lacrosse. A collection of Taíno artifacts, as well as a garden with typical Taíno crops, including *yautía, yuca,* and corn, are also located here. Open daily 9:00 A.M. to 4:30 P.M. No admission charge.

Here also is the awesome **Arecibo Observatory** (end of Route 625; 787–878–2612), home to the world's largest radar/radio telescope. The telescope is 305 meters in diameter and is dramatically set in a depression surrounded by a ring of the stunted limestone mountains of Karst Country. Cornell University scientists operate the facility to search for radio emissions from across the galaxies. To follow their work more closely, go to their Web site at www.naic.edu, with links to the observatory, Cornell University, and the National Science Foundation. Portions of the famous SETI project, a search for intelligent life in the universe through the sending of radio signals, were conducted here. It was also the setting for much of the movie *Contact,* in which Jodie Foster contacts an alien presence.

The approach to the observatory is one of the most dramatic you're likely to see—a science fiction movie prop set against the lush green and twisted hillsides. The **Angel Ramos Foundation Visitors' Center** makes the observatory more accessible than ever. Through exhibits, videos, telescopes, and other presentations, the observatory puts you on intimate terms with the solar system and the universe. The observatory is open Wednesday through Friday noon to 4:00 P.M.; Saturday, Sunday, and holidays, 9:00 A.M. to 4:00 P.M. Admission is $3.50 for adults, $1.50 kids/seniors. To get there take Route 129 to Route 134. From Route 134, take Route 635, and then it's on to Route 625, which ends at the observatory.

The North Coast

Trivia

Quebradillas's professional basketball team is called **The Pirates,** *in homage to the town's pirate past.*

As Highway 22 spills into Highway 2, the expansive blue Atlantic seems to spill across the highway. The casual traveler might think she or he has rounded the corner on the last curve to the west coast in Camuy, but the illusion is created by the highway curving inland along with the incline of the bay. Playa Sardinera and Playa Marina are located alongside the highway, off to the right.

You'll know you've reached **Hatillo** when you see the statue of a guy with a pig (a caricature of *el jíbaro*). The area by the highway is marked by fast-food joints. A good bet is **Wenchy's,** which features a restaurant, antiques, and miniature golf. Closed Monday.

Farther west lies **Quebradillas,** a stunning settlement of cliffside ocean overlooks with a seafaring and pirate past. You'll pass **Parador El Guajataca** (Highway 2, km. 103.8; 787–895–3070 or 800–964–3065; www.elguajataca.com), which overlooks the northern coast on a bluff at the point where the Guajataca River empties into the Atlantic. There's a pool, tennis courts, and a restaurant here. Also nearby is **Parador Vistamar** (Highway 2, km. 7.8; 787–895–2065 or 888–391–0606), another hilltop *parador* with a pool, tennis and dining areas, and weekend entertainment. You'll also pass the oceanfront **Pedro Albizu Campos Recreation Area,** a wonderful place to stop for great views of both the cliffs and water. For a good look at the dramatic north coast scenery, feel free to pull off at one of the rest stops off Highway 2.

Quebradillas is known for **Guajataca Beach,** a pretty area located alongside what is called **El Túnel,** a railroad tunnel for a train that ran from San Juan to Ponce from 1907 until the mid-1950s. El Túnel has an eatery and picnic area bordering the beach.

Puerto Rico's Northwest Corner

Beyond Quebradillas, visitors who want to see one of the most beautiful and undeveloped coastal areas in the Caribbean will take the exit for Route 113 and **Isabela.** Immediately after leaving the highway the roadway cuts through dense forest. Butterflies flutter between the branches of the almond trees, and greenery surrounds.

The forest quickly gives way to a strip of farmland, residences, and scattered commercial establishments. The next commercial area at **Playa Jobos** is a good forty-minute drive down this double-lane country road, which soon turns into Road 4466, a hardened dirt roadway that passes rows of beautiful but deserted beaches.

Isabela has been hit by more than its fair share of natural disasters, including a 1918 earthquake that destroyed the town. In the town's Aresnales sector, there are many *paso fino* horse farms. Before turning into an undeveloped coastal area, the roadway comes to Isabela's town plaza. In general, stay to your right and try to exit the town center going downhill toward the coast.

Just down the coastal road out of town is the **Costa Dorada Beach Resort** (900 Emilio González; 787–872–7255), a great setting on a mile-long beach. One of Puerto Rico's best locally run small hotels, all fifty-two rooms face the ocean. You'll also find pool areas, tennis and basketball courts, bars, and restaurants here.

Beyond this resort the roadway leaves its asphalt behind and becomes hard-packed sand as you move into some of Puerto Rico's most pristine, isolated areas. Here you'll find miles of undeveloped beachfront property, much of it fronted by agricultural fields, with wild cotton plants blooming along wooden fences backed by towering trees.

As you approach the colorful beach cottages of **Villas Del Mar Hau** (Road 4466, km. 8.3; 787–872–2045; www.villahau.com), you'll be

The Train

*E*l *Túnel is one of the best kept remains of the famous, and notoriously slow, train that ran from San Juan to Ponce from 1907 until the mid-1950s. The train line, originally commissioned in 1888 by the Spanish crown, was not completed until after the American invasion of 1898. It was purchased by the American Railroad Company in 1910 and subsequently grew to include 420 miles of track. For most of its history, the train line was primarily used to ship agricultural products such as sugarcane from the farm to the mill and from the mill to the ports. Because it lacked restaurant cars, people debarked at train stations to buy food*

from vendors. As a result, towns began to develop reputations for the particular types of food served at their train stops.

In the early 1940s, Jack Delano, an accomplished photographer, writer, artist, and musician, published The Train (El Tren), *a photographic essay of a train voyage. His essay not only provides the most realistic account of train travel at the time but also delves into the enormous changes in Puerto Rican society in the 1940s, when poverty forced the move from an agri-cultural-based to an industrial-based economy.*

Paso Fino

struck by its Shangri-La-like appearance, since this thriving but low-key resort surrounded by towering Casuarina pines lies in the middle of desolate beachfront. Located at Playa Montones, a beautiful white-sand beach, the colorful cottages are built in the traditional Puerto Rican *casita* style (with a wide front porch) and are linked by a boardwalk that runs across the edge of the beach. Just about everything is here, from a convenience store to fax and photocopy services.

Puerto Rico is famous for long-maned, strong-legged **paso fino *horses.*** *The name* paso fino *literally translates to "fine step," a reference to the graceful, dance-like movements of well-trained members of the breed.*

There are game rooms, laundry rooms, basketball and volleyball courts, a pool, as well as scuba, snorkeling, and horseback riding tours. There's also a cocktail lounge and restaurant.

Playa Jobos is one of the bigger settlements on the northwest corner of Puerto Rico, a several-block stretch of businesses that front a beautiful beach. It is located about a mile west of Villas del Mar Hau and is the first settlement you'll come to after passing Costa Dorada. Although there are several good spots in town, the place that's a cut above the rest for food, lodging, and entertainment is the ***Ocean Front Hotel and Restaurant*** (787–872–0444 or 3339; www.oceanfrontpr.com). It has two restaurants, the Ocean Front and Ocean Deck Bar & Grill, both with good seafood and Puerto Rican specialties, entertainment, and beach views. The rooms are clean and comfortable, and the hotel has a nice rooftop deck, one of the best vantage points for sunset-viewing. Beyond Jobos the road passes several other beaches, including ***Shacks,*** a surfing favorite, and Surfers Beach.

The dirt Road 4466 eventually passes into Route 110 as Isabela passes into ***Aguadilla.*** Although this area is more developed, the coastline remains unspoiled. One nice spot to stay or eat is the ***Villa Montaña Resort*** (Road 4466, km. 1.9; 787–872–9554 or 888–780–9195; www.villamontana.com), which has sixteen oceanfront villas on two miles of secluded beachfront. There are tennis courts, a pool, and an open-air bar and restaurant, ***Eclipse*** (787–890–0275), which cooks up gourmet continental fare. The shrimp with mushroom sauce and double-baked filet mignon, as well as the crispy calamari salad and shark salad, are recommended. This is really one of the least known resorts of quality in Puerto Rico. Also nearby is ***Tropical Trail Rides*** (787–872–9256), where you can rent horses for up-to-two-hour tours of secluded beaches and tropical trails along cliff sand caves. Expect to pay between $40 and $80 per person (special rates for groups).

Rafael Hernández

Rafael Hernández, whose prolific output has been called the "highest expression of Puerto Rican popular music," was born in Aguadilla in 1891. Hernández's musical talent was evident at an early age, and as an adolescent he penned his first melody, **Mi Provisa.** *He went on to compose dozens of songs, many of which have been etched into Puerto Rico's popular culture, including* **Preciosa, Lamento Borinquen,** *and* **Cumbanchero.**

Heading into Aguadilla, Route 110 passes pizza shops, Mexican restaurants, bars, and hotels. Most of these places are worth a stop, including *La Cima* (Route 110, km. 9.2; 787–890–5077), a restaurant, bar, and hotel. For nightlife try *La Cabaña* (Route 110, km. 21.5; 787–882–3070) or *Woopy's* (Highway 2, km. 118.4; 787–891–0388). A suburban community has sprung up outside the gates of the old Ramey Airforce Base. The roadway leaves the well-kept suburbs and then passes the ghostly remains of the base. A portion of the base is the *Rafael Hernández Airport,* named after the famous Puerto Rican composer. During the winter high-tourism season, U.S. carriers run direct flights here from popular stateside destinations such as New York.

Beyond the airport the road meets with Route 107 as it winds around the northwest corner of Puerto Rico's coast. There are a number of nice beaches along this stretch, including Wilderness, Gas Chambers, and Crashboat. Here is where you'll find the ruins of *La Ponderosa,* an old Spanish lighthouse, as well as *Punta Borinquen,* a lighthouse at Puerto Rico's northwest point.

Beyond the airport Route 107 merges back into Highway 2. Downtown Aguadilla, farther down Highway 2, has the rough and tumble feel of a port town, but with dramatic cliffs towering above and a beautiful coastline. Aguadilla is known for its *mundillo* work, the delicate white bobbin lace that adorned turn-of-the-century dresses, as well as other woven products.

Aguadilla has more than its fair share of hotels, including *Parador El Faro* (Route 107, km. 2.1; 787–882–8000 or 888–300–8002), a modern hotel with a pool near the airport; *Hotel Cielo Mar* (84 Montemar; 787–882–5959), which offers a view of Puerto Rico's west coast from almost every room. *Hotel Hacienda El Pedregal* (Road 111, km. 0.1; 787–891–6068 or 888–568–6068) is built on the estate of General Esteves, the first Puerto Rican to make the rank of general in the U.S. armed forces. Nice grounds, and some rooms have Jacuzzis.

Punta Borinquen Lighthouse

The original **Punta Borinquen Lighthouse** *was built in 1889 as part of an island-wide lighthouse system. The octagonal structure, which was painted red with white detailing, was destroyed in the earthquake of 1918. In 1920 the U.S. Coast Guard built another structure on the same location, keeping true to the original's architectural components.*

Just inland of Aguadilla, nearby **Moca** is an old sugar plantation town that retains its history. Among the sites here are **Nuestra Señora de la Monseratte Church,** built in 1772; the **Palacete Los Moreau,** a French Provincial–style mansion; **Los Castillos Meléndez,** which is constructed in the manner of a medieval castle; and **Hacienda Enriqueta,** a private museum of colonial artifacts that is open to the public. The town holds an annual **Mundillo Lace Festival** on Thanksgiving weekend each year.

Rincón and Aguada

arther south along Highway 2 an unassuming cutoff onto Route 115 leads to one of the most beautiful parts of Puerto Rico. Although Rincón is undoubtedly the final destination and main attraction, Aguada is such a pleasant surprise that it becomes much more than just a town you drive through.

Downtown **Aguada** is one of those super-clean, small Puerto Rican towns that seems so far away from San Juan. This isn't a bad spot to grab some lunch. **El Túnel Pizzeria** (214 Colon; 787–868–5430), just north of the plaza, is a busy, unpretentious place that draws a loyal local clientele. As you enter town there is a public parking lot right behind the main plaza, so park there if you don't find a spot along the street. The plaza, fronted by a pretty pastel-blue church, is a nice place to stroll.

Beyond town the road to Rincón passes through a hilly forested area that stretches out to the coast. Look for **Cheers & Beers** (Route 115, km. 21.4; 787–484–5922), a huge nightclub with outdoor huts and bars run by local merengue sensation Elvis Crespo.

The approach to Rincón may be disorienting for two reasons: The town's main road runs in a circle, and there's water on all sides, making it difficult to tell north from south and east from west. It's a good idea to pick up a Rincón tourist map, available for $1.00—or sometimes free—at many of the town's restaurants and guest houses. It's an excellent guide to town and is sure to save you many hours of aimless wandering.

Rincón is Spanish for "corner," and the name fits this town's geographic location in a corner of land overlooking Puerto Rico's west coast. But the name actually stems from Don Gonzalo Rincón, a

Columbus's First Stop

Aguadilla and neighboring Aguada have a running historical argument over where Christopher Columbus actually landed when he "discovered" Puerto Rico in 1493. Aguadilla residents argue that Columbus and his crew first stopped to get water from a spring that is now the site of Parque El Parterre. To back its claim, Aguada erected the **Parque de Colón** *in the center of the 2,500-foot Playa Espinar, a sight beautiful enough to warrant the historical occasion.*

sixteenth-century landowner who allowed poor families to reside on his land. The town is located on a flat peninsula of *La Cadena Hills,* the most western offshoot of the Cordillera Central that runs through Puerto Rico. The dramatic meeting of mountain and coast makes for awesome views all around town, and the white-sand beaches that surround the town are just as beautiful.

Rincón has a worldwide reputation for its powerful waves, and it's been a haven for surfers from the Caribbean and the States since at least 1968, when this small town was the host of the World Surfing Championship. The town continues to be the surfing capital of the Caribbean and boasts a lively nightlife.

While beachfront guest houses have long catered to the surfer culture by offering basic accommodations at rock-bottom prices, Rincón has become a haven for beach and nature lovers of all stripes, and the quality of the restaurants and lodgings within town have dramatically improved in recent years. As Route 115 crosses into town, you'll pass the entrance to the new Punta Del Mar, a development of beachfront villas. After this, bear to the right and take Route 413, Rincón's main road, which winds through the center of the municipality on the back of a rising hillside. To keep your bearings, think of Rincón as a circle that spreads out from this road. You may get the sense that you are leaving Rincón as the road winds its way into increasing heights, but you're actually entering its elusive heart.

Off to the right is the gorgeous *Sandy Beach* area, which can be accessed by taking any one of the turnoffs on the right side between the Velázquez Shell Station and the Nieves Mini-Market and Puntas Bakery. If you take the road straight until it drops off to your left, you'll get to the lighthouse area or the low road into the town proper and its equally pretty southern end.

Taking the first turn after the gas station will allow you to take the entire beach road. The first stop of note is *The Landing* (Sandy Beach Coast Road; 787–823–3112), a sprawling bar and full-service restaurant that is one of the best and most reliably open (from 11:30 A.M. to 11:00 P.M.) restaurants in town. Surf, turf, jerk-chicken sandwiches, and inventive appetizers such as the "exploding onion" are served here. The wooden interior is decorated with a seafaring and mariner theme, and it looks as if it could be located in any New England coastal town until you walk out onto the huge back porch overlooking a nice stretch of palm-lined beach. In Rincón this is nothing special; beaches line three sides of the town. But the view from here—especially when you're enjoying the surprisingly good fare, which also includes a delicious vegetarian lentil soup, yellowfin tuna with black bean corn salsa, and lobster kabobs—is particularly good. Live music on weekends.

Going past the restaurant the road passes a cutoff that leads to the *Rincón Surf & Board Caribbean Surfari Guest House* (787–823–0610 or 800–458–3628), which boasts a backyard jungle. Farther along the lower road that runs along Sandy Beach is the *Beside the Pointe Guest House* (787–823–8550; www.besidethepointe.com), which must be one of the most charming, affordable guest houses in the Caribbean ($60 to $100 nightly, depending on the season). Room No. 8, which has an ocean view, is particularly nice. Room No. 7, with a small kitchenette and deck, isn't bad either. The guest house also includes the Tamboo Tavern, which hops on many nights.

Beyond Nieves Shell Station and the Brisas Bar cutoff, Route 413 continues to climb high, lined with beautiful homes and small businesses. *The Lazy Parrot Inn & Restaurant* (Route 413, km. 4.1; 787–823–5654 or 800–294–1752; www.lazyparrot.com) is a restored home on a hill with views of the water all around. Each room has a different tropical theme and a small outdoor deck. The restaurant has outdoor and indoor eating areas, and the inn opens up onto a beautiful waterfall pool set on the hill. A nice place run by a friendly couple from Texas, it's close to several beaches. Rates from $95 to $125.

The road passes by some small bakeries and *colmados* (food shops), which are good places to buy provisions if you're heading for a beachfront apartment. *Desecheo Divers* (787–823–0390) runs scuba and sportfishing trips. A two-tank dive costs less than $100, and a full-day fishing trip is a little more than $500, lunch and beer included.

Route 413 then drops down. Turning right will take you to the 1892 *Punta Higuera Lighthouse,* which is open to the public. El Faro Park, one of only two whale-watching parks in the world, fronts the restored lighthouse. Off the western coast of Puerto Rico is the winter playground of humpback whales, which come from as far as Newfoundland and New England to frolic and mate in the warm Caribbean waters. In the winter bring your binoculars to see whales breaching off the coast. The 170-foot-long *Viking Starship* (787–823–7068) gives whale-watching tours, as well as scuba and boat tour excursions. Also visible offshore is 360-acre *Desecheo Island,* a federal wildlife reserve located 13.3 miles off the coast of Rincón.

The road continues past a forested area of towering pine and palm trees as it approaches the *B.O.N.U.S. Thermonuclear Energy Plant,* Latin America's first nuclear power plant, which ceased operation in 1974. The

B. O. N. U. S. Thermonuclear Energy Plant

dull turquoise-domed structure cuts an eerie presence on this majestic coastline. The adjacent **Domes Beach,** one of the more popular with surfers, draws its name from the reactor.

After coming down from Route 413 to the Calypso Inn, turn left on Route 413 to the south side of Rincón or downtown. You'll immediately pass **Little Malibu Beach,** where a 1616 brass astrolabe (an instrument used before the invention of the sextant) was discovered by local divers just a quarter-mile offshore. A small marina here is the home of **Moondog Charters** (787–823–7168), an outfit that specializes in fishing, diving and whale-watching trips, as well as sunset cruises. Remember this is the West Coast of Puerto Rico, and the sunsets here are every bit as pretty as California. There's also **Tanks-A-Lot Charters** (787–823–6301), which specializes in scuba and other trips aboard the *Island Queen.*

Down the road is the **Rincón Cultural Museum** (Route 13; 787–823–5120), filled with Taínos artifacts that were unearthed in the area. Open Thursday through Sunday 9:00 A.M. to 2:00 P.M. You'll also see the **Tourism Information Center** (Route 115, after the post office; 787–823–5024. Open Monday through Friday 8:00 A.M. to 4:30 P.M.).

Continuing straight along the road you will eventually pass a church that is just down the block on Route 414 from the downtown plaza. The open-air plaza, with a church and town hall, is a lot like other small Puerto Rican towns. But because this is Rincón, there's a surf shop, too: *West Coast Surf Shop* (Muñoz Rivera; 787–823–3935).

Taking the road to the right before the cultural museum winds around the coast as it passes a school, a low-cost housing project, and a *balneario.* Indian artifacts from A.D. 475, including pottery and other remnants of Taíno culture, were recently unearthed in this area. Beyond the *balneario,* the road leads back into Route 115, which exits town through the southern route.

Just before the road splits around an island of three towering mango trees lies the cutoff for Route 429, which leads to a beautiful coastal road and some of this town's better lodging options. The landscape here evokes the Mediterranean, which must have been an inspiration to the owners of the *Horned Dorset Primavera Hotel* (Route 429; km. 3; 787–823–4030, 787–725–6030, or 800–633–1857; www.horneddorset. com), one of the Caribbean's most luxurious resorts. You might think you're lost as you drive through a rural barrio, but the hotel's discreet entrance lies further along the road. The resort is built in the style of a Spanish villa complete with seaside terraces, hand-painted tiles, and blooming gardens. The grounds are lush, filled with birds and *coquís,* Puerto Rico's famous singing tree frogs. The resort's restaurant is regarded as the best in western Puerto Rico, and it attracts diners from across the island. While staying at the resort ($380 per night; minimum stay of four nights) or eating at the restaurant will cost you a bundle, it's well worth it.

For more reasonably priced accommodations, try *El Quijote Beach Cabañas* (Route 429; 787–823–4010), which has two fully equipped oceanfront beach units for rent. There's a beachfront area with hammocks and barbecue pits. The restaurant here, open Friday through Sunday specializes in Spanish and Puerto Rican food, with good *paella, tapas,* and sangría.

Beyond this Route 429 hooks back up to Route 115. This is the quickest way back to Highway 2 and every major point in Puerto Rico. If you're continuing on to Mayagüez, turn right on Route 115.

One last spot you should get to in Rincón is *Pico Atalaya,* also known as *La Bandera,* a mountaintop from which rugged Mona Island can be seen. While you're here, stop by *La Cima Burger,* a restaurant with a view, serving *mofongo,* steak, seafood, burgers, and sandwiches.

Mayagüez

Mayagüez, the island's third largest city, is known as the "Sultan of the West." Smack in the middle of the west coast, it's always had a California air about it. Its name is derived from a Taíno word meaning "place of many streams." The main river, the Yagüez River, runs through town, and much of Mayagüez is open to the sea as it sits on its wide-mouthed bay.

Mayagüez isn't the tourist town you think it might be, located as it is halfway down Puerto Rico's enviable west coast. There is no beach here (although plenty surround the city), and many visitors probably feel that it's more convenient to stay elsewhere. But Mayagüez is a nice city, small and warm enough to more appropriately be called a town.

Entering Mayagüez from Highway 2 south takes you past its two most established hotels. The **Holiday Inn Mayagüez** (2701 Highway 2, km. 149.9; 787–833–1100) lies a mile from downtown. The hotel bar and disco are jammed on weekends, and behind the hotel is a lively string of bars and restaurants that fill up for weekend happy hours. The best place to stay if you're looking for a big hotel is the recently renovated **Mayagüez Resort & Casino** (Route 104; 787–832–3030 or 888–689–3030), the former Mayagüez Hilton. The hotel features a casino and restaurant and sits on a clifftop overlooking Mayagüez Bay on more than twenty acres of tropical gardens. It's right off Highway 2 on the way into town. **Parador Hotel El Sol** (9 Santiago Riera Palmer; 787–834–0303 or 888–765–0303), with fifty-two clean, modest rooms and a pool, is located two blocks from the center of town and is much cheaper than the name-brand hotels.

Mayagüez's elegantly tiled **Plaza Colón** is dominated by a monument

Mayagüez's Unique Architecture

Although Mayagüez was founded as a Spanish settlement in the eighteenth century, aside from the small historic district surrounding the plaza, this west coast town is filled with the sunburned hulks of pre-1930s wooden homes. While not known for its historic districts, Mayagüez owes its unique architecture to a series of disasters that led to successive rebuildings of the town. First there was the Great Fire of 1841 and, in 1862, a second fire ravaged the city's waterfront district. These two disasters were but preludes to 1918, when a large earthquake destroyed most of the town.

I'll Drink to That

*F*rom Guánica to Mayagüez is Puerto Rico's **sangría** country. The Spanish import has flourished on the island, and several wildly unique local varieties are offered here. Fido's in Mayagüez and Coño in La Parguera are just two of a group of sangría makers who jealously guard their special recipes.

The refreshing drink is made with red wine, limes, and a variety of liquors (either dark or light rum or vodka) mixed with fruit—anything from apples to mangos to grapes to canned peaches. The beverage goes well with the island's plentiful seafood dishes— it's also likely to be the cheapest drink in town.

to Christopher Columbus. There are several architecturally interesting buildings on the central plaza, including **La Alcadía,** Mayagüez City Hall, which is constructed in a neo-Corinthian style. Other historic sites include the Art Deco **Teatro Yagüez** and the roaring 1920s Post Office, both of which are located on McKinley Street.

Mayagüez also has a historic waterfront district that features a restored 1920s Custom House and large warehouse district. This is also the site of two tuna processing plants. A few years ago, this town canned more than half the tuna consumed in the United States.

The adventurous might want to check out **La Sangría de Fido's** (Dullievre Street; no phone) in the town's barrio Balboa. It's a bar with a lot of character that also serves as the base office of the 3,000-gallon-a-month sangría business, **Sangría Fido: La Tradicional Wine Cocktail.** Seventy-two-year-old Fido (Wilfredo Aponte Hernández) has been making his potion since 1964. In 1997 he revealed his secret for success to the *San Juan Star*: "I was selling rice and beans, but people don't pay for food. People will pay for drinks."

Mayagüez is also where you'll find a the campus of **Recinto Universitario Mayagüez,** a branch of the University of Puerta Rico. A convenient city trolley runs between downtown sites, the university, a municipal stadium, and the city zoo. The campus grounds, located near the roadway heading up into the western mountains, are beautiful, and the university itself easily mixes modern and neo-classical styles. Next door to the campus are the beautiful botanical gardens of the **Tropical Agriculture Research Station** (787–831–3435), which feature wild fruit trees and bamboo, ornamental flowers, and timber trees. Free maps are available at the station. The research station is open 7:00 A.M. to 4:00 P.M. weekdays only; no admission charge. Across the street is the pretty Patriots Park. A budget hotel on campus, *Hostal Colegial,* run by RUM, (787–832–4040), is the best deal around for visiting students and educators.

The forty-five-acre *Mayagüez Zoo* (787–834–8110), nearby on Route 108, has 300 species, including an African Savannah with lions, giraffes, hippos, rhinos, and large reptiles. A Caribbean exhibit with jaguars, pelicans, and flamingos is also in the works. Open Wednesday through Sunday 9:00 A.M. to 4:00 P.M.; $3.00 admission.

Just south of Mayagüez is *Hormigueros,* a pretty town in the hillsides of the west coast. Its *Cathedral of Our Lady of Montserrat,* with its ivory columns and crimson-domed top, is a simple yet forceful presence rising above the town. Every September during the patron saint celebration of the church's namesake, thousands of pilgrims travel here for a religious procession. The church is named after the Virgin of Montserrat who, according to legend, found and protected the eight-year-old daughter of local farmer Giraldo González for fifteen days in the sixteenth century. The dark-skinned virgin is popular throughout the Spanish Caribbean.

Puerto Rico's Pirate Past

*W*hen Spain all but stopped trading with Puerto Rico from 1640 to 1750, the island experienced a minidepression. To compensate, islanders began illegally trading food products and other goods with Spain's enemies, including the neighboring French, Dutch, and British islands. Coastal towns from Cabo Rojo to Fajardo bustled in contraband goods, and the booming trade not only attracted trading partners, but rogues and pirates as well.

Many pirates used Puerto Rico as their base of operations or sold their loot on the black market on the island's east coast. Many also took refuge from their high-seas adventures on the island's shores. The offshore island of Mona, in the Mona Channel between Hispaniola and Puerto Rico, was a favorite place to lay low. In fact in1698 *Captain Kidd* hid here. Kidd's biggest hoist had occurred earlier that year, when he captured the Quedagh Merchant, *an Armenian ship bound for Bengal with a hull full of silk, guns, spices, and valuable metals.*

While Kidd was eventually hanged for his crimes, the whereabouts of much of the Quedagh Merchant *loot* remains a mystery. Some speculate it might still be buried on Mona Island or on the neighboring island of Hispaniola (the Dominican Republic and Haiti).

The Natural Islands

oth Desecheo Island, 13.3 miles off the west coast, and Mona Island, 48 miles southwest of Rincón, are protected wildlife reserves with only rustic accommodations for overnight stays. While Desecheo can be visited for an afternoon of snorkeling, visiting Mona requires an expedition.

Mona Island has been called the Caribbean Galapagos, a natural reserve in the middle of the rough Mona Channel. Although the island is uninhabited today (except for transient and hardy campers and rotating personnel from the Department of Natural and Environmental Resources), it was settled centuries ago by the Taíno Indians, as the petroglyphs and ancient ceramic shards in the ruins of ceremonial ballparks attest. When Columbus and Ponce de León stopped here, in 1494 and 1508 respectively, both encountered a well-established Taíno community. In later years, pirates used the island as a base. Captain Kidd used it as a hideout, and the famous Puerto Rican pirate Cofresí also operated from here. Today the lure of still-buried treasure continues to attract an assorted mix of fortune hunters. For a time the island was home to settlers who mined for guano, a mixture of limestone and bat manure used as fertilizer. Today the nature reserve attracts campers, spelunkers, scuba aficionados, and nature buffs. Teams of researchers and scientists also use it as a natural laboratory.

Many visitors' first glimpse of the island is *Playa Sardinera.* This is the first stop for many boats, as it has a lighthouse and primitive showers. The beach also is home to an old colonial jail and a cave. Here you'll find some of the calmest waters on Mona.

Two-hundred-foot-tall limestone cliffs ring the island, which also has thick mangrove forests and what is thought to be one of the largest ocean-formed cave systems in the world. The bean-shaped, 7-by-4-mile island is home to 650 plant and tree species, including 78 endangered species. There are some twenty endangered animal species here, including three different types of sea turtles that nest on its shores. The island is filled with yard-long iguanas, and flocks of sea birds, such as the red-footed booby. It is surrounded by coral reefs in waters teeming with marine life, including tropical fish, lobster, queen conch, barracuda, dolphin, tuna, and five different species of whale. Just offshore the ocean is filled with black coral and patch reefs, as well as underground caverns. Large sea sponges, spoor, and groove growth are found here. Visibility in the Mona waters stretches out 200 feet, which makes for great diving. In addition to abundant marine life, there are also eleven known shipwrecks, including old Spanish galleons, buried in the surrounding waters.

Basic camping, where all necessities must be packed in and all garbage packed out, is still the only way to stay at the nature reserve. Camping permits are available through the Department of Natural and Environmental Resources (787–723–1616 or 787–721–5495). Although there is no electricity on the island, a solar research project is now underway that should have the entire island running on solar power from panels erected on top of the *Mona Island Museum,* an outdoor permanent exhibit about the island's animal and plantlife.

Today scuba divers can make it out for a full-day dive in Mona's waters and back with no need to stay over. Several socially oriented groups, such as the Natural History Society and El Fondo de Mejoramiento, run trips to Mona, as do educational organizations such as the University of Puerto Rico. A number of private tour and travel companies also organize trips here, such as *Encantos Ecotours* (787–272–0005), the Mayagüez-based *Conozcamos a Puerto Rico* (787–831–0865), and *Adventours* (787–831–6447). Depending on the number of people involved and the types of activities planned, a weekend trip can range in price from $300 to $1,000 per person. Since planes are no longer allowed to land on Mona, most people get here via a three-hour boat trip. (Although it is possible to hire a seaplane, this is both a costly and rare service. At press time, there is no commercial service based in Puerto Rico.)

A 4-mile road from the beach leads to *Playa Uvero,* where you can camp among low-lying trees running across the beachfront. A cave in the area, *Cueva de Doña Geña,* was named after a woman who lived in it for thirty-three years while working as a cook for guano miners. A small trail off Uvero leads to the ruins of ceremonial Taíno ball courts.

Desecheo Island is much smaller than Mona and lies just 12 miles off Puerto Rico's coast. The island is most used for its sandy beaches, and its coastline is rimmed by coral and clear waters. The island, an unforgiving land of scrub forest, sand, and rock, looks a lot like a Middle Eastern desert. Like Mona, Desecheo is now a federally protected nature reserve. This is also a favorite spot of divers and snorkelers (see above for tour organizers).

PLACES TO STAY ON THE NORTH COAST AND IN THE WEST

AGUADA

Ann Wigmore Spa
Route 114
(787) 868–6307

Cabañas el Palmer
Route 115
(787) 868–6307

Parador JB Hidden Village
Route 416, km. 9.5
(787) 882–5960

Pino Mar
Route 115
(787) 868–8269

AGUADILLA

Hotel Cielo Mar
84 Montemar
(787) 882–5959

Hotel Hacienda El Pedregal
Road 111, km. 0.1
(787) 891–6068 or
(888) 568–6068

La Cima Hotel
Route 110, km. 9.2
(787) 890–2016

Parador Borinquen
Route 467, km. 2
(787) 891–0451

Parador El Faro
Route 107, km. 2.1
(787) 882–8000 or
(888) 300–8002

CAMUY

Posasa El Palomar
Route 119, km. 7.5
(787) 898–1060

DORADO

Hyatt Dorado Beach Resort
and Country Club
Route 693, km. 12.8
(787) 796–1234;
www.hyatt.com

Hyatt Regency Cerromar
Beach Resort and Casino
Route 693, km. 12.9
(787) 796–1234;
www.hyatt.com

ISABELA

Costa Dorado Beach Resort
900 Emilio González
(787) 872–7255 or
(877) 975–0101;
www.costadoradobeach.
com

Ocean Front Hotel
Road 4466, km. 0.1
Playa Jobos
(787) 872–0444;
www.oceanfrontpr.com

Parador Villas del Mar Hau
Road 4466, km. 8.3
(787) 872–2045;
www.villahau.com

Villa Montaña Resort
Road 4466, km. 1.9
(787) 872–9554 or
(888) 780–9195;
www.villamontana.com

MAYAGÜEZ

Holiday Inn Mayagüez
2701 Highway 2, km. 149.9
(787) 833–1100

Tourist Information for the North Coast and West

Aguadilla Tourism Information
Rafael Hernández Airport
(787) 890–3315

Arecibo Tourism Office
offices at City Hall and Lighthouse Museum
(787) 879–2232 or (787) 878–2299

Camuy Tourism Information
Route 119, km. 4.8
(787) 898–2240

Dorado Tourism Information
City Hall
(787) 796–5740

Mayagüez Tourism Information
City Hal
(787) 834–8585

Rincón Tourist Information Center
Route 115
(787) 823–5024
www.rincon.org

Hotel El Embajador
111 Este Ramos Antonini
(787) 833–3340

Mayagüez Resort and
Casino
Route 104, km. 0.3
(787) 832–3030 or
(888) 689–3030

Parador Hotel El Sol
9 Santiago Riera Palmer
(787) 834–0303 or
(888) 765–0303

QUEBRADILLAS
Parador El Guajataca
Highway 2, km. 103.8
(787) 895–3070 or
(800) 964–3065;
www.elguajataca.com

Parador Vistamar
Highway 2, km. 7.8
(787) 895–2065 or
(888) 391–0606

RINCÓN
Beside the Pointe Guest
House
Sandy Beach
(787) 823–8550;
www.besidethepointe.com

Coconut Palms Guest
House
Route 115
(787) 823–0147

Desecheo Inn
Route 413, km. 2.5
(787) 823–0390

El Quijote Beach Cabañas
Route 429
(787) 823–4010

Horned Dorset Primavera
Hotel
Route 429, km. 3
(787) 823–4030,
(787) 725–6030, or
(800) 633–1857;
www.horneddorset.com

Lazy Parrot Inn and
Restaurant
Route 413, km. 4.1
(787) 823–5654 or
(800) 294–1752;
www.lazyparrot.com

Lemontree Waterfront
Cottages
Route 429, km. 4.1
(787) 823–6452;
www.lemontreepr.com

Parador Villa Antonio
Route 115, km. 12.3
(787) 823–2645;
www.villa-antonio.com

Pipóns Resort
Route 413, km. 3
(787) 823–5106;
www.piponsresort.com

Pools Beach Cabañas
Verdes
Pools Beach
(787) 823–8135

Rincón Surf & Board
Caribbean Safari Guest
House
Sandy Beach
(787) 823–0610 or
(800) 458–3628

Sandy Beach Inn and
Restaurant
Route 413, km. 4.3
(787) 823–1146

Sunset Paradise Villas
Route 115
(787) 823–7183 or
(800) 875–6399;
www.sunsetparadise.com

Villa Cofresí
Route 115, km. 12
(787) 823–2450;
www.villacofresi.com

**PLACES TO EAT ON
THE NORTH COAST AND
IN THE WEST**

AGUADA
Cheers and Beers
Highway 115, km. 21.4
(787) 484–5922

El Tapatío Mexican
Restaurant
Highway 115, km. 20.1
(787) 868–1160

El Túnel Pizzeria
214 Colon
(787) 868–5430

Las Colinas
Road 4416, km. 1.3 at
Parador J.B Hidden Village
(787) 868–8686

AGUADILLA
Dario's Gourmet
Restaurant
Route 110, km. 8.8
(787) 890–6143

Eclipse
Road 4466, km. 1.2
at Villa Montaña Resort
(787) 890–0275

New Golden Crown
Route 110, km. 9.2
at La Cima Hotel
(787) 890–5077

Tres Amigos
Route 107, km. 2.1
at Parador El Faro
(787) 882–8000,
extension 225

CAMUY
Casa del Playa
Highway 2
(787) 989–3850

El Fogón de Abuela
Route 485, km. 3.1
(787) 262–0781

Johnny's Barbecue
Highway 2
(787) 262–5059

DORADO
El Ladrillo
334 Méndez Vigo
(787) 796–2120

El Malecón
Route 693, km. 8.2
(787) 796–1645

El Navigante
385 Méndez Vigo
(787) 796–7177

Jewel of Dorado
Route 693, km. 8.1
(787) 796–4644

La Terraza
C–1 Marginal
(787) 796–1242

Mangére
Route 693, km. 8.5
(787) 796–4444

Yukiyu Sushi Bar
Route 693, km. 8.5
(787) 796–4477

HATILLO
El Buen Café
381 Highway 2, km.
84 at Parador El Buen Café
(787) 898–3495,
extension 129

ISABELA
Happy Belly's
Playa Jobos
(787) 872–6566

Ocean Front Restaurant
Road 4446, km. 0.1,
Playa Jobos at the
Ocean Front Hotel
(787) 872–3339

Olas y Arenas
Playa Montones
(787) 830–8315

Sonia Rican Seafood
Playa Jobos

MAYAGÜEZ
Brazo Gitano
101 Méndez Vigo

El Estoril
100 Este Méndez Vigo
(787) 834–2288

Mesón Español
525 Jose González
Clemente
(787) 833–5445

Restaurant Don Pepe
58 Este Méndez Vigo
(787) 834–4941

Repostería y Cafetería
Franco
3 Manuel Pirallo
(787) 832–0070

Ricomini Bakery
202 Méndez Vigo
(787) 832–0565

QUEBRADILLAS
Casabi
Highway 2, km. 103.8
at Parador El Guajataca
(787) 895–3070

Historíco Puente Blanco
Road 4484, km. 1.09
(787) 895–1934

Parador Vistamar
Highway 2, km. 7.9
(787) 895–2065

RINCÓN
Ann Wigmore Living Food
Off Route 115 at km. 19.9
(787) 868–6307

The Black Eagle
Route 115
(787) 823–3510

Calypso Tropical Café
Route 413
(787) 823–4151

El Bambino
Route 115
(787) 823–3744

El Flamboyán
By Pools Beach

El Molino del Quijote
Route 429, km. 3.3
(787) 823–4010

El Tapatío
Route 115, km. 20.1
(787) 868–1160

Horned Dorset Primavera
Route 429, km. 3.0
at The Horned Dorset
Primavera Hotel
(787) 823–4030 or
(800) 633–1857

La Cima Burger
Route 411 on way to
Aguada

The Landing
Route 413, km. 2.5
(787) 823–3112

Larry B's
Route 413, at Tamboo
Tavern, Beside the Pointe
(787) 823–3210

The Lazy Parrot Inn and
Restaurant
Route 413, km. 4.1
(787) 823–5654 or
(800) 294–1752;
www.lazyparrot.com

Paradise Restaurant
Route 115
(787) 823–1226

Sandy Beach Inn
Off Route 413
(787) 823–1146;
www.sandybeachinn.com

The Central Mountains

The Cordillera Central mountain range runs through the center of Puerto Rico in an east-west direction like a mammoth spinal column. At an average height of 1,000 to 3,000 feet, several peaks push their way higher, such as Cerro de Punta, Puerto Rico's highest point at 4,398 feet.

Central Puerto Rico is a land of dramatic beauty rarely seen by most visitors. The people and their way of life here seem more traditional than their coastal counterparts. A few multi-lane highways pass through the Cordillera Central as quickly as possible, connecting major points to coastal cities such as San Juan, Ponce, and Arecibo. But the only real way to explore the region is via winding country roads. The central mountains are home to a rain forest, several lakes, and state forests. This lush countryside, which on many roads forms a tall green canopy overhead, also has dazzling views stretching from the dry southern coast to the green northern coast. Wooden homes and road-side businesses are perched precariously at the edge of steep drop-offs, and the rural roadways switch back and forth around mountains, dropping suddenly and then climbing again. Expect to see lots of dogs, chickens, goats, cattle, and horses. The folks you run into are quite friendly to visitors; you're sure to meet them in the rustic bars and eateries along the mountain roads.

The *Panoramic Route (la ruta panorámica),* is a tangled network of more than forty country roads that stretches some 165 miles and goes directly through much of the region. It can be driven at a leisurely pace over three days, from its beginnings outside the east coast town of Yabucoa on the Caribbean to its end in the damp cool of coffee country between Maricao and Mayagüez. Alternate routes through the mountains are also enjoyable, however, and it's possible to pick up portions of the Panoramic Route outside major roads, such as Highway 52 or Highway 10. Another good idea is to combine a trip to the mountains with a visit to a beach town on the coast near that mountain region. This chapter follows, more or less, the Panoramic Route, although it detours to points of interest off the route.

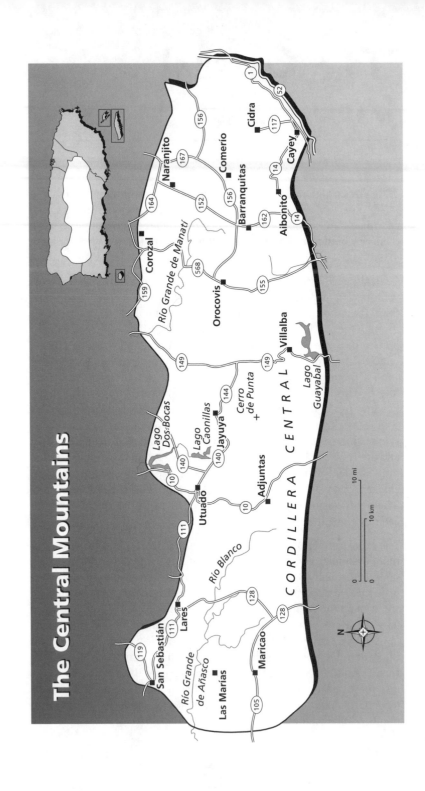

The Central Mountains

Although lodgings are not as abundant as on the coast, several comfortable country inns are scattered throughout the mountains. The region is a perfect lure for the more low-key traveler, who may be genuinely surprised by how much the Caribbean can feel like New England, even if it is a wild, tropical New England.

The Eastern Mountains

The Panoramic Route begins right outside the city of **Yabucoa**, where steep cliffsides rise up out of deep blue water, their vast undersides eaten away by the glaring sun, the wind, and the pounding of sea and salt. A center of the sugar industry in its heyday, this city on a hill is beautiful. A new

> **AUTHOR'S FAVORITES IN THE CENTRAL MOUNTAINS**
>
> **Guavate,** *Cayey*
>
> **Lago Guineo (Banana Lake),** *Orocovis*
>
> **Cerro de Punta,** *Jayuya*
>
> **La Piedra Escrita,**
> *The Written Rock, Jayuya*
>
> **Castañer,** *Lares*
>
> **Maricao Fish Hatchery,**
> *Maricao*

El Jíbaro

El **jíbaro** *is a mythic figure, a cultural icon in Puerto Rico that is on par with the cowboy in the United States. Today,* sanjuaneros *call anyone not from San Juan* jibaros, *in much the same that a New Yorker is likely to think of everything west of the Hudson as wilderness.*

The term el jíbaro *dates back to the start of the eighteenth century when it referred to rural dwellers, especially in the mountains. The word is believed to have stemmed from the days when the last of the Taíno Indians fled into the mountains to escape the Spanish. The machete-wielding jíbaro of Puerto Rican folklore is an honest, hard-working, independent man—an owner of a mountain farm who can always provide for his family.*

The rise of the sugar plantation economy in the early 1900s, followed by the industrialization that began in the

1940s plus the increased lure of emigration stateside, drew thousands of jíbaros from the central mountain region. Today, the true jíbaros found in Puerto Rico live mostly in the central mountains.

Still, el jíbaro continues to be a figure in Puerto Rican arts and culture. The brooding and excellent Ballad from Another Time, *by José Luis González, does much to scrub off the idealized veneer on the portrait of the jibaro. The hapless jíbaro, lost in the big city, has provided endless fodder for skits on television comedy shows.*

Look for sculptor Tomás Batista's "al jíbaro puertorriqueño," the monument "to the Puerto Rican Jíbaro," as Highway 52 crosses over the Cordillera Central. It stands in the shadow of the huge twin-peaked mountain of **Cayey,** *which locals call Las Tetas, or the "Breasts of Cayey."*

expressway, Highway 53, is your quickest route from Fajardo. From San Juan take Highway 52 to Highway 30; at Humacao, you can catch Highway 53 or Highway 3 south to Yabucoa.

The road quickly heads away from the coast, passing through the beautiful hilly and forested region of *Patillas.* As on much of its length, the road here is shaded beneath a canopy of trees and towering bamboo. The Panoramic Route then segues into Route 7740. In Patillas, *Las Casas de la Selva* (787–839–7318) is a campground and inn in a natural reserve on the edge of the Carite Forest. Dirt-cheap rustic lodgings and planned adventures are the main draw. Call ahead to arrange your visit, which could be a half-day guided hike, a full-day trek with picnic and swimming, or a trek and overnight stay with meals. Your host is Richard Druitt. At his place, back-to-nature instincts and events such as Summer Solstice parties are the norm. South of Las Casas lies *Lake Patillas,* a beautiful body of water surrounded by green mountains.

Al HBARO PUERTORRIQUEÑO

Monument to the Puerto Rican Jíbaro

The Panoramic Route next takes you to the *Carite Forest Reserve,* a 6,000-acre nature reserve (Route 184, Cayey) with picnic and camping areas and 25 miles of hiking trails. To reserve a campsite, contact the Department of Natural and Environmental Resources in San Juan. (See Introduction for more details.) Two areas accommodate sixteen tents and have bathroom facilities. The reserve's main feature is *Charco Azul,* or Blue Pond, a natural pool named for the color of its water. It's an easy mile hike from the parking area alongside the road to the pond. The roadside picnic area has a nice stream running through its grounds.

The forest, filled with mahogany and *yagrumo* trees, towering ferns, and sierra and royal palms, is full of trails. *Carite Lake* is also in the reserve, just down Route 742. The artificial lake is stocked with bass and other fish. Another

THE CENTRAL MOUNTAINS

TOP ANNUAL EVENTS IN
THE CENTRAL MOUNTAINS

Coffee Harvest Festival,
mid-February, Maricao

**Barranquitas
Artisan's Fair,**
mid-July, Barranquitas

Flower Festival,
late June-early July, Aibonito

Chicken Festival,
August, Aibonito

El Grito de Lares,
September 23, Lares

Indian Festival,
mid-November, Jayuya

picnic area with restrooms, barbecue pits, and covered eating areas sprawls out across a hilly stretch of forest farther along the roadway, right before the Ranger's Office.

Just south of the Carite Forest Ranger Station, along Route 184, is a string of lechoneras in Guavate (actually part of Cayey). Many *puertorriqueños* trek here regularly from the San Juan area to enjoy roasted pig. Eating here at the open-air restaurants is a memorable experience for visitors. Those looking for a more formal dining experience might try **La Casona de Guavate** (Route 184, km. 28.5; 787-787-5533). The place is a hodgepodge of architectural styles, and the food can be just as inventive. There's very good basic Puerto Rican and Spanish fare, but the kitchen also experiments: for example, Filete Tropical, a filet mignon stuffed with lobster.

This is one of the quickest and easiest trips to the mountain region from San Juan and is easily accomplished in a single afternoon. The Guavate exit is about forty minutes south of San Juan on Highway 52.

Pigging Out on Lechón

*L*echón—roast suckling pig—draws islanders to Guavate on the weekends for an afternoon orgy of eating, drinking, and socializing. Although food is served at the numerous outdoor eateries every day of the week, Sunday is the most popular time to make the pilgrimage. There are at least a dozen lechoneras on Route 184, but the highly recommended ones are those concentrated around km. 27 on the route. Look for Lechonera El Rancho Original, there for thirty years and claiming to be the first of its kind. La Reliquia, El Monte, El Mojito, and El Rancho Numero Uno all get good reviews. Din-

ers load up their plates with slices of juicy pork that marinated for days before its slow roasting, basted with orange juice, leaving a golden, crispy-skinned and smoky meat. It is accompanied by vegetables such as cassava or plátanos, and arroz con gandules (rice with pigeon peas) or red beans with calabaza (pumpkin). Morcilla (blood sausage) and longaniza (chicken and pork sausage) could be on the side. Cost is determined by the weight of your plate; a hearty meal can be had for $10.00. Good food, cold beer, and lively island music combine for a festive atmosphere and happy crowd.

Folk Music

*T*he mountain region and the jíbaro *gave birth to Puerto Rican folk music,* décima.

Based on the old Spanish seis, *it is called the* decima *because it is sung in ten-line rhyming cadences, either in an expression of great joy or sorrow. Verbal improvisation is key to this music,* and often a group of singers will perform the décima, *each taking a line and trying to outdo those who came before. Today this music, which makes use of guitars of various strings, maracas,* guíro, *and other gourd percussion instruments, informs the ballads and protest songs of singer Andrés Jiménez, who is known as "El Jíbaro."*

North of Guavate and directly south from San Juan on Highway 52 are a few other mountain towns of note. The first one is **Aguas Buenas,** just south of Caguas, the southern border of the San Juan metropolitan area. Route 156 begins climbing immediately after leaving Caguas on this northeastern shoot of the Cordillera Central. This town brings the mountains very close to San Juan, and many *sanjuaneros* who work in the city live here. The town is also home to the **Aguas Buenas Caves.** While The Department of Natural and Environmental Resources no longer runs tours through here, it is still a favorite spot of experienced spelunkers.

A bit south, along Route 172, is **Cidra**, a small mountain town that is one of the fastest growing municipalities on the island, mainly because of new housing developments and an influx of *sanjuaneros.* Thankfully, Cidra still retains its small-town flavor. The road to Cidra is filled with vegetable, fruit, and flower vendors, and its central plaza is charming with its historic buildings and many trees. Five-mile-long Lago Cidra is a manmade reservoir with good fishing.

Cayey is the next major mountain town you'll encounter on a southern route from San Juan. It's located on the northern slope of the Cordillera Central near its summit in the **Sierra de Cayey,** Puerto Rico's central mountain range in this area.

A **University of Puerto Rico** campus is located here, which lends this mountain town a larger cultural life than many of its neighbors. The fine **Museo Pío Lopez Martinez** (787–738–2161, extension 2191 or 2209) is located on campus. A permanent collection features the work of Ramón Fraube (1865–1954), a Cayey painter whose realistic works depict everyday scenes from Puerto Rican mountain life.

Open Monday through Friday 8:00 A.M. to 4:00 P.M.; free admission. *Parroquia San José,* a Catholic church built in 1813, anchors Cayey's charming central plaza.

Outside of the town center, on the road to *Jájome,* you'll find *The Sand and the Sea* (Route 714, km. 5.2; 787–738–9086), a charming out-of-the-way restaurant serving local cuisine staples in an inventive way. A few minutes on the restaurant's back terrace is all it takes to realize that the drive here is worth it. The view extends down to the south coast and the sparkling Caribbean.

Another nice restaurant in a rural setting is the *Jájome Terrace* (Route 15, km. 18.6; 787–738–4016). Flower gardens surround this mountain perch with views of the distant sea. French-influenced local dishes are served on an open-air terrace. Also in this area, on Route 15, is one of the beautiful official vacation residences of the Puerto Rican governor (not open to the public).

From either Cayey or Guavate, Route 14 picks up the baton of the Panoramic Route and takes you to the mountain town of *Aibonito.* The best time to visit the town is during the annual *Flower Festival* (June) or the local festival run by chicken producer *To-Rico* (August). While flowers and food are the main attractions, respectively, like most Puerto Rican parties, there's also live music and a lot of dancing.

Mountain Walks

A really wonderful thing for visitors to try is one of the walking adventures of the local group **El Fondo de Mejoramiento** (P.O. Box 364746, Correo Central, San Juan, PR 00936-4746; 787-759-8366), administered by the very capable Gabriel Ferrer. Every spring the non-profit group organizes hikes along a different stretch of the Panoramic Route. The day-long, 10-mile hike trips are very popular with professional sanjuaneros. The entire route is covered over successive weekends over three months. A modest reservation fee, which pays for refreshments, is charged. All walks are accompanied by support vehicles with water, emergency medical equipment, and a van to pick up stragglers.

The group's purpose is to heighten awareness of Puerto Rico's natural resources. The group also organizes walks elsewhere in Puerto Rico and the Caribbean. Ferrer says that one of the organization's goals is to forge an Antilles Trail on existing roadways and walkways that would run through much of the Caribbean.

Aibonito is a must-stop, even though the Panoramic Route doesn't come directly here. At 2,500 feet, Aibonito is the highest town in Puerto Rico, a place where temperatures have been known to plummet to 40 degrees Fahrenheit. The town's name apparently stems from an account of a hapless seventeenth-century wanderer who stumbled on the town and remarked, "¡Ai, que bonito!" ("Oh, how pretty!") For a time, the town also served as Puerto Rico's capital, when Spanish troops moved here from San Juan to stomp out an *independentista* uprising circa 1867.

Aibonito is surrounded by hills, chicken farms, and flower nurseries. It was once a summer retreat for the wealthy, and many stately residences remain. The plaza, with a movie theater and diner, has a nice lived-in air about it. There's also **Parroquia San José,** a bright-white nineteenth-century wooden church with two towers. One of the best establishments in town is **La Piedra Restaurant** (Route 7718, km. 0.8; 787–735–1034), a mountaintop restaurant with a view. Much of the produce and many of the herbs used in the restaurant are grown on the premises. This is healthy *comida criolla* with a gourmet touch. *Mofongo* is a specialty. Helicopter transportation is available from San Juan. The owners suggest you bring a sweater.

The Central Mountains

The **San Cristóbal Canyon,** Puerto Rico's deepest gorge, lies between Aibonito and Barranquitas. The canyon, with sheer walls that shoot up 700 feet, was formed by the raging **Río Usabon,** a giant gash in this mountainous terrain. Route 725 gets you closest to the canyon. You'll know you're getting close because of the great number of businesses with *El Cañon* in their names. **Bar El Cañon** (Route 725, km. 4) has cold cheap beer and a good jukebox. A trail from here leads to the canyon floor, but it's a rough hike. Farther along the road, at km. 5.5, a narrow side road takes you closer to the top of the canyon. From here it's a much shorter hike to the bottom, which features a 100-foot waterfall.

The area surrounding the canyon was recently bought by the Puerto Rico Conservation Trust, which has started a clean-up and tree-planting campaign here. There are hundreds of plant species and about seventy-five bird species that claim this as their habitat, which is much dryer than many mountain forests. To protect the ecosystem, the non-profit group wants to eventually limit canyon use to only guided tours.

Barranquitas, which overlooks the San Cristóbal Canyon, has the look of a European town, with closely built houses and narrow winding streets surrounded by hills. The focal point of the town's plaza is the white, red-roofed church, **Parroquia San Antonio Padua,** that rises above the townscape. Barranquitas is set at an elevation of 1,800 feet and is just as cool and refreshing as Aibonito. It is best known as the birthplace of Luis Muñoz Rivera, who struggled for autonomy from Spain. It is also the final resting place of his son Luis Muñoz Marín, the governor of Puerto Rico from 1948 to 1964 and the seminal Puerto Rican political figure of the twentieth century.

The birthplace of Luis Muñoz Rivera is now the **Muñoz Rivera Library Museum** (Calle Muñoz Rivera between Tonia Vélez and Padre Berríos Streets; 787–857–0230), located one block west of the town's plaza. The library's contents belonged to Muñoz Rivera, and the house provides a glimpse into life among Puerto Rico's elite at mid-century. There's also much here about his son, Muñoz Marín. Open Monday through Saturday 8:30 A.M. to 5:00 P.M. Free admission.

Just around the corner is the mausoleum where Muñoz Rivera, his son, and their wives are buried (Padre Berríos Street).

Every year a huge three-day craft fair takes place around Muñoz Rivera's July 17 birthdate. It's one of the biggest fairs on the island and

San Cristóbal Canyon

draws artisans from across the island who set up their wares in the town's shaded plaza.

A bit northwest of Barranquitas lies **Orocovis,** probably the most isolated town on the island, located dead center in the island's mountainous middle. To the south is **Villaba,** which can be reached most directly from Route 149, which travels south to Highway 52 near Ponce at Juana Díaz. Both towns have spectacular views extending to the coasts.

The Panoramic Route goes west along Route 143 from Barranquitas, passing through the Corozal mountain range and dissecting the awesome **Toro Negro Forest.** This 30-mile stretch between Barranquitas and Adjuntas to the west is the longest on the Panoramic Route and among the most beautiful. Traveling along the mountainous backbone of the Cordillera Central, it's possible to see both the north and the south coasts. A look north, the mountains fall off into the tightly

Luis Muñoz Marín

*B*orn in 1898, the year the American troops landed at Guánica, **Luis Muñoz Marín** literally mirrored the life of modern Puerto Rico. In fact no single person has had as much of an effect on modern Puerto Rico.

The son of Luis Muñoz Rivera, the top Puerto Rican leader at the end of the nineteenth century, Muñoz Marín was well suited for the role. In his youth he traveled in bohemian circles in his adopted home of New York City. Urbane and proficient in English and Spanish, he also proved a deft politician who easily mixed with jíbaros in rural Puerto Rico.

At the age of forty, Muñoz and a group of liberal colleagues created the Popular Democratic Party in his father's birthplace of Barranquitas. The party controlled Puerto Rico for decades under Muñoz's leadership

with their slogan of "Bread, Land and Freedom." Rather than concentrating on resolving Puerto Rico's political status question, the new party focused its energy on improving economic and social conditions.

This effort reached its apex in the advent of Puerto Rico's current commonwealth status, called Estado Libre Asociado, or "free associated state," which was established on July 25, 1952, the anniversary of the U. S. invasion of Puerto Rico.

Muñoz reigned as top Puerto Rican leader for twenty-four years. During this time, Puerto Rico went from being "the poorhouse of the Caribbean" to the "showcase of the Caribbean." Even today Puerto Ricans will tell you how they were able to afford their first pair of shoes under Muñoz's leadership.

The Long and Winding Route

*S*an Juan–based travelers wanting to visit **Aibonito** or **Barranquitas** may want to take the long and winding route from Bayamón, just west of San Juan via Kennedy Avenue, which runs into Highway 2. Take Route 167 from traffic-clogged Bayamón and, before you know it, you'll be passing through forested mountainsides. The route is lined with lechoneras that offer live music on weekends. A short jaunt on this road may be enough for most people, but it's possible to take the road all the way to Barranquitas (at Comerio, take Route 156). Be aware that the 30-mile drive over winding, two-lane country roads is likely to take you a lot longer than you might think. On weekdays a private bus company plies this route in weathered school buses from Old San Juan to Barranquitas. One of the buses, La Flecha Vengadora, or the "Vengeful Arrow," leaves between 9:00 A.M. and 10:00 A.M. Since the bus company has no telephone number for information, make sure to ask drivers for schedules and rates. Also, be sure to ask what time the last bus leaves for San Juan. The trip is slow and not very comfortable, but it costs less than $1.00 to get there and back. Visitors with the time will appreciate this close-up view of everyday Puerto Rican life.

formed Karst hills just before the Atlantic. Vast plains stretch south of the mountain range to the distant Caribbean. You can even see offshore islands, such as Ponce's Caja de Muertos, from here. Often, however, this mountainous road is draped in mist, and one gets the impression of traveling through a vast, impenetrable cloud forest.

Sandwiched between the mountain towns of Villalba and Jayuya, and Adjuntas and Orocovis, the **Toro Negro Forest Reserve** encompasses 7,000 acres in the heart of Puerto Rico. The reserve is every bit as impressive as the more famous El Yunque (Caribbean National Forest) in Rio Grande-Luquillo. It, too, has some characteristics of the rain forest, but its jungle-like vegetation is at higher elevations. Multitudes of mountain streams with names like Salto de Inabón, Indalecia, Guayo, and Matrullas, lace the reserve. Adjacent narrow footpaths offer hikers a quick way to get off the beaten path. Bamboo, giant ferns, *tabonuco*, trumpet trees, and towering royal palms fill the forest.

The main entrance to the forest is at the **Doña Juana Recreational Area** (Route 143, km. 32.4), which features a picnic area and an S-shaped swimming pool filled by the cold mountain streams. The area, which is the starting place of many trails in the reserve, also has a campground, with wooden lean-tos to help protect from the rain. Stop by the Ranger Station (787–844–4051) for orientation and a trail map. The Ranger Station is open most predictably during the summer from 8:00 A.M. to noon and 1:00 to 4:00 P.M. on weekdays. Just outside the recreational area is *Las Cabañas de Doña Juana* (Route 143), a rustic, friendly place offering tasty mountain barbecue and other fare. The ribs are recommended. Also try the side dish of rice with white beans, unique in Puerto Rico, where most people prefer pink beans. Food can be eaten under the small *cabañas* that give the place its name.

The recreational area looks like a final outpost of civilization, with the dense forest looming at all turns. From here it's about a 2-mile hike to a lookout tower and the nearby *Doña Juana Falls,* which come crashing down 200 feet over a cliffside. The half-paved trail is a pretty easy hike, but take care: The constant rain makes for a slippery surface.

> **OTHER ATTRACTIONS IN THE CENTRAL MOUNTAINS**
>
> *Cerro Maravilla, Jayuya*

West of the recreation area, Route 143 passes *Lago Guineo,* or Banana Lake, Puerto Rico's highest. This round lake, created by damming the Toro Negro River, is almost completely hidden by dense forest growth, notably towering bamboo, and is ringed by steep, slippery, red-clay banks. Those who come here will be greeted by fresh mountain air, the singing of the *coquí,* and little else.

Farther west lies *Cerro de Punta* (Route 143, km. 16.5), Puerto Rico's tallest peak at 4,398 feet. It's possible to drive to the top on an extremely steep, 10-mile-long, single-lane gravel road, but most visitors will prefer to hoof it. However you get there, the view is worth it. Up top you can see all the way over to the capital city of San Juan and most of the Atlantic Coast. At other times the peak is wrapped in swirling mist, giving it an otherworldly, lunar quality.

North of the Toro Negro area are several towns and other attractions that are definitely worth a visit. Continue west along Route 143 beyond the cutoff to Ponce at Route 139. The next exit to the north will be Route 140, which leads to a mountain crossroads. Turn right on Route 144 to get to *Jayuya,* a mountain town resting in a valley beneath the imposing Cerro de Punta and surrounding mountains. Route 144 is the only way into Jayuya from either the west or the east. The town is surrounded by a lush valley, which in turn is circled by many of the highest peaks in the Cordillera Central. The town is filled with old coffee estates, as well as Taíno ruins and artifacts.

Parador Hacienda Gripiñas (Route 527, km. 2.5; 787–828–1717 or 800–981–7575), built on the grounds of an old coffee plantation, is one of the best places to stay in Puerto Rico's interior. Built in 1853 by coffee baron and Spanish nobleman Eusebio Pérez del Castillo, the former plantation home was turned into an inn in 1975, and it retains the elegance and grandeur of its past. A wide porch, gorgeous gardens, and twenty acres of coffee fields surround it. Ceiling fans and hammocks point the way to laze away a few days here, and the chorus of chanting *coquís* lulls you further into relaxation. There is also a pool and an excellent restaurant. A small 2-mile trail from here leads to the summit of Cerro de Punta.

Jayuya is known for the Taíno relics found here. The *Cemí Museum* (787–828–5000) in town has a collection of Taíno pottery and *cemís,* Taíno ceremonial objects. Off Route 144 is *La Piedra Escrita,* "The Written Rock," a huge boulder with Taíno petroglyphs. Located next to a stream, it's a wonderful picnic spot. In November the town hosts an annual *Indigenous Festival,* which combines native crafts with music and food.

North of here lies *Utuado* (take Route 140 to Route 111). The town is the unofficial center of the mountain district. Now that Highway 22 has been completed, it's also one of the most accessible towns in the region. Eventually, the highway will cut completely across the Cordillera Central and connect with the south coast at Ponce.

The place to stay in Utuado is *La Casa Grande* (Route 612, km. 0.3; 787–894–3939 or 888–343–2272; www.hotelcasagrande.com), located just off Route 140 in the town's lake district. The hotel is set on 107 acres of tropical forest. Another former coffee plantation, the hotel has twenty rooms, each with private bath, balcony, ceiling fan, and hammock. There's also a restaurant, *Jungle Jane's,* (featuring local and international dishes), a bar, and a pool. Yoga classes are offered every morning.

Casa Grande is close to both *Lago Dos Bocas* and *Lago Caonillas,* two artifical lakes built as part of the same system. (In all, there are about six lakes making up this system. At one time all had been connected by underground piping but these connections have become unusable through neglect.)

Route 10 swings to the shore of *Lago Dos Bocas,* a popular, U-shaped lake ringed by restaurants. Small ferry boats take visitors on rides around the lake, and fishing is also a favorite pastime here.

Utuado makes a good base to explore many of the attractions in the interior of Karst Country and its mountainous adjacent regions (these are described in more detail in the North Coast and West chapter).

The Western Mountains

offee country actually starts in Jayuya, but it flourishes in the western Cordillera Central. After passing the Toro Negro Forest Reserve, the Panoramic Route (now called Route 143) continues on to **Adjuntas**, known as the "town of the sleeping giant," as its silhouette suggests that illusion. Here the majestic peaks of the central mountain range give way to more roughly formed mountains and hills.

Adjuntas is an agricultural town surrounded by coffee fields, but citron, an ingredient processed from citrus fruits that is used in cakes, is by far the biggest crop here. In fact, the town is one of the world's leading producers of it.

West of Adjuntas, the Panoramic Route continues on Route 518. You'll pass by several private farms before reaching **Guilarte Forest Reserve**. The forest reserve has a beautiful picnic area beside a eucalyptus grove, and there are five cabins available for overnight rentals. Call the Department of Natural Resources (787–724–3724) for reservations. The cabins are in the eucalyptus forest, providing a scenic setting. Within the reserve is the 3,950-foot-tall **Monte Guilarte,** one of the few peaks on the island that isn't loaded down with serious media and telecom equipment. It's only 400 feet shorter than the island's highest point, and the lack of clutter makes a hike up here far more rewarding.

Trivia
Puerto Rico's own **Rita Moreno** was the first actress to win all four of the entertainment industry's highest awards: the Oscar, Emmy, Grammy, and Tony.

Just west of the forest reserve the Panoramic Route passes the settlement of **Castañer**, one of the most remote parts of the town center and main settlement of Lares. This beautiful, one-road community is filled with friendly residents. Despite its isolation, there are some North American and other foreign settlers in the area.

Lares, an hour north along Route 128, is known as the birthplace of the largest uprising in Puerto Rican history. In 1868 Ramón Emeterio Betances, a distinguished physician and prominent voice in Puerto Rican politics, masterminded the rebellion, which was dubbed **el grito de Lares,** literally "the shout of Lares." Though a republic of Puerto Rico was briefly declared, it was smashed back by the Spanish when the insurgents attempted to march on San Lorenzo.

Today Lares is a beautiful mountain town. The town's traditional New World Spanish central plaza, **La Plaza de la Revolución**, is where thousands of *independentistas* gather each September 28 to celebrate the anniversary of *el grito.* As with most Puerto Rican political rallies, it's a surprisingly easily digestible mix of political speeches, live music, and stimulating and silly conversation. There's plenty of beer and food, and scores of artisans come to sell their work. The town also jumps during its annual patron saint festival in early December.

The plaza's towering trees and scattered gardens obscure the view across the plaza but provide much needed shade and fresh air. (If only San Juan plazas were the same.) Fronting the plaza is *Heladería Lares* (787–897–2062), a highly recommended ice cream parlor that has dreamed up such unique ice cream flavors as *habichuelas* (bean) and *plátano* (plantain).

Beyond Castañer, the Panoramic Route (now Route 128) continues past magnificent views and Lago Guayo. The road becomes Route 365 and then Route 366 before turning into Route 120 and the *Maricao Forest.* A 2,600-foot stone observation tower a half-mile beyond the forest entrance affords great views of much of the island's western coast. Also in this area is the *Maricao Fish Hatchery* (Road 105 and Intersection Route 444), where many freshwater fish species are raised to stock Puerto Rico's more than twenty island lakes. The hatchery is open weekdays 7:30 A.M. to noon and 1:00 to 4:00 P.M.; weekends 8:30 A.M. to 4:00 P.M. Free admission.

The town of Maricao is the smallest on the island in terms of population. A visit here will immerse you in a peaceful, isolated place that is lush in vegetation and blessed with dramatic vistas. Maricao is home to coffee plantations, including a former one now run as an inn, *Parador Hacienda Juanita* (Route 105, km. 23.5; 787–838–2550; www.haciendajuanita.com). There are simple accommodations here, along with a game room, pool, and basketball and tennis courts. The resident chickens will scoot around you in the morning as you head to the verandah for breakfast; good coffee and local fruit are always available as well as heartier options. The restaurant, *La Casona de Juanita,* is a *meson gastronómico* recognized for fine meals of *criollo* cuisine. Room rates include breakfast and dinner.

Another lodging option is to rent a cabin from the *Centro Vacacional Monte de Estado* Route 120, km. 131.1; 787–787–5632). It is necessary to reserve ahead, contacting the Recreation Development Department (787–722–1771 or 888–767–4732), a government agency in San Juan. Cabins accommodate six; the center has a pool, picnic area, observation tower, and basketball court.

Holidays bring more visitors to Maricao; Monte de Estado is its busiest when Puerto Ricans are vacationing. One event that always attracts a crowd is the coffee harvest festival in mid-February, with coffee and crafts featured, but plenty of music and dancing as well.

North of Maricao is **Las Marías,** another coffee-country town that offers more rural splendor for the traveler looking to get away from the hustle and bustle that informs much of Puerto Rican life. While Maricao feels like it's so far away from it all, it's actually quite close to Mayagüez—maybe a thirty- to forty-five-minute drive. The most pleasant route to Maricao is Route 120, which rises up into the mountains from Sabana Grande in the south.

Closing this book of possible adventures while in the mountains of Puerto Rico not only leaves it on a high note but in a special place of inspiration, awe, and majesty. Hopefully this book has shown you the wealth of choices and adventures that await you on *la isla.* Your visit can provide you with the experiences of new sights, sounds, and tastes as well as relaxation and a good time. You can feel challenged, enriched, and renewed from your time here. *Saludos y buen viaje—* have a great trip!

WHERE TO STAY IN THE CENTRAL MOUNTAINS

ADJUNTAS
Monte Río Hotel
18 César González
(787) 829–3705

Villas de Sotomayor
Route 123, km. 36.8
(787) 829–1717

AIBONITO
Las Casitas Hotel
Route 162, km. 4.8
(787) 735–0180

BARRANQUITAS
Hacienda Margarita
Route 152, km. 1.7
(787) 854–0414

JAYUYA
Hotel Posada Jayuya
49 Guillermo Esteves
(787) 828–7250

Parador Hacienda Gripiñas
Route 527, km. 2.7
(787) 828–1717 or
(800) 981–7575

LAS MARÍAS
Gutiérrez Guest House
Route 119, km. 26.1
(787) 827–2087

MARICAO
Centro Vacacional Monte de Estado
Route 120, km. 13.1
(787) 873–5632

Hacienda Juanita
Route 105, km. 23.5
(787) 838–2550;
www.haciendajuanita.com

PATILLAS
Las Casas de la Selva
(787) 839–7318

UTUADO
Hotel La Casa Grande
Route 612, km. 0.3
(787) 894–3939 or
(888) 894–3532;
www.casagrande.com.

WHERE TO EAT IN THE CENTRAL MOUNTAINS

ADJUNTAS
Las Garzas
Route 123, km. 36
(787) 829–1717

Terraza Tropical Restaurant
Route 123, km. 24
(787) 829–0348

AGUAS BUENAS
El Sirimar
Route 156, km. 45.2
(787) 732–6012

AIBONITO
La Piedra Restaurant
Route 7718, km. 0.8
(787) 735–1034

BARRANQUITAS
Bar Plaza
Calle Barcello at the plaza
(787) 857–4909

CAGUAS
Chalet Jordano Ristorante
Route 172, km. 4.9
(787) 286–0085

El Paraíso
Highway 1, km. 29.1
(787) 747–2012

La Cántara
D–6 Degetau
(787) 743–0220

Marcos' Restaurant
3 Muñoz Rivera
(787) 743–2306

México Lindo
8 Muñoz Marin
(787) 746–9066

Mochomo's
Gautier Benitez Avenue,
corner of !st Street
(787) 286–9181

CAYEY (INCLUDES GUAVATE)
El Cielito
Route 715, km. 3
(787) 738–1805

El Mesón de Jorge
Highway 1, km. 57
(787) 263–2800

El Mojito
Route 184, km. 27,
Barrio Guavate
(787) 738–8888

El Rancho Numero Uno
Route 184, km. 27,
Barrio Guavate
(787) 747–7296

Jájome Terrace
Route 15, km. 18.6
(787) 787–4016

La Casona de Guavate
Route 184, km. 28.5,
Barrio Guavate
(787) 747–5533

Martin's BBQ
Highway 1; Cayey exit off
Luis Ferré Expressway
(787) 738–1144

Siempre Viva
Route 715, km. 5.1
(787) 738–0512

The Sand and the Sea
Route 714, km. 5.2
(787) 738–9086

CIALES
La Estancia Restaurant &
Inn
Route 615, km. 4.5
(787) 871–4541

JAYUYA
Don Pedro
Route 527, km. 2.5 at
Parador Hacienda Gripiñas
(787) 828–1717 or
(800) 981–7575

El Dujo
Route 140, km. 7.8
(787) 823–1143

LARES
Criollo Buffet and Salad
Bar
Route 129, km. 19.6
(787) 897–6463

El Taíno
Route 129, km. 20
(787) 645–4591

Las Cavernas
Route 129, km. 19.6
(787) 897–6463

Tourist Information for the Central Mountains

Adjuntos Tourist Information
Plaza Aristides
(787) 829–3310

Jayuya Tourism Information
Route 144, km. 9.3
(787) 282–5010 ext. 9704

Maricao Tourism Information
Town Hall
(787) 838–2290

Orocovis Tourism Information
Town Hall
(787) 867–5060

MARICAO

La Casona de Juanita at
Parador Hacienda Juanita
Route 105, km. 23.5
(787) 838–2550;
www.haciendajuanita.com

OROCOVIS

Las Cabañas de Doña Juana
Toro Negro, Route 143

UTUADO

Don Alonso
Route 621 to Lago Dos
Bocas dock
(787) 894–0516

Doña Fela
Route 123, next to the
cemetery
(787) 894–2758

El Fogón de Abuela
Route 621 to Lago Dos
Bocas dock
(787) 894–0470

Jungle Jane's at Hotel La
Casa Grande
Route 612, km. 0.3
(787) 894–3939 or
(888) 894–3532;
www.casagrande.com

Index

INDEX

INDEX

About the Author

John Marino is city editor at the *San Juan Star*. He writes frequently about Puerto Rico and the Caribbean for *The New York Times*, Reuters news agency, *Newsday*, the *Economist Intelligence Unit,* and other publications.

About the Editor

Tina Cohen is a research librarian at Deerfield Academy in Deerfield, Massachusetts. She writes about islands and Latin America.